A TACIT ALLIANCE

France and Israel from Suez to the Six Day War

VOLUME 7

The Modern Middle East Series
Sponsored by The Middle East Institute
Columbia University, New York

A complete listing of publications of
The Middle East Institute appears
at the end of this book.

Sylvia K. Crosbie

A TACIT ALLIANCE

France and Israel from Suez to the Six Day War

PRINCETON UNIVERSITY PRESS

PRINCETON, NEW JERSEY

Published by Princeton University Press, Princeton and London
LCC: 73-18310
ISBN: 0-691-07557-3

Library of Congress Cataloging in Publication data will
be found on the last printed page of this book

This book has been composed in Linotype Baskerville

Printed in the United States of America
by Princeton University Press,
Princeton, New Jersey

To My Parents
May and David Kowitt
and
To My Husband
Angus Duncan Crosbie IV

Contents

Preface

WHEN ONE deals with recent events, especially where national security, the defense establishment, and military industries are concerned, little official documentation is available to confirm circumstantial evidence. This is particularly true of Israel, where severe and wide-ranging censorship prevails on security questions. Thus, in researching this study, I was often forced to glean bits and pieces of information from professional journals in the defense-related aircraft and electronics industries, scientific periodicals, newspapers, and government debates. Despite occasional lapses in accuracy or flights of journalistic fancy, these sources proved generally reliable. In addition, numerous books have appeared which deal with the period of the Suez crisis. Much of this literature is in the form of personal memoirs which shed considerable light on the problems I have dealt with. A great deal has also been written on civil-military relations in France and in Israel and on French nuclear policy. But by far the greatest contribution to this study came from the principal architects of the tacit alliance, whom I interviewed in the spring and summer of 1969. A list of those individuals who gave permission for their names to be used appears in the bibliography, along with a brief description of their public careers.

In France, former ministers, bureaucrats, and army officers of the Fourth Republic who were no longer in government service were particularly willing to discuss the relationship with Israel and talked with relative freedom about the issues I raised. However, in almost every instance I was granted an interview on the condition that no verbatim record would be made of the discussions, and most of my sources asked that no remarks be directly attributed to them. While those interviewed often confirmed certain facts to support my assumptions, in several cases where secrecy was guarded only the broadest hints could be elicited. As a group, the people I met who had served the Fourth Republic were largely hostile to the policies of the Fifth Republic and Charles de Gaulle, especially in light of the General's words and deeds in the aftermath of the 1967 Arab-Israel war. As for servants of the Fifth Republic, the timing of my interviews in May and June 1969 raised certain difficulties. Although de Gaulle had just resigned as President of the Republic, no new trend in French politics had yet manifested itself. Many people felt it might be politically unwise to discuss Gaullist policies before the future of Gaullism could be fully ascertained.

Israeli officials in Paris were extremely guarded in their remarks while the situation remained in flux. Within Israel itself, in light of continuing hostilities with the Arab states and the activities of the Palestine guerrillas, government officials were overworked, tense, security-conscious, and concerned with the pressing needs of defense. With the French embargo on arms deliveries to Israel still in force, they feared that any disclosures might further endanger relations with France and threaten future supplies. When they did feel free to speak, their unhappiness at the dissolution of the partnership with France often precluded a candid assessment of past events and future prospects. It was somewhat easier to gain access to the highest levels of government, for officials there were more fully aware of what could or could not be said without infringing upon security regulations. I was also able to rely on several former colleagues in the Israel Ministry for Foreign Affairs. At lower operational levels, however, many officials preferred to remain completely silent rather than to risk divulging secret information.

Apart from the official censorship in Israel, one also encounters a pattern of secretiveness that occasionally pervades the bureaucracy and is in part a vestige of the pre-independence fight for statehood. Furthermore, because of the narrow membership of the ruling elite and the relative lack of turnover at the top, many of the individuals who had been in power for the whole period of the tacit alliance were still in government. Thus they showed a notable reluctance to criticize policy decisions or to divulge classified information about a system in which they still participated. This difficulty particularly hindered discussions of how the change in regime under Levi Eshkol's premiership might have affected foreign relations with France. Within the ruling Israel Labor Party, to which both Eshkol and former Prime Minister David Ben Gurion belonged before their split in 1964, I found a general desire to let old wounds heal in order to maintain labor unity in the election campaign for the *Histadrut* (General Federation of Labor) and *Kneset* (Israel parliament), which was in progress.

Despite these limitations, the interviews did elicit a wide-ranging exchange of views and clarification of facts, and I am sincerely grateful for the cooperation and kindness of those French and Israeli officials I had the pleasure of meeting.

Acknowledgments

Grateful acknowledgment is made to Professor J. C. Hurewitz, Director of the Middle East Institute of Columbia University, under whose patient guidance this study was undertaken. I am also indebted to the late Professor Philip E. Mosely, Director of the European Institute of Columbia University, for his friendship and help and to Professor Gerson D. Cohen, formerly Director of the Center for Israel and Jewish Studies of Columbia University, for having granted me a Hadassah Traveling Fellowship.

A TACIT ALLIANCE

France and Israel from Suez to the Six Day War

Introduction

ALMOST immediately after Israel declared its independence on May 14, 1948, France embarked on what amounted to a policy of military and scientific cooperation with the new state. Yet the official position of the French government at that time was pro-Arab, designed to maintain some measure of French influence in the Arab heartland, while under the terms of the Tripartite Declaration of 1950 France was obligated to abide by a limitation on arms supplies to the Middle East. Such French-Israeli cooperation also ran counter to the predilections of Israel's timorous and tradition-bound Foreign Ministry. Wedded to their pre-independence ties with the English-speaking countries, Israeli diplomats hoped for United States security guarantees and saw little diplomatic advantage to be gained from involvement with France. Nonetheless, by the time of the Suez crisis in 1956, when Israel and France embarked on the joint invasion of Egypt, it was apparent that a special relationship had indeed been forged between the two powers. That relationship has never been publicly defined. Although collusion at Suez was generally admitted, and the planners of the attack have often alluded to a military alliance for joint action against Egypt, no formal state-to-state arrangement was signed. Apart from a brief period of overt political cooperation late in 1956 and in the first half of 1957, the France-Israel association appears to have operated in unorthodox ways, largely outside the public arena.

When, after 1956, France became the major arms supplier to the Israel Defense Forces, most commentators assumed that Israel was merely helping France recoup the influence it had lost in the Middle East after the Algerian revolt and the disastrous Suez adventure. Despite predictions that French support for Israel would cease when the Algerian war ended, cooperation with Israel persisted and broadened even while France gradually recovered its interests in the Arab world. It was only in the aftermath of the Arab-Israel war of June 1967 that the special relationship that had endured for slightly more than a decade was ruptured brusquely and unilaterally by President Charles de Gaulle.

Obviously, this was no ordinary diplomatic relationship but something which implied more than friendship and less than an official government-to-government contract. One cannot assume that the two countries were impelled only by the Algerian rebellion and mutual hostility to Gamal 'Abd al-Nasir of Egypt. As a result of the interplay of international and regional politics, French and Israeli interests were converging before as well as after French power in North Africa ceased to be at issue. Certain factors in the domestic systems of the two nations created the possibility for a close working relationship between specific elements within them. In effect, a tacit alliance existed between the defense establishments of France and Israel, rooted in the military and technological cooperation which antedated the political relationship and which managed to outlast it for many years.

It was within the framework of the complex and often confusing interplay of the international, regional, and domestic systems that the tacit alliance arose, evolved, and survived for more than a decade before transformations within the systems forced the allies apart. With the possible exception of the political system in Israel, where the change was less fundamental, there were radical transformations at all three levels. Although the tacit alliance apparently survived the internal changes within both governments, its functioning was undoubtedly affected by the transition from a period of strong leadership in Israel and weakness in France to one of indecisiveness in Israel as vigorous leadership was being reasserted in France. Meanwhile, changes on the international and especially the regional levels directly contributed to its demise.

I

The International and Regional Settings

AFTER a century or more of fierce competition with the British for hegemony in the region, France effectively ceased to be a Middle East power at the close of the second world war. In 1946 pressures from Great Britain and the United States forced France's retreat from Syria and Lebanon, where a long tradition of trade and the "civilizing mission" of its educational and religious ties had created permanent enclaves of French culture. At the same time France came under increasingly agonizing pressures for independence in the Arab West, where it had been installed for more than a century.

With France occupied in the Maghrib, Britain alone had to assume the burdens of protecting western oil interests in the Arab world, guarding communications with the Commonwealth through the Suez Canal, and attempting to shore up the region's unstable regimes, particularly where the vulnerable oil fields and exposed pipelines were located. But it had already become apparent soon after World War II that this burden was too onerous for the United Kingdom. As the United States began to assume a broader share of Middle East responsibilities, Cold War rivalry became the basic feature of political life in the region. The Truman Doctrine of March 12, 1947, and the inclusion of Greece and Turkey in the NATO alliance were the first step. Then attention was no longer concentrated solely on the northern states—Turkey, Greece, and Iran—where

Soviet pressure was most apparent, but on the Arab heartland as well.

In pursuing its own goals, the United States could not ignore French protests that the remnants of its economic and cultural influence in the Arab East were being further eroded. Projecting its classic image as defender of the rights of man and protector of the Christian minorities in Syria and Lebanon, and tenaciously holding its grip on the territories still under French control in the Maghrib, France deeply resented any attempt to deny its status or to exclude it from western policy decisions which might affect the region. Especially important, the French argued, was their dependence on Middle East oil for approximately one-fifth of their energy needs. Extraordinarily sensitive to every indication that a special exclusive relationship might exist between Britain and the United States, France fostered the principle of tripartite consultation.

Primarily out of courtesy to a NATO ally and partly in consideration of the Anglo-French wartime entente, Britain and the United States included France in the Tripartite Declaration of May 25, 1950. While peace in the area may not have been the parties' overriding interest, they did at least aim at preserving the status quo and preventing the Arab-Israel arms race from eluding western control. The Tripartite Declaration stated:

> The three governments recognize that the Arab states and Israel all need to maintain a certain level of armed forces for the purposes of legitimate self-defense of the area as a whole. All applications for arms or war materials for those countries will be considered in the light of these principles.[1]

[1] United States *Department of State Bulletin,* vol. 22, n. 570 (1950), p. 886.

Detailed requests for arms under the terms of the declaration were handled by the Near Eastern Arms Coordinating Committee (NEACC). Composed of representatives of the three signatories, the NEACC was moderately successful in monitoring a relatively balanced flow of arms to the area from 1950 to 1954. Although the tripartite mechanisms were not absolutely obligatory, the signatories usually kept one another informed of arms transactions. As Pierre Maillard of the French Ministry for Foreign Affairs explained, there was "real cooperation among the powers, for no one country wanted to be the sole supplier." [2] The United States, however, as a rule preferred to remain only a marginal supplier, leaving Britain to manage the Arab-Israel arms market in the zone until 1955.

One aim of United States policy had been to establish a collective security system for the Middle East. France had been included in the first, unsuccessful attempt to link both Turkey and Egypt in such a system. But France was ignored when, in 1953-1954, the United States began in earnest to foster a series of bilateral agreements between Britain, Turkey, Iran, Iraq, and Pakistan that eventually became known as the Baghdad Pact. France's involvement in colonial wars apparently made it an unacceptable partner.

The French complained bitterly that their exclusion violated the spirit of the Tripartite Declaration and that French interests in Syria were apt to be harmed since the pact would make Iraq the most highly armed Arab nation. According to Maurice Schumann, whose views reflected those strongly and widely held in France, Iraq was "the most violent and most tenacious adversary of French interests" and posed a threat to Syrian inde-

[2] Interviewed in Paris, June 24, 1969.

pendence.[3] In particular, the French feared an increase of British influence in the Middle East through their position in Iraq and viewed with alarm the possibility that a Greater Syria under the Hashimite label might emerge with British support. The French correctly predicted that the issue of the pact would split the entire area and pit an anti-Iraq, anti-Hashimite axis revolving around revolutionary Egypt, Syria, and Saudi Arabia against the kingdoms of Iraq and Jordan.

The French believed that Secretary of State John Foster Dulles suffered from "pactomania," and that his complete misunderstanding of Middle East strategic realities would eventually split the region. Worse, by insisting on a formal northern tier alliance, Dulles would, in effect, be inviting the Russians into the Middle East. The Israelis tended to concur with the French point of view.[4] At this juncture France, which had shipped arms to both Lebanon and Syria in 1950 and supported Syria in the United Nations when border fighting erupted over Israel plans to drain the Lake Hulah swamps, openly began to find a common interest with Syria's enemy—Israel. The notion began to take shape that, in any contest between Iraq and Egypt for influence over Syria, Israel might effectively serve France as a balancer.[5]

As the French had foreseen, the Soviet Union viewed the Baghdad Pact, finally signed in February 1955, as a

[3] *Journal Officiel de la République Française. Débats Parlementaires. Assemblée Nationale. Compte Rendu,* Oct. 16, 1956, 2nd sess., p. 4145. Unless otherwise stated, all translations from French and Hebrew sources are the author's.

[4] See Walter Eytan, *The First Ten Years: A Diplomatic History of Israel* (London: Weidenfeld & Nicolson, 1958), p. 141.

[5] See Guy Wint & Peter Calvocoressi, *Middle East Crisis* (Harmondsworth, Middlesex: Penguin, 1957), pp. 48, 51-54.

threat to its security. If the center of the Cold War had shifted from Europe to the Far East with the outbreak of the Korean War in June 1950, the Baghdad Pact negotiations now moved the main arena to the Middle East. An arms deal between the Soviet Union and Egypt was negotiated in mid-February 1955, completed in May, and formally announced by Gamal 'Abd al-Nasir on September 27, 1955.[6]

Since 1951, the Soviet Union had repeatedly expressed interest in arming Egypt as a means to neutralize the western monopoly in the Middle East. If it could not set up a series of buffer states on the East European order, it could at least "jump over" the potentially dangerous northern tier alliance along its borders. Moreover, on the assumption that Egypt could not absorb vast quantities of sophisticated matériel, the Soviet leadership probably saw arms deliveries to Egypt as the means of indirectly providing weapons for and gaining influence in other Arab states. This policy was reinforced when the Twentieth Congress of the Communist Party of the Soviet Union, in February 1956, approved support for nationalist leaders—a departure from their dictum that only Communists could lead the struggle for national liberation.

Egypt found the Soviet offer an attractive alternative to American aid, which, apart from the problem of credits, was subject to the conditions of the Tripartite Declaration and to Congressional restrictions that arms be used only for internal security, legitimate defense, or

---

[6] The following account draws heavily on Uri Ra'anan, *The USSR Arms the Third World: Case Studies in Soviet Foreign Policy* (Cambridge: M.I.T., 1969). Ra'anan points out that by January 12, 1955, the world knew of the impending signature of the Baghdad Pact, and he presents a cogent argument for the timetable outlined above.

in support of regional defense arrangements. These limitations were at odds with 'Abd al-Nasir's regional objectives.

Soviet actions effectively upset the balance of Middle East power by providing some $200 million worth of arms to Egypt.[7] The way was now open for great power competition in feeding the local arms race, since the West could no longer regulate the supply of arms to Arabs and Israelis. Whether Washington liked it or not, the era of tripartite diplomacy had ended and four-power rivalry had begun.

Military men in France had viewed with alarm the signs of growing Soviet influence in Egypt as early as 1954-1955. A change in the direction of Egyptian trade toward the USSR was already discernible, and Russian advisers had replaced German experts by the end of 1955.[8] It was part of a Russian conspiracy, the French said, to force the Americans to abandon the total war concept, to threaten western oil supplies, and to encircle Europe by way of the Middle East and North Africa.[9] At the same time, the United States attitude toward the Atlantic alliance and its intolerant moralizing on French colonial struggles became more and more baffling to the French. Foreign Minister Christian Pineau remarked in October 1956:

> I apologize for saying it, but it is very difficult for us—I weigh my words—always to understand completely the line of American foreign policy I

[7] *Ibid.,* p. 157.

[8] Merry & Serge Bromberger, *Les Secrets de l'expédition d'Egypte* (Paris: Aymon, 1957), pp. 111-112.

[9] See *Le procès des généraux Challe et Zeller: textes complets des débats réquisitoires—plaidoiries, annèxes* (Paris: Nouvelles Editions Latines, 1961), pp. 257-258.

must say, in effect, across these meanderings of American policy, we sometimes have had the impression that the United States does not completely understand in the same way as we the meaning of the Atlantic alliance.[10]

When, the French wondered, would the United States stop ignoring the true priorities and begin to recognize the strategic importance of French holdings in Africa? "When the Cossacks water their horses in the fountains of the Tuilleries—before, after or never?"[11]

Within this complex setting, Israel during the first years of statehood sought a permanent peace through direct, individual negotiations with the Arab governments. But the failure of negotiations for a peace settlement at Lausanne in 1949 and the assassination of King 'Abd 'Allah of Jordan in July 1951 made it apparent that peace was a chimera. The festering conflict took several forms. The most comprehensive measure was the Arab boycott of Israel, which eventually included a blockade of all goods bound for Israel via the Suez Canal and the Gulf of 'Aqabah. Egyptian gun emplacements at Sharm al-Shaykh, which guarded the entrance to the Strait of Tiran, stifled the development of Israel's southern territory, and along Israel's borders an undeclared war was fought with light weapons and occasional mortars. Continuous Arab harassments eventually produced spontaneous reprisal raids by the Israelis.

Like any small state threatened with isolation and encirclement, Israel turned to the major powers for protection. Earlier, Israeli leaders had refused to identify their state with either superpower, partly in recognition of the Soviet Union's initial support for the

[10] *Journal Officiel,* Oct. 16, 1956, 2nd sess., p. 4154.
[11] Jean Legendre in *ibid.,* 1st sess., p. 4132.

Jewish State and partly in the vain hope that the Soviets might allow Russian Jewry to emigrate to Israel. The anti-Semitic outrages of Stalin's last days, the doctors' plot, and the final breakdown in Soviet relations with Israel in February 1953 put an end to all illusions on that score, however. For a brief period there was the hope that the western system of Middle East defense alliances might be extended to include a guarantee of Israel's security. But although Israel may have been convinced of its own value as a possible ally, its hope for membership in such a system was unrealistic. No other state in the Middle East would consider entering an alliance in which Israel was a partner. Moreover, the United States—which might have offered a bilateral treaty—felt that such a guarantee would jeopardize the American position in the Arab world "or give formal recognition to the armistice lines as permanent legal boundaries." [12] Nor could Israel find a place within the third world as the Afro-Asian bloc crystallized at the United Nations in the 1950s.

The Baghdad Pact negotiations added to Israel's difficulties. Although Turkey, Iran, and Pakistan were not among Israel's enemies, the arming of Iraq or any other Arab state with expensive ultramodern weapons meant the intensification of the arms race in the area and the threat that the balance of military power might come to favor the Arabs. Israel's isolation and insecurity hardened the belief fostered by the Nazi holocaust and the independence struggle that, in the last analysis, Israel and the Jewish people could depend for survival only upon themselves. In October 1953,

[12] John C. Campbell, *Defense of the Middle East. Problems of American Policy,* rev. ed. (N.Y.: Praeger, for the Council on Foreign Relations, 1960), p. 239.

Israel inaugurated a policy of active defense with the bloody Qibya reprisal raid against Jordan—the first major retaliatory operation to involve regular army units. What Israel now needed was more sophisticated equipment, the military means by which it could secure its own future. Arms purchases became Israel's major priority, and the Israelis were ready to ally themselves with whatever power could furnish the needed matériel. France proved to be that power.

France's isolation on the international scene had created a common political purpose with Israel in opposition to big power aims in the Middle East. Mutual enmity to Egypt and Gamal 'Abd al-Nasir now bound the two states together. In the first two years after the Egyptian coup d'etat of 1952, there was relative quiet on the Egyptian borders while the Revolutionary Command Council concentrated on consolidating its position. Although 'Abd al-Nasir emerged from the power struggles as the Egyptian leader, his control was still somewhat in doubt, for he had to counter the prestige of the ousted President General Muhammad Nagib, to contend with the activities of the Muslim Brotherhood, and, above all, to deal with the continued British presence in Egypt. But as a result of the July 27, 1954, agreement (effective October 19, 1954) for the withdrawal of British troops from Suez, Egypt, not Britain, now sat astride the Suez Canal. The balance of power in the Middle East was bound to change.

Israel would be faced with the threat of a direct Israel-Egypt confrontation in Sinai once the last of the 80,000 British troops was evacuated from Egypt in the fall of 1955 and the British buffer was removed. Tensions mounted as Israel's policy of active defense was increasingly directed against Egypt. An Israeli raid against Gaza in February 1955 pointed up Egypt's military weakness.[13] Matters reached a fever pitch in August 1955, when the *fidaiyun* or Arab commando forces were launched with the official blessings of the 'Abd al-Nasir government. Then, one month later, on September 27, came the official announcement of the "Czech" arms deal with Egypt, with its dire implications for the Middle East arms balance. Threatened by such superiority in weaponry, Israel would have to act before Egypt could absorb the new Soviet equipment.

As A. H. Hourani observed:

> Once the Agreement of 1954 gave Egypt freedom to act as she pleased, she began a policy of building up her diplomatic and military strength, while not binding herself by any agreement with Great Powers. This involved the creation around Egypt of as large a hinterland as possible free from the direct control of the Great Powers, and able to deal with them from a free and relatively strong position. It involved also an attempt to control the oil-resources of the Arabian Peninsula, both as a means of putting pressure on the Powers, and in order to make the royalties available for economic development in the countries which most needed capital. For these purposes Egypt set herself to appropriate and control the two movements which would arouse an echo in every Arab country: the movement towards Arab unity, and that to assert the rights of the Arabs in Palestine . . . .[14]

[13] Kennett Love, *Suez: The Twice-Fought War. A History* (N.Y.: McGraw Hill, 1969), pp. 9-10 & *passim*, exaggerates the importance of the Gaza raid in leading to the Suez-Sinai war. The raid must be seen as merely one development in the interplay of regional and international forces.

[14] "The Middle East and the Crisis of 1956," *St. Antony's Papers*, no. 4, Middle Eastern Affairs, no. 1 (London: Chatto & Windus, 1958), pp. 24-25.

The Baghdad Pact issue provided 'Abd al-Nasir with the first real opportunity to assert his leadership. While the western powers had originally envisioned a security arrangement based on Egypt and linked to the Arab League collective security pact, the bilateral nature of the northern tier arrangement conflicted with Egypt's desire for a leading role in any regional alignment. 'Abd al-Nasir's direct appeal to the Arab people for support against the Baghdad Pact profoundly radicalized regional politics, and he became a symbol of Arab unity for the masses.

Prior to the Egyptian coup d'etat, Arab harassment of Israel had had little ideological content. 'Abd al-Nasir's revolutionary attraction, however, worried security planners in Tel-Aviv, for any increase in Arab unity would decrease Israel security.

France, meanwhile, despite its embarrassing departure from Syria and Lebanon, had retained some voice in Middle East affairs because of its North African territories. There was no question of surrendering such prized possessions. Algeria, the heart of French power and influence in the Maghrib, had been tightly integrated into metropolitan France, while French interest in the other lands across the Mediterranean was rooted in French fears of the historic vulnerability of its southern coastline.

When the Algerian struggle for independence erupted in violence on November 1, 1954, France was gripped by the fear that the spreading Arab independence movements signaled the end of French presence in the region and would remove once and for all any illusions that France could retain its position as a global power. The remains of French influence in Syria had declined further after February 1954, with the ouster of the pro-

French military dictator, Colonel Adib al-Shishakli, and Syria's drift to the left; French interests in Tunisia and Morocco eroded progressively. Visions of a pan-Islamic danger to French Black Africa rode with the spectre of a hostile coalition on France's exposed southern flank. All this was aggravated by American and, particularly, John Foster Dulles' moralizing on French colonial troubles.

Foreign Minister Christian Pineau (February 1956-May 1958) and other French leaders were later to accuse 'Abd al-Nasir of actually fomenting the rebellion. Algerian rebel headquarters were established in Cairo, where the Arab League mustered world opinion against France, establishing a permanent service for the North African question on January 16, 1954, and a League for the Independence of the Arab West on April 4. Radio Cairo regularly supported the rebels with inflammatory broadcasts inciting hatred of the French. Arms shipments as well as propaganda emanated from the Egyptian capital, and Algerians at al-Azhar were regularly required to take military training and induced to join the struggle.[15]

Increasingly under the influence of India's Nehru after 1953, 'Abd-al-Nasir had "moved from a temporary and tactical non-commitment to a neutrality of principle," but a new, virulent, anti-western neutrality.[16]

[15] See *United Nations General Assembly Official Records* (UNGAOR), 11th sess., 1st ctte., 831st mtg., Feb. 4, 1957, paras. 18-21; 12th sess., 1st ctte., 913th mtg., Nov. 27, 1957, paras. 30, 33-34; Raymond Aron in *Le Figaro,* Feb. 21, 1956; and Jacques Soustelle, *A New Road for France,* trans. by Benjamin Protter (N.Y.: Speller, 1965), pp. 69, 98, note 6. For Egyptian and Syrian denials, see UNGAOR, 12th sess., 1st ctte., 913th mtg., Nov. 27, 1957, paras. 55-56.

[16] Hourani, "Middle East and Crisis of 1956."

Even though French interests in Africa and Asia differed in-kind and degree from those of Britain, both nations came to view 'Abd al-Nasir as a threat. The knowledge that the Egyptian dictator could control the canal once Britain departed from the Canal Zone had little appeal for France. Probably France hoped to step into the strategic vacuum created by British withdrawal. French military circles, convinced that the Suez Canal was strategically vital, from 1954 on had their eyes on Israel, which was located not only atop the Red Sea, and so on a line with Djibouti, but on the other side of the canal.[17]

When 'Abd al-Nasir's *Philosophy of the Revolution* appeared in 1955, it was immediately regarded by French strategists as a revised edition of *Mein Kampf.* Colonel Louis Mangin first made the analogy between 'Abd al-Nasir and Hitler which became so popular at the French Ministry of Defense. *Assemblée Nationale* debates are full of illustrations drawn from the interwar period and dire warnings of the fruits of appeasement. If history were allowed to repeat itself, another Munich would lead to global warfare. The Egyptian press hardly helped matters with such comments as that of *El Tahir,* on April 10, 1956, "Each Egyptian is proud to be a Goebbels." [18] As 'Abd al-Nasir's negotiations with the Americans for a loan to build the Aswan Dam entered a difficult phase in the spring of 1956, the "Munich complex" grew. In fact, France fully expected some act of

[17] See articles commemorating the tenth anniversary of the Suez invasion in *Le Monde,* Nov. 4, 1966; for views held by Admiral Barjot, commander of the French fleet, see Henri Azeau, *Le Piège de Suez (5 novembre 1956)* (Paris: Laffont, 1964), p. 356.

[18] Cited by Maurice Schumann, *loc. cit.* On the theme of appeasement, see Pierre de Chevigne, *ibid.,* Aug. 2, 1956, p. 3843; and Hugh Thomas, *The Suez Affair* (Liverpool: Weidenfeld & Nicolson, 1966), p. 20.

defiance in reaction to United States' withdrawal, on July 15, 1956, of its offer to help finance the dam, and French Ambassador to Egypt Maurice Couve de Murville had long and correctly anticipated the form that might take.[19]

Once 'Abd al-Nasir controlled the canal and then nationalized the French-controlled Suez Canal Company on July 26, 1956, the French feared he might use his power against France as well as Israel. One-half of France's oil imports were received via Suez. Moreover, the threat that 'Abd al-Nasir might cut off France from its interests in Africa and Asia could prove an effective weapon in the Algerian campaign.[20] The canal had to be safeguarded. At no time in the past had any of the great powers ever seriously attempted to help the Israelis use the canal, and they had hardly raised a collective eyebrow when an Israeli ship, the *Bat Galim,* was refused passage on September 28, 1954. They were unlikely to help France now.

In addition to its primary objectives, action against 'Abd al-Nasir at Suez may also have been designed in some indefinite way to facilitate France's return to its previous economic influence in Egypt. Forty percent of France's Middle East trade had been with Egypt. In 1950, France had been Egypt's third largest client and second largest supplier after Great Britain. By 1956, however, it had lost ground in the fierce competition for Egyptian markets with the United States, the USSR, West Germany, and Britain.[21]

[19] See Herman Finer, *Dulles over Suez. The Theory and Practice of His Diplomacy* (Chicago: Quadrangle, 1964), p. 47.

[20] See *Journal Officiel,* Dec. 18, 1956, 3rd sess., p. 6117; and Dec. 19, 1956, *passim.*

[21] See *ibid.,* Oct. 16, 1956, 2nd sess., pp. 4140, 4135; and *The Economist,* vol. 180 (Aug. 4, 1956), p. 413.

After the humiliation of France and Britain at Suez, the United States had formally assumed responsibility for the Middle East under the Eisenhower Doctrine, enunciated on December 31, 1956. While Britain's sphere of influence was reduced to Aden and the Persian Gulf, France was faced with inevitable defeat in North Africa. If the protection of Israel had originally been little more than a pretext for French involvement at Suez, many French leaders came to realize, as the Suez crisis deepened, that by protecting Israel they had found a key to influence in the Middle East and Africa. France could threaten to aid Israel in retaliation for aid given to Algeria. Its friendship with Israel could be used as a means by which France would have to be appeased not only by the Arabs but by the great powers. This latter consideration seems to have been of primary importance during the last years of the Fourth Republic and especially in the first years of the Fifth Republic under General Charles de Gaulle. Convinced that many of the present conflicts in the area could be settled or reduced if the western nations coordinated their policies, de Gaulle, like the leaders of the Fourth Republic, insisted upon tripartite consultation. Because of France's profound knowledge of the area and its historical experience in the Arab world, he argued that a French presence was indispensable whenever the future of the Middle East was in question.

De Gaulle realized that not only could he influence Middle East developments indirectly, but at the same time he could counter American influence in the region, and he used France's relationship with Israel as a lever in negotiating the French relationship with the United States. Washington's failure to consult with France before the 1958 Anglo-American intervention after the upheavals in Iraq, Jordan, and Lebanon; American refusal to countenance an independent nuclear deterrent for France; and the growing technological gap which threatened France with a new form of American economic imperialism, as well as de Gaulle's own wartime experiences, all contributed to a definite anti-Americanism in the General's world view. Convinced that any American success would increase the world's imbalance and further the trend to polarization, de Gaulle counseled Israel in 1958-1959 to remove itself from complete dependence upon Washington. Instead he encouraged Israel to establish closer ties with West Germany and Europe.[22]

While the Fourth Republic had tended to base foreign policy on the premise that two blocs existed, one free and one totalitarian, de Gaulle was consistently guided by only one consideration—what was best for France. As early as 1958-1959, he disallowed an exclusive alliance relationship with Israel and, rejecting the traditional French policy that excluded the Soviet Union from Middle East diplomacy, he placed his hopes for area stability in four-power agreement. This complicated matters for Israel, however, when the East/West impasse of 1958 failed to mature into a superpower detente, and from 1962 to 1967, superpower rivalry in the Middle East contrived to pull France and Israel apart.

After the Cuban missile crisis of 1962, the Soviet Union intensified its efforts to establish a continual naval presence in the Mediterranean with a view to neutralizing the American Sixth Fleet. De Gaulle saw

[22] See *ibid.*, vol. 192 (July 11, 1959), p. 88; vol. 207 (June 15, 1963), p. 1120; and Erel Ginay, "De Gaulle and Israel," *New Outlook,* vol. 11 (Jan. 1968), p. 15.

in Soviet influence a potential check on American policy and, to a certain extent, on Nasirist extremism in the region. However, the Russian arms deliveries to the radical military regimes tended to polarize the Arab nations into Soviet- and American-sponsored camps. A quantitative and qualitative escalation of the arms races ensued, which transformed the Arab-Israel arms balance, altering Israel's foreign and defense priorities and fostering changes in its relationship with France. After a new Egyptian arms deal with the USSR in 1962, Israel signed a contract with Washington in 1963 for short-range ground-to-air Hawk missiles, with delivery to begin in 1965.[23] By broadening Israel's sources of arms, Premier David Ben Gurion was able to lessen dependence upon any one country for military hardware and assuage those political opponents who, in criticizing his defense policies, had advocated closer ties with the United States.

Friction with France was inevitable once the exclusiveness of France-Israel ties had ended. The French argued that this would be only the initial step in Israel's return to Washington's tutelage since, unlike France, the United States was known to attach political conditions to its arms sales.[24] Moreover, both de Gaulle and the French arms industry resented American competition. Apart from obvious economic and technological implications, there was a political element as well. Once

[23] See the *Jerusalem Post* and *Ha-Arets,* Sept. 27, 28, Nov. 2, 1962; April 3, 5, 8, June 25, 1963; and Nadav Safran, *From War to War. The Arab-Israeli Confrontation, 1948-1967* (N.Y.: Pegasus, 1969), p. 134. The terms were 10% down with interest at $3\frac{1}{2}$% and ten years to pay in annual installments. The cost was not publicized.

[24] Maillard, interview cited; and General Paltiel Makleff, interviewed at Israel Aircraft Industry near Lydda, Israel, August 14, 1969.

de Gaulle in January 1963 had rejected the possibility of nuclear dependence on the United States, which had offered Polaris missiles, he accelerated his drive for equality in matters of defense within the Atlantic alliance and on other questions of common interest. An independent arms industry could provide the technological and scientific developments to ensure French independence from Washington. While the United States was attempting to arrive at a common western policy toward arms dispersals, France tended to display "a dispassionate commercial approach" to regional arms sales once the Algerian war had ended in 1962, seeking only to gain its "fair share" of the market.[25]

In 1965 Washington agreed to sell Israel Skyhawk light bombers on easy terms out of a desire to balance American and British arms aid to the Arabs. This placed American-made weapons designed essentially for an attack role in the hands of Israel for the first time.[26] France had been unable to offer a comparable system, but de Gaulle could hardly have been pleased by this development, particularly since Franco-American relations were further complicated by the Viet-Nam issue after 1965.[27] The General saw American actions as

[25] Michael Howard & Robert Hunter, "Israel and the Arab World: The Crisis of 1967," *Adelphi Papers,* no. 41 (London: Institute for Strategic Studies [ISS], 1967), p. 42.

[26] See J. C. Hurewitz, *Middle East Politics: The Military Dimension* (N.Y.: Praeger, 1969), pp. 480-481; *Jerusalem Post,* May 20, 22, 1966; and *The Jewish Observer and Middle East Review* (JOMER), vol. 15 (May 27, 1966), p. 4, for reports that the United States State Department erroneously inferred that Israel would have to stop buying French arms as a condition to the sale.

[27] Price was not a factor in Israel's decision for, although American electronics equipment often cost half the price of French matériel, French planes were generally less expensive.

likely to harden Cold War rivalry, polarize the Middle East, upset the intra-Arab regional arms balance, and add to the threat of local war and even of a global conflict involving the superpowers in support of their various clients.

Even while dismissing the "contradictory" and "hypocritical" policies of the United States in the Middle East, France sought to secure a foothold in the area and, by spearheading a third force, to reverse the trend toward regional polarization. This meant carving a policy in the Middle East independent both of the United States and Cold War rivalry. De Gaulle may have felt sympathy for the concept of a Jewish State in the framework of support for local nationalism, but his primary goal was to increase his popularity among the nonindustrial states—a large number of which were Israel's enemies. To do this he encouraged France's image as an impartial mediator in the Arab-Israel dispute because of its good relations with both sides, while at the same time he reinforced traditional French ties with the Arab world. This gave France greater maneuverability in the area than either Britain or the United States and thus strengthened de Gaulle's claim for consideration in any approach to Middle East problems by the other major powers.

The sense of humanitarian moralism, of the mission of Christian France, of responsibility to history and of cultural nationalism, which formed part of the political culture of France, was accentuated in the Gaullist Fifth Republic. That there was a measure of altruism in this cannot be denied, but one of the few means of influence remaining to France in the Middle East was the educa-

---

Makleff, interview cited above. Cf. Ben Porat & Uri Dan, *Mirage Contre Mig* (Paris: Laffont, 1967), p. 86.

tional and cultural activities which had perpetuated French influence by training successive generations in the spirit and language of French civilization.

Immediately after Suez, France had quickly acted to reestablish its educational and commercial interests in the Arab world, even before other matters were negotiated. By emphasizing the ability of France to provide needed goods and services while stressing the irrelevance of his political stance in continuing to supply Israel's military needs, de Gaulle was able to make inroads into countries not traditionally within the French sphere of influence, such as Iraq, Iran, Jordan, and Saudi Arabia.

After the Algerian settlement, France resumed normal diplomatic contact with Syria, Jordan, and Saudi Arabia in 1962, and with Iraq and the UAR in 1963. The reentry of France into the Middle East was signaled by a succession of Arab visitors to Paris, culminating in the 1965 visit of Egyptian Field Marshal 'Abd al-Hakim Amer. Obviously, the Arab states hoped to weaken the French commitment to Israel, but, according to reports, Egypt, for example, adopted a flexible policy to which France agreed, which asked only that France explain the extent of its ties to Israel. Indeed, some French firms such as Schneider-Creusot, which was designated to execute specific projects in conjunction with joint French-USSR grants of $30 million over ten years to Egypt for industrialization, also had substantial dealings with Israel.[28] The Arab states—and particularly the Soviet clients—acquiesced to French commitments to Israel primarily to lessen their own dependence on the superpowers, and they welcomed de Gaulle's at-

[28] JOMER, vol. 14 (Oct. 22, 1965), pp. 2-4; *The Near East Report,* vol. 9 (Nov. 2, 1965), p. 87; *Le Monde,* Oct. 17, 1965; and Patrick Seale in *Jerusalem Post,* April 8, 1966.

tempt to open a third alternative option in the big power competition. Having stimulated superpower rivalry in the area, the French helped undermine client-superpower relations while gaining a new source of diplomatic maneuverability. By 1965 France began exploiting its revitalized contacts with the Arab world in the hope of finding new outlets for its arms industries.

At first Israeli officials were quick to follow the French cue. Stressing France's traditional and not negligible influence and interest in the Middle East, they pointed out that closer French-Arab relations could stabilize tensions. Beneath their public optimism, however, they recognized their lack of choice in accepting a French posture of outward impartiality instead of a close political alliance which would have increased Israeli security but which might have hampered France's diplomatic freedom. The Israelis correctly predicted, moreover, that any expansion of exports to the Arab world would lessen French dependence upon the Israeli market, resulting in further disintegration of the special relationship between the two countries.

Increasingly throughout the 1960s, Cold War rivalry and regional events negated bilateral considerations in the France-Israel relationship. With the Arab states divided into radical or revolutionary and conservative or traditional camps, each with its superpower patron or great power supplier, the Arab-Israel dispute grew more and more intractable as it became a central issue in intra-Arab struggles. As the concept of regional unity increasingly questioned Israel's right to exist, the opportunities for mediating a settlement or maintaining a middle ground narrowed. Both sides planned for the long-range—Egypt for weapons of ultimate destruction and Israel for defense against all contingencies. They demanded new sophisticated weapons.

After July 1963, warfare in the Arab-Israel zone reached a new level of violence as advanced weaponry of Israel, Egypt, and Syria was put into use. Air battles became increasingly common, accompanied by massive infusions of Russian aid to Egypt and Syria. With the Arab summit meetings of 1964-1965 and the establishment of the United Arab Command in 1964, guerrilla activity along the borders of Israel was revived and became a major issue in internal Arab struggles. Enmity to Israel was the single unifying factor in Middle East politics. Tensions escalated steadily until January 1965, when *al-Fatah* (Organization for the Liberation of Palestine) guerrillas further raised the level of violence in a succession of incursions from Jordanian territory. Israeli retaliation against Jordan in May ended the tacit truce that had existed since the Sinai Campaign and precipitated a series of border clashes—against Syria in August, Jordan in September, Lebanon in October, and Jordan again in November. The February 1966 left-wing coup d'etat in Syria aggravated matters by bringing to power the Ba'thist government of General Salah Jadid, which actively sponsored al-Fatah activities. In November 1966, the signing of a Cairo-Damascus defense pact, which was designed to strengthen the Syrian regime in the face of internal unrest, posed a further threat to Israel by raising the possibility of a two-front attack.

On November 13, Israel staged a major raid against al-Samu' in Jordan, supposedly in reprisal for al-Fatah activities. At the United Nations all four great powers concurred in condemnation of the Israeli action. France was unequivocably opposed to the attack, and seemed genuinely anxious to effect a conciliation as nine acts of terrorism in the next two weeks raised tensions. But events outpaced diplomatic efforts; air battles with Syria raged after al-Samu'. On April 7, 1967, Israeli planes struck at Syrian artillery positions, shot down six Syrian planes, and nearly flew over Damascus, causing a serious threat to the Syrian regime. At this juncture, the Soviet Union sought to push Egypt into a closer commitment to Syria's security. The opportunity arose in May, when the Russians hinted to the Egyptians that they had reliable knowledge of Israeli contingency plans for attacking Syria.

It was this series of events which led to 'Abd al-Nasir's bellicose threats against Israel, accompanied by his dramatic moves to oust the United Nations Emergency Forces stationed on Egyptian territory and to reinstate the blockade of the Gulf of 'Aqabah. Israel, believing itself threatened, responded with a preemptive strike, defeating the Arabs in six days in June 1967. Forced at last to make a choice, General de Gaulle chose to pursue France's traditional interests and strengthen the French role in the Arab world. The tacit alliance between France and Israel collapsed.

II

Unorthodox Diplomacy

IN the years immediately after World War II, France's relations with the nascent State of Israel were curiously irregular. On an official diplomatic level, the French government was often cool, if not hostile to aspirations for a Jewish State, though many high officials within the government actively supported the Jewish struggle for independence. Powerful links had been forged out of the Nazi occupation, when Frenchmen developed a new knowledge and understanding of the Jewish people and their role in history. Because of their exploits within the *Résistance* and in the Free French Forces, large numbers of Jews could count on the support of leading figures in the *Rassemblement du Peuple Français* and the Gaullist government.

Ben Gurion and other *Haganah* (Jewish underground defense army) leaders had established their headquarters in Paris in 1946, after the British cracked down on their activities in Palestine. The Jewish underground ran training camps, established a radio station, and built an intelligence network, all with the quiet acquiescence of French authorities. *'Aliyah Gimmel* (illegal postwar immigration) was also directed from France with the tacit approval of the French government. The French army and police aided the refugees and often kept British agents from interfering with their attempts to reach Palestine. The Ministry of Interior usually provided the refugees with false papers and facilitated

the transit to the southern ports of some quarter of a
million East European Jews, permitting another 120,000
to settle permanently in France.[1] When, in July 1947,
British authorities in Palestine forced the *Exodus* to
return to its French port of embarkation crowded with
refugees determined to reach Palestine at all costs, their
plight aroused a great deal of sympathy. The refusal of
officials such as Interior Minister Edouard Depreux to
accede to Bevin's demands that the Jews disembark in
France, made it easier for many Frenchmen to aid the
Jewish cause openly.

Immediately after the war, the Haganah had combed
France for arms and ammunition. The Résistance became a major source of weapons, and, as French forces
withdrew from Syria, much of their equipment also
found its way into Jewish hands. In 1947, due to the
intervention of Jules Moch, Minister of Public Works
and Transport and Minister of Interior (1947-1950), a
heavy traffic in arms flowed toward Palestine from
Corsican airfields. Landing rights were granted only
with a password, and no official papers were demanded.
Only Moch's personal staff and the commander of the
Ajaccio airport in Corsica were apprised of the deliveries, although Moch indicated that they did have the
approval of the Prime Minister.[2]

The Zionist Directory meeting in Paris openly collected money to purchase arms, while the Paris police
closed their eyes to the comings and goings of underground leaders. When the police chanced upon an
arms cache and surprised three Jewish agents, they
quickly released not only the conspirators but the arms

[1] Jules Moch, Minister of Interior (1947-1950), interviewed in
Paris, June 2, 1969; and *Jerusalem Post,* April 24, 1964.

[2] Interview cited.

as well on orders from the Minister of Interior.[3] According to one anecdote, when the French Zionist leader André Blumel flew to Prague to negotiate for arms on behalf of Israel, the plane he used was put at his disposal by the French government.[4] Arms destined for a dissident guerrilla group, the *Irgun Zvai Leumi* (National Military Organization), were "obtained" with official concurrence from French arsenals, and a French military convoy delivered the weapons to the *Altalena* on June 11, 1948.[5] French sources also helped the Haganah purchase airplanes and twenty light aircraft guns, which were used as anti-tank weapons during the independence

[3] Albert Stara of the Revisionist Organization in France, interviewed in Paris, June 5, 1969. Presumably this occurred during 1947.

[4] Michael Bar-Zohar, *Gesher 'al ha-Yam ha-Tikhon. Yahasei Tsarfat-Israel, 1947-1963* (Bridge over the Mediterranean. France-Israel Relations, 1947-1963; Tel-Aviv: 'Am ha-Sefer, 1964), p. 30. The author gives no date, but Czech arms began arriving in April 1948. Although Bar-Zohar supplies few sources to document his assertions and the footnotes are often misleading, he supposedly had access to both the Israel Ministry of Defense archives and Ben Gurion's private papers.

[5] There was at least one other similar instance, according to Stara, interview cited. See also *Jerusalem Post*, Feb. 23, 1964. An interesting sidelight to the struggle between the Irgun and the Haganah which led to the sinking of the *Altalena* was told to the author by Jules Moch. Bidault had asked Moch to let the arms destined for the Irgun pass without informing the Jewish authorities. Moch, as Minister of Interior, did inform the Haganah, on the grounds that it was the organ of the official representatives of the Jewish government. This resulted in the seizure of the arms, a most significant contribution in the struggle to construct a national army in Israel out of the diverse and often competitive military organizations. The sinking of the *Altalena* helped David Ben Gurion effectively to eliminate the threat of a major dissident group.

war, albeit "not very effectively." [6] By a secret agreement in 1948, some rather ancient tanks and other relics
"of bygone days" were bought from France as part of a
trickle of weapons from diverse sources which reached
the Jewish forces as soon as the state was proclaimed.[7]

Despite these activities, the French attitude on the
Palestine issue at the United Nations was, according to
the Jewish representative Moshe Sharett (Shertok), "cold
and doubtful." [8] Only after much angry dissension
within foreign policy councils did France vote for the
partition resolution on November 29, 1947. In 1948,
while Jewish forces were fighting for survival and there
was little doubt weapons supplied to any Arab state
would find their way to the Arab armies attacking them,
there was some discussion in the French cabinet of
shipping arms to Lebanon. One member of the government who opposed the move leaked news of the secret
deliberations to Albert Stara of the Revisionist Organization, however, and he was then able to enlist
the press in a successful campaign to "postpone" the
arms shipments indefinitely.[9]

These seeming contradictions in French policy can
be explained largely by the difficulties that plagued
the government of the Fourth Republic: authority was
fragmented, responsibility diffused, and the execution of
policies was often sporadic, inconsistent, and hesitant.
Different, sometimes contradictory policies were pursued by various branches or levels of the hierarchy.

[6] Benjamin Kagan, *Combat Secret pour Israël* (Paris: Hachette,
1963), pp. 75, 204. No further details are offered by the author.

[7] Michael Bar-Zohar, *The Armed Prophet: A Biography of Ben
Gurion,* trans. by Len Ortzen (London: Barker, 1967), p. 139.

[8] Cited by Bar-Zohar, *Gesher,* pp. 25-26.

[9] Stara, interview cited.

Within the cabinet, each minister tended to treat his ministry as an independent domain, executing policies divergent from those of other cabinet members. Generally, the diplomatic branch of government was pitted against the Interior and Defense Ministries on the question of support for the Jewish State. When the issue reached the Prime Minister, it was usually decided in favor of Israel, as when Robert Schumann (1947-1948) saw to it that arms and volunteers reached Palestine.

More subtle factors were also at play. The policy of Georges Bidault, who was Minister of Foreign Affairs from the Liberation until mid-1948, except for one month, often diverged from that of his own ministry. Like many of his colleagues, Bidault was a discreet friend and supplier of arms to the Jewish cause, particularly through the Irgun, which was tied to the Revisionist Organization of France.[10] It seems unlikely, as has been suggested by Bar-Zohar, that Bidault was seeking only to protect Catholic institutions in Palestine by striking a bargain with the Irgun, a group which represented a secondary element in the Jewish underground.[11] His support of the more extreme terrorists, and hence the more anti-British group, was probably based on his hope of seeing leaders friendly to France and opposed to Britain established in Palestine. But such maneuvers had to be surreptitious and clandestine. On the surface, France was committed to its western allies and had no wish to defy openly the United States and Britain. Nor could it necessarily withstand pressure

[10] The Revisionists had close contacts with the *Ligue Française pour la Palestine Libre,* which included among its members René Capitant, Alfred Coste-Floret, Raymond Schmittlein, and Maurice Schumann.

[11] See *The Armed Prophet,* p. 142.

from them. The Corsican transit flights, for example, had been stopped at the United States' urging.[12]

Once Israel proclaimed its independence, France granted de jure recognition on May 21, 1949, only after Israel agreed to pay reparations for damages suffered by French religious establishments during the war and granted special status to French educational activities and interests in the holy places. According to a semi-official Israeli view put forward by Bar-Zohar, this delay resulted from Roman Catholic pressure: the leaders of the unstable French government were particularly sensitive to the position of the Church, which was "alarmed by the destruction and requisitioning of their mission stations in Palestine." [13] It is true that Georges Bidault did vote in the National Assembly against a Foreign Affairs Commission decision to recognize the Jewish State on January 1, 1949. Rather than attributing this to the influence of the Church, however, it is more likely that his attitude was due to the opposition of the North African territories. Bar-Zohar alludes to an unwritten agreement between Habib Bourguiba of Tunisia and the Queuille government (1948-1949). The alleged understanding guaranteed that the Arab countries would not attack France at the United Nations on the issue of independence for Tunisia and Morocco, so long as France delayed its recognition of Israel.[14]

France showed a similar reluctance to admit Israel to the United Nations. It also participated in the Palestine Conciliation Commission, which was generally sus-

---

[12] Jon & David Kimche, *Both Sides of the Hill. Britain and the Palestine War* (London: Secker & Warburg, 1960), p. 205.

[13] *The Armed Prophet,* pp. 155-156.

[14] *Gesher,* pp. 31-32.

pected in Israel of a pro-Arab bias.[15] On December 31,
1949, when Premier David Ben Gurion announced the
transfer of the state capital to Jerusalem, France placed
a motion of censure before the United Nations. While
Vatican influence may have made itself felt, it is more
likely that France was merely trying to protect one of its
historic interests in calling for the internationalization
of Jerusalem. Not until September 1952 did France
raise its legation in Israel to the embassy level.

Despite early unofficial arms aid in the late 1940s, and
a French loan to Israel in 1950, there was little willingness to treat Israel as a friend or ally during the years
in which tripartite consultation was strongest. In 1952,
however, Israel supported France in the United Nations
vote on the issue of self-determination for Tunisia and
Morocco. It may be that Israel simply feared any
worsening of relations with France. More likely, a
community of interests was developing between the two
countries in opposition to a British-animated Greater
Syria and an Anglo-American-managed Baghdad Pact
and in recognition of the mutual isolation of France in
international and Israel in regional politics.

French arms markets similarly began to open up to
Israel in the early 1950s. After the failure of peace
negotiations with the Arabs in 1949 and 1951, fighting
along the Jordanian border soon made it obvious to
Israelis that relations with London were bound to be
troublesome. An association with France, however, presented a more hopeful picture. Accordingly, Premier
David Ben Gurion's aides in the Ministry of Defense
began to look for key pressure points in the French

[15] Ben Halpern, *The Idea of the Jewish State* (Cambridge:
Harvard, 1961), p. 399.

military, political, and scientific establishments.[16] The segmented structure of the French government and the alienation of the military establishment facilitated their efforts.

Inertia, *immobilisme,* and caution characterized the successive governments of postwar France, partly as a result of proportional representation and a multiparty system based on undisciplined groupings without cohesion or power. Compromise coalitions faced a constant threat of disruption as each party, no one of which could hope to attain a majority or implement a program alone, pursued its own electoral interests in the hopes of a marginal advantage in its bargaining position. Since the perpetual coalitions obscured responsibility, change in government became an end in itself as ministers sought to further their own careers at their colleagues' expense. Frequent cabinet crises and the ambition for ministerial office stimulated further crises. Cabinet solidarity was thus practically nonexistent and with no basis of agreement among the parties, to stay in power coalitions avoided any contentious issues.

As for the vacillating indecisive National Assembly, it was rarely involved in actual policy decisions, supreme only in its ability to paralyze the executive and obstruct the government, reducing its power and preventing any strong exercise of authority. Little attention was given to foreign policy debates and even less to military expenditures, except during occasional moments of crisis and for treaty arrangements.

---

[16] Professor Ernst Bergmann, former Chairman of the National Committee for Space Research and head of the Defense Ministry Scientific Department, interviewed in Jerusalem, July 29, 1969. See also Peter Calvocoressi et. al., *Suez Ten Years After. Broadcasts from the BBC Third Programme* (Frome & London: Butler & Tanner, 1967), p. 59.

Nor did parliament fulfill its potential for effective criticism. While debate on budget matters and interpellations were devices for controlling the executive, they were used more to embarrass ministers and to stalemate the government than for positive action. Despite the constitutional provisions that no bill could be debated in the house before being discussed or reported by the committees, the latter were little more than institutional façades for interest groups, more often concerned with checking administrative abuses than in drafting legislation.

On the other hand, a cabinet minister was often able to treat his ministry as an independent domain. It was not uncommon for a minister to be at odds with his entire ministry, for each was a closed institution possessing a particular historical or partisan outlook. Socialist Christian Pineau, for example, found little support for his policies among the lower echelons of the Quai d'Orsay during his term as Foreign Minister from 1956 to 1958, and this was particularly true with regard to relations with Israel. There were also traditional rivalries between ministries, such as the enmity which existed between the high-spending Defense Ministry and the powerful inspectorate of the Finance Ministry. These rivalries touched even the fragmented and competitive security services that were attached to the different ministries. The SDECE (*Service de documentation extérieure et de contre-espionnage*), for example, was directly responsible to the Prime Minister.

Given parliamentary inertia, *immobilisme,* obstruction, the rapid succession of ministerial crises, and executive paralysis, technocrats and bureaucrats actually moved France. They not only made the countless daily decisions that gave policy its major direction but often devised constructive long-range policies which were then passed on to the politicians. Administrators could stop or sabotage laws through delays in drafting the decrees necessary for enforcement, or they would simply not implement a distasteful policy. Bureaucrats would often reopen policy debates after decisions had been reached, by judicious leakages of privileged information. In the case of the army and the overseas bureaucracies, policies were effectively imposed on the metropolitan government.

The immensely powerful civil service was by no means monolithic. Like other French institutions, the bureaucracy was fragmented by internal divisions and traditional rivalries among the competitive *grands corps* of the prestigious civil services. Since the *grands corps* drew their personnel from one of the *grandes écoles* directly controlled by the different ministries, old school ties further fragmented the bureaucracy. Many members of the *grands corps* were promoted or seconded to senior diplomatic posts or other public duties or, through the system of *pantouflage,* found their way into executive business positions. Their influence was considerable.

In addition to being attached to parliamentary committees, high civil servants increasingly staffed ministerial cabinets. Although designed to coordinate liaison among the directorates of the various ministries, the cabinets, whose members often pursued their minister's career goals, assumed tremendous importance by making ad hoc policy decisions. The head of a ministerial cabinet who followed his minister through various portfolios might acquire a great deal of power. For example, Abel Thomas, director of Maurice Bourgès-Maunoury's cabinet in the Defense and Interior Ministries, was a key man in the Fourth Republic. It was at this level of the bureaucracy that pressure could be most effectively exerted for the consideration of special interests, and Israeli leaders took the fullest advantage of openings for unorthodox diplomacy.

Many naval officers and members of the French Interior and Defense Ministries were anti-British and violently anti-Arab, especially those with Free French or Résistance backgrounds. They were sympathetic to the Israeli army, which had defeated both Arabs and British, and felt that the Israeli victory at Faluja had delayed the North African rebellion for almost ten years.[17]

Among Israel's friends were such highly regarded national leaders as Generals Pierre Koenig and Diomède Catroux, Jules Moch (who during his term as Defense Minister had helped Israel acquire 75 mm. guns), Edouard Depreux, Maurice Fischer, Pierre Gilbert (the French Ambassador to Israel from 1953-1959), and Paul Reynaud (who in 1954 helped overcome Quai d'Orsay opposition to the sale of 155 mm. guns to Israel). Among lower-level officers, one colonel, acting in an unofficial capacity, arranged for the transfer to Israel of one hundred reconditioned, obsolete Sherman tanks in 1955.[18] Other friendships were painstakingly cultivated as Israeli officers attended French staff schools, French officers lectured in Tel-Aviv, and naval ships exchanged courtesy calls. André Monteil recalled that in 1950-1951, the first French war matériel was sold to Israel, consisting of "a few PT boats." [19]

In 1950, when Colonel Benjamin Kagan sought jet

[17] Israel Ambassador to France Ya'akov Tsur (1953-1959), citing General Augustin Guillaume, Chief of the General Staff of the Armed Forces (1954-1956), interviewed in Jerusalem, August 13, 1969.

[18] Bar-Zohar, *Gesher,* pp. 75-76.

[19] André Monteil, Secretary of State for the Navy in the Pleven and Queuille governments (1950-1951), interviewed in Paris, June 20, 1969.

planes to shore up the Israel Air Force, his mission received unofficial cooperation and assistance from the French Air Force, Nord Aviation, and the Ministry of Defense, where Jules Moch was minister.[20] French Mosquitos originally acquired from Great Britain and a variety of old Messerschmidts were reconditioned and transferred to Israel.[21] Jacques Piette laughingly recalled that, in order to avoid difficulties with its tripartite allies, France concocted the unlikely story that the planes had been shipped from Israel to France for repairs.[22] In acquiring new jets, however, Israel encountered numerous difficulties. Although initially hesitant to buy French planes, the Israelis had few options. The Sud Aviation Mistral, a French variation of the Vampire, was eliminated because it was produced under British license and export was dependent upon British approval. The French Air Minister Diomède Catroux was willing to help and at first offered the Triton SO-6000. When that model was taken out of production, Catroux showed Kagan the Dassault Ouragan fighter-bomber in June 1950. With certain instrument changes, the Ouragan satisfied the Israel Air Force.

The Israelis reasoned that the French planes would be cheaper than an American equivalent designed for greater distances, that they would be sold without political strings attached, and that it would be simpler to deal

[20] Although the Prime Minister was specifically responsible for defense under the constitution, the power was often delegated to the Minister of Defense. Under Article 47, the Premier's decisions on defense matters required the countersignature of the Minister of Defense. Some ministers, like Jules Moch (July 1950-August 1951), managed to enjoy wide freedom of action.

[21] Kagan, *Combat Secret pour Israël*, pp. 229-235.

[22] Piette, President and Director-General of the *Société Nationale de Constructions Aéronautiques du Nord* (1951-1955), interviewed in Paris, June 6, 1969.

with the French bureaucracy. Moreover, the French offered complete instruction for pilots and maintenance crews. Catroux hoped that the sale of the Ouragan would inject fresh orders into the French aviation industry, which had been floundering since World War II, and was then working at only about thirty-five percent of capacity.[23] The Air Ministry's orders were too small to support the industry and, because of government instability, too subject to revision, postponement, and cancellation. France's colonial troubles limited both the markets and finances available, while the failure of the European Defense Community wrecked hopes for a European-scale industry or French-German integration. Overseas sales not only would prove the superiority of French wares to NATO members and offer an alternative to United States equipment, providing a source of needed dollar revenue, but might open up markets throughout Europe.[24]

The French military establishment, once its continuing need for conventional weapons became apparent, actively promoted arms sales as a means of supporting domestic, military industries and easing the balance of payments. Economies of scales were especially vital to the impoverished French military establishment, aspiring to independence after the war. This is not to suggest that economic arguments superseded political motives. As General Pierre Billotte pointed out, since the United States was aiding the reconstruction of the European aircraft and armored industries through NATO, "money was no object." [25] Independence was, and an overseas client would be able to in-

[23] *Idem;* see also *Time,* vol. 66 (July 18, 1955), pp. 90, 92.

[24] Max Lazega, "Quelques aspects de la politique israélienne," *Revue de Défense Nationale,* vol. 22 (July 1966), pp. 1031-1032.

[25] Interviewed in Paris, May 29, 1969.

fuse convertible currency into the industry's economy without any concomitant commitment to American policies.

In June 1952, a protocol with Israel was signed which covered three Nord-2500 transports and twenty-five Ouragans, costing between OF 2-3 million each (roughly $50,000-$70,000). Payment, according to terms fixed by the Finance Ministry, was to be in United States dollars, with approximately fifteen percent in advance. Although the number of planes to be purchased was insignificant out of a series of some two hundred, Israel was the first foreign client of the French air industry. Piette and other aviation officials saw this as France's first step toward becoming a major exporter of military equipment.[26]

Despite Defense Ministry interest in the sale, the French government officially refused to honor the June 1952 protocol and, on July 29, 1952, acquiesced to a negative tripartite decision. However, under the guise of the mutual defense system, Britain had already upset the Middle East arms balance of 1950 by lucrative sales of jets and other modern weapons to Egypt, Syria, Lebanon, Iraq, and Jordan. When the United Kingdom proceeded to offer Israel Gloster Meteors for 1953-1954 delivery, the French were rankled and intensified their efforts to sell military equipment to Israel.[27] With Israel spending between $50 million and $100 million a year from 1950 to 1955, France was losing an important arms market and possible source of hard currency for its struggling industries.[28] General Paul Stehlin has out-

[26] Interview cited.

[27] Kagan, *Combat Secret pour Israël,* pp. 236-247.

[28] Shim'on Peres, Director-General of the Ministry of Defense until 1959, Deputy Minister of Defense (1959-1965), interviewed

lined the new initiatives taken by the export office in
1953; the aircraft builders turned to the government to
eliminate customs duties on machines and materials
used in building airplanes, to grant long-term credits to
foreign purchasers of aircraft, and to simplify export
regulations.[29]

Israeli initiatives began to meet with increasing success. In order to overcome the Quai d'Orsay's reluctance
to approve the purchases under the 1952 protocol without tripartite agreement, and to placate Pierre Maillard
of the Levant desk, there was some juridical juggling.
With the support of the defense establishment, Maurice
Schumann, Secretary (or Minister) of State for Foreign
Affairs, and Paul Reynaud, President of the Finance
Commission, brought pressure to bear until the Quai
d'Orsay agreed that, if the tripartite powers did not
specifically express their disagreement with the sale,
France could deliver the planes. After more than two
years of negotiations the Ouragans (by then retired from
the French inventory) finally made their way to Israel.[30]

At the end of 1952, talks were under way for the sale
of AMX-13 light tanks from the nationally owned
Ateliers d'Issy-les-Moulineaux, and, according to an

in Tel-Aviv, July 31, 1969, put the figure at about $100 million
a year; Nadav Safran, *From War to War. The Arab-Israeli Confrontation, 1948-1967* (N.Y.: Pegasus, 1967), pp. 157-158, suggests
$87 million; Tsur, interview cited above, and General Pierre
Billotte, Minister of National Defense and the Armed Forces
(1955-1956), place the amount at between $50 and $100 million.
Interview cited.

[29] Paul Stehlin, Chief of the General Staff for the Air Force
(1960-1963), and Vice President of the Superior Council for the
Air Force (1962-1963), interviewed in Paris, June 28, 1969. See
also *Aviation Week and Space Technology* (AWST), vol. 59
(Nov. 23, 1953), p. 34.

[30] Piette, interview cited.

agreement signed in 1953, Israel began to receive
Howitzers and light arms at a cost of approximately $1
million.[31] Continued pressure was necessary to ensure
actual deliveries, however, until the tanks began arriving in 1954.[32]

Almost immediately upon his accreditation as Ambassador to Israel late in 1952, Pierre Gilbert had suggested to the Israel Ministry for Foreign Affairs that it
base its foreign policy on cooperation with France
against pan-Arabism. He received little encouragement
from Israeli diplomats, however. Moshe Sharett, in particular, could not envision France playing any role in
defense of Israel. The Israel Foreign Office was largely
"Anglo-Saxon" in orientation as a result of pre-independence experience; French diplomats complained of
the "typical British coolness and snobbery" of Israeli
officials, most of whom were either of British background or education or had served in the British administration of Palestine. Diplomatic relations with
France, meanwhile, were hampered by Israeli actions
against French missions, the transfer of the capital to
Jerusalem, Arab pressures, a lack of Israeli interest in
French culture and limited scope for a French economic
presence. Undaunted, Gilbert turned instead to the
Israeli Defense Ministry, where officials, needing a
source of weapons supply, listened closely.[33] Gilbert
pointed out that regular diplomatic channels were likely
to be closed to Israel and suggested instead that Israel

[31] Shim'on Peres, *David's Sling. The Arming of Israel* (London:
Weidenfeld & Nicolson, 1970), p. 51; and Bar-Zohar, *Gesher*,
p. 59.

[32] Tsur, interview cited.

[33] French Ambassador to Israel Pierre Gilbert (1953-1959), interviewed in Paris, June 11, 1969.

pursue relations with the French defense establishment directly. Shim'on Peres, Director-General of the Defense Ministry, championed this idea, despite Foreign Office reluctance to engage in unorthodox diplomacy.[34] It was largely because of Peres' insistence that Israel opted for French weapons rather than following the tortuous path of endless negotiations for American arms. After seeking Ben Gurion's approval (although he was in retirement), and apparently with little reference to Defense Minister Pinhas Lavon, Peres and Gilbert met and planned General Moshe Dayan's 1954 visit to Paris.[35]

In late July 1954, Israel Chief of Staff Dayan was invited to Paris on an official visit by General Augustin Guillaume, French Chief of Staff (1954-1956). Overriding the opposition from the Quai d'Orsay, Guillaume promised Dayan bazookas and introduced him to Generals Pierre Koenig and André Zeller, who were later to figure prominently in the Israel alliance.[36] After lengthy secret talks, a formal agreement in principle was signed early in August by Air Minister Diomède Catroux and Shim'on Peres, with the full accord of Premier Mendès-France (June 1954-February 1955). Israel was to purchase Ouragan fighters, Mystère IIs, with an option on twelve Mystère IVs, AMX tanks, radar equipment, 75 mm. cannon, anti-tank missiles and other weapons. The arms purchases were kept secret

[34] Peres, interview cited.

[35] Bar-Zohar, *Gesher,* p. 61; in *The Armed Prophet,* p. 191, Bar-Zohar notes that Lavon's suspicious attitude brought to the brink of rupture the first negotiations with France for the purchase of tanks.

[36] General Augustin Guillaume, correspondence with the author, June 23, 1969.

until April 1956.[37] Although Ben Gurion instructed Peres always to inform the Foreign Minister of his actions, there is evidence that the Foreign Office increasingly was left in complete ignorance of the arms mission's activities.[38] Its officials were often irritated to see the Defense Ministry's representatives engaging in direct diplomacy as they negotiated with the French for the purchase of equipment.

Relatively little matériel actually passed into Israel's hands before 1954—some tanks, cannon and surplus World War II planes worth a total of no more than about $5 million, according to Peres.[39] Yet in 1954 the French attitude changed. Many French officials later justified their willingness to arm Israel by referring to the Algerian rebellion. General Guillaume, for example, said that the decision to arm Israel in 1954 was taken as part of the fight against 'Abd al-Nasir and the Algerian rebels.[40] Yet given the fact that France had agreed to open negotiations between one and two years before the Algerian rebellion began, Algeria alone could not have been the sole rationale. Moreover, most French leaders at first were relatively unconcerned about the revolt. "We thought it would be quickly suppressed, like the Constantine rebellion of 1945," said former SDECE Director-General Paul Grossin. "It was only

[37] Merry & Serge Bromberger, *Les Secrets de l'expédition d'Egypte* (Paris: Aymon, 1957), p. 46; Simha Flapan, "Swords Across the Sea," *Atlas,* vol. 8 (Sept. 1964), p. 85; E. B. Childers, *The Road to Suez: A Study of Western-Arab Relations,* 2nd ed. (London: MacGibbon & Kee, 1966), p. 172; and J.-R. Tournoux, *Secrets d'état* (Paris: Plon, 1960), p. 158, note 2.

[38] Premier David Ben Gurion, interviewed in Tel-Aviv, July 30, 1969.

[39] Interview cited.

[40] Correspondence cited.

toward the end of 1955 that we realized it could not be put down by local authorities." [41]

In all likelihood, a whole range of emotional factors, including shame at France's decreasing role in postwar regional and international developments, were at play in the defense establishment's willingness to supply Israel with arms. Ever since the debacle of Vichy during World War II, the command structure and almost the entire armed forces of France had felt themselves at variance with the civilian leadership and alienated from political and social institutions. In order to "save France," they had been led to rebel against the system in 1940 and were to rebel against it again in 1958, and in 1960. Often directly opposed to the foreign policy of the Quai d'Orsay and increasingly disillusioned by the civilian leadership, they worked for a European defense community and the rearmament of France within that wider framework, only to see the diplomats nullify their efforts. They won France's colonial wars on the battlefield, only to see their victories frittered away at the conference table by diplomatic defeats.

With other like-minded individuals, this group defended the interests of the armed forces whenever they were challenged. Eventually, they developed the *guerre révolutionnaire* school of thought—the official doctrine of the French army and the pattern of action for Algeria which had grown out of the defeat in Indochina. They would see Middle East developments as a Communist phenomenon, assume that Arab nationalism was Com-

[41] General Paul Grossin, attached to Prime Minister Guy Mollet (1956-1957); Director-General of the *Service de documentation extérieure et de contre-espionnage* (SDECE) (1957-1962); member of the Superior War Council (1957), interviewed in Paris, June 25, 1969.

munist subversion in another guise, and believe that the
Algerian war, the Suez invasion, and support for Israel
were integral to a global crusade against Communism.
Some were Gaullists, while almost all tended to be activists and, as such, were particularly in tune with
Israel's philosophy of political behavior and active
military defense.

Most important, the military were the first to recognize Israel's potential as a balancer of power in the
Middle East and to regard the military establishment of
Israel as a future ally, an instrument for remote control
in the area. It should not be forgotten that at this
juncture practically all the weapons sold Israel would
have had to come from the French army's own stockpile. Only much later was Israel permitted the luxury
of ordering merchandise from the drawing-boards.

In advocating an Israel-Arab arms balance that would
guarantee Israel's security, the military often found itself at odds with the diplomatic corps, which brandished
the specter of the Tripartite Declaration whenever the
question of arms for Israel was discussed, pursued the
traditional policy of friendship with the Arab world,
and held up export licenses long after decisions to arm
Israel were reached.[42] The diplomatic branch of government was slower to realize the possibilities inherent in
such a relationship and slower to relinquish traditional
ideas in favor of this uncommon diplomacy. Their
main concern was to preserve French ties with the Arab
world, especially with Syria. Bar Zohar describes French
insistence that AMX tanks sent to Israel be used only in
the Negev, i.e. against Egypt, and not against Syria.[43]

[42] General Paul Ely, Chief of Staff, President of the Committee
of Chiefs of Staff (1954-1955), interviewed in Paris, June 5, 1969.
[43] Bar-Zohar, *Gesher,* p. 43.

After 1953 Quai d'Orsay acceptance of Israel eased as Egypt, not Syria, became Israel's main enemy.

Arms questions were decided by an interministerial committee composed of at most four or five key ministers and the Chiefs of Staff. Where there was conflict or disagreement, the rival ministers, with the aid of the bureaucrats, could circumvent the dissenters often without recourse to a decision at the Prime Minister's level. Maurice Bourgès-Maunoury wielded considerable influence on the committee as Minister of Interior in 1955 and was able not only to supply Israel with arms but to divert a shipment of tanks destined for Egypt.

It is hardly a coincidence that Bourgès-Maunoury and his *chef de cabinet,* Abel Thomas, were the two men who did most to arm and otherwise support Israel within the French government. As graduates of the *Ecole Polytechnique* which traditionally produced many of France's military and civil engineers, and as former *Résistants,* they both had close ties to the armed forces which were reinforced by long tenure in defense posts. An unofficial Israeli source has stated that,

> Since 1955 there was something in France which was called "The Club" and which was composed of some Ministries which were in very close touch with anything which was connected with Algeria. There were also some generals, and some military people, in this Club, and they were sure that Egypt was the main force behind the rebels. They came to the Israelis and asked them to create special relations between themselves and this French Club, whose common enemy they pretended was Nasser. I may add to this: some members of this Club were members of the French government, as a matter of fact.[44]

[44] Michael Bar-Zohar, cited in Calvocoressi et. al., *Suez Ten Years After,* p. 60.

It was the segmentation and fragmentation of the internally weak Fourth Republic which permitted Israel to capitalize on the reservoir of pro-Jewish sentiment that existed in France. With the executive paralyzed by a domineering legislature, which was in turn immobilized by its own failings, there was widespread freedom of action at various levels in the bureaucracy. This enabled a relatively small group of individuals in the defense establishment and related ministries to cooperate intimately with Israel without any formal arrangement, sometimes in opposition to official government policy. Acting independently and often autonomously, they were in essence conducting their own foreign relations directly with the Israel Defense Ministry. It was this group which created what amounted to an alliance between war ministries that was already taking shape as early as 1954.

III

Forging the Alliance

THE NATURE of government under the Fourth Republic had enabled influential French politicians in the defense establishment to strengthen Israel in accordance with their own view of Middle East necessities. When the Suez crisis developed, its most profound effect was to transform the special relationship between France and Israel into official policy. What had begun as a series of informal, unofficial, and unorthodox contacts, ripened into a full military alliance as Israel's strongly centralized leadership asserted its policy of active defense. Of course, at no time was it a question of a formal state-to-state alliance. Nonetheless, commitments were made so that a durable entente emerged from Suez to replace the earlier amorphous system of ties.

Although ostensibly governed by a multiparty system based on proportional representation, Israel experienced little of the instability evident in France after World War II. The Israel Labor Party (*Mapai*), with David Ben Gurion at its head, dominated a series of cohesive coalitions after the formation of the first cabinet in 1949 and, despite concessions exacted by its coalition partners, remained to all intents and purposes the governing party. Stability was built into the system, for majority rule and collective responsibility obligated ministers and deputies belonging to the coalition parties to vote for government policy. Moreover, turnover in cabinet personnel was limited: some fifty people filled the 275 incumbencies in nineteen years and fifteen governments.

Until June 1967, except for one brief period from 1953 to 1955, the Prime Minister headed the Defense Ministry in successive governments, on the assumption that its activities were so ramified that only he was in a position to coordinate them. There is actually no legal framework for civilian control of the military in Israel, although all proposed legislation must have cabinet approval. By law, the Defense Minister is commander-in-chief of the armed forces and is not required to consult with the cabinet or to obtain parliamentary approval for major policy decisions. Even such serious matters as mobilizing the reserves must merely be brought to the attention of the Kneset (Israel parliament) Foreign Affairs and Security Committee, which can confirm the mobilization order or not within fourteen days.[1] The committee, whose deliberations are not made public, has usually served as little more than a rubber stamp for actions already initiated by the Defense Minister and has rarely functioned as a controlling or decision-making body. Moreover, the budget of the ministry does not go to the floor of the Kneset but is dealt with in the Foreign Affairs and Security Committee. Since the budget must have the approval of the Minister of Finance, however, budgetary control can be used to supervise the spending of the military establishment and indirectly to influence defense policy.

[1] See J. C. Hurewitz, "The Role of the Military in Society and Government in Israel," *The Military in the Middle East. Problems in Society and Government,* Sydney Nettleton Fisher, ed. (Columbus: Ohio, 1963), pp. 89-104; and Asher Zidon, *Kneset. The Parliament of Israel,* trans. by Aryeh Rubinstein & Gertrude Hirschler (N.Y.: Herzl, 1967), p. 209.

In order to consolidate his power and to establish his primacy in defense matters, Ben Gurion had immediately sought to create a national defense establishment out of the diverse military units that had fought the war of independence. Purging the army of men, practices, and cliques that stood in the way of creating a professional officer corps, he allocated key functions to his supporters and placed them under his direct supervision. Widely respected for his expertise in military matters, Ben Gurion made all the supreme political decisions on defense from 1948 to 1963. Consulting only a few key personal advisers, he often failed to inform the party and the cabinet on military policy, and, when they expressed disagreement, he simply overruled them. Ben Gurion would argue that the key to safeguarding Israel's security lay in decisive leadership. Daily operational direction of *Zahal* (Israel Defense Forces) was left to its commanders, and, since he shared a very close personal relationship with the Chief of Staff and senior officers, they tended to reflect Ben Gurion's views closely.

In view of Israel's precarious security situation, military policy to a large extent determined foreign policy. By the early 1950s, when peace negotiations had failed and strategic thinking was forced to cope with the reality of Arab encirclement, Ben Gurion had become the undisputed champion of the reprisal policy advocated by the young, chauvinistic, tough-minded *sabra* (native-born) leadership in the army. Foremost among those who called for relentless activism in dealing with Arab guerrilla attacks, he was often opposed by Moshe Sharett and the Foreign Office. Sharett tended to conceive of Israel diplomacy as a passive, powerless diplomacy and, rejecting force, he sought security through great power guarantees.

Aware that he was losing his struggle for control of defense policy when the Qibya reprisal raid of October 1953 evoked bitter debate, Ben Gurion retired in December. First, however, he assured cabinet approval for his security program. Pinhas Lavon became Minister of Defense, Moshe Dayan was Chief of Staff, and Shim'on Peres, Director-General of the Ministry of Defense. Dayan and Peres often acted independently of Lavon, partly as a result of habits acquired during Ben Gurion's tenure and partly in order to fend off reforms that threatened the division of labor Ben Gurion had established between the army and the Defense Ministry. Although the relationship between the army and the ministry had been ill-defined in the first years of statehood, General Dayan had relieved the army of administrative and logistical duties and separated it from the armament industries, in order to strengthen its role as a swift and highly mobile strike force. The ministry assumed control over supply and manufacture of armaments, and, except for highest policy decisions, Ben Gurion generally had left its administration to the Director-General.

Undoubtedly Peres and Dayan were also concerned about the deteriorating security situation. Lavon often moved independently of the cabinet in his attempts to follow Ben Gurion's example and to assume full responsibility for military policy-making. His pride in being more activist than Ben Gurion led to the naïve attempt to secure passage for the *Bat Galim* through the Suez Canal and the disastrous plot to blow up the American information office in Cairo, which resulted in the discovery and capture of an Israeli spy network in Egypt on October 1, 1954. Both events upset the unofficial balance of functions between army and ministry and stirred up a hornets' nest that later rocked the Israel government as the "Lavon affair." As Lavon, Dayan, Peres, and the army struggled for power, Prime Minister Moshe Sharett and Walter Eytan of the Foreign Ministry exercised less and less control over foreign policy.[2]

Lavon suddenly resigned and Ben Gurion returned to the Defense Ministry on February 17, 1955. While retaliation continued to be the major approach to the military situation, strict supervision by senior officers was imposed on all operations, curtailing responsibility previously held by middle and junior-level officers. This enabled Ben Gurion to coordinate reprisals such as the February 28 raid against Gaza within the framework of larger policy goals.

Ben Gurion immediately began to strengthen the army in preparation for a second round with the Arabs by acquiring desperately needed armored and aerial equipment. To fend off any motorized breakthrough across Israel's narrow neck would require a strategy based on an anticipatory attack or a counteroffensive by mobile armored columns. Speed and mobility on the ground would require air power, and to control the skies, Israel would have to acquire planes capable of preemptive strikes at Arab airfields. Ben Gurion also decided to expand the Defense Ministry's scientific efforts and armament industries and to develop a nuclear

[2] On this period and the Lavon affair, see my M.A. thesis, Columbia University, 1961, "The Influence of the Military Establishment on Israeli Politics"; and Amos Perlmutter, "The Institutionalization of Civil-Military Relations in Israel: The Ben Gurion Legacy and its Challengers (1953-1967)," *The Middle East Journal,* vol. 22, no. 4 (1968), pp. 415-432. See also Jon Kimche, "La politique extérieure d'Israël," *Evidences,* vol. 6, no. 45 (1955), pp. 3ff.

option as a deterrent to Arab aggression. The ministry acquired enormous influence as it came to control production of military equipment for Zahal, as well as the scientific research conducted by the Atomic Energy Commission.

Ben Gurion deliberately set out to consolidate ties with France—heretofore Israel's only major supplier of modern weaponry and the center for scientific training for Israel's nuclear researchers. As early as January 1955, there had been signs that the pace of the rapprochement between the two states was accelerating. Secretary of State for Air Diomède Catroux confirmed French willingness to sell the Mystère IV to Israel, despite British arguments that the transonic jet was more advanced than any plane in the inventories of Israel's immediate neighbors. Preliminary accords were also to be signed for the Vautour bomber, plans for which were entering the final stages. Toward the end of the month, European press reports of a growing "military alliance" between France and Israel were lent credence by Israel's denunciation of the Baghdad Pact and the mild French reaction to Israel's offensive in Gaza: the French argued that the Baghdad Pact had upset the military balance in the region, forcing Israel to adopt a policy of aggressive defense.[3]

Upon his return to the Defense Ministry in February, Ben Gurion wrote directly to General Pierre Koenig, Edgar Faure's Minister of Defense, explaining his decision to adopt French equipment in the armed forces and outlining Israel's weapons needs.[4] In April 1955,

---

[3] See Ya'akov Tsur, *Prélude à Suez: journal d'une ambassade, 1953-1956* (Paris: Cité, 1966), p. 150.

[4] *State of Israel Government Yearbook 5716 (1955)*, p. 189; and Michael Bar-Zohar, *Gesher 'al ha-Yam ha-Tikhon. Yahasei Tsarfat-*

the sale of the Mystères was approved.[5] When Shim'on Peres arrived in Paris in May with new requests for arms, he found that Yosef Nahmias of the arms purchasing mission had already made friendly contacts with Abel Thomas and Louis Mangin of Interior Minister Bourgès-Maunoury's cabinet. Probably as a result of their considerable pressure, in June the Council of Ministers decided to accede to Israel's requests. The fact that negotiations were simultaneously underway for a considerable arms sale to Egypt undoubtedly strengthened Israel's bargaining position.

Abel Thomas has explained that Bourgès was not alone among Frenchmen in fearing that any arms shipped Egypt would eventually find their way to the Algerian rebels. A consignment of 100 AMX tanks and 75 mm. guns due to leave Marseilles in September as part of a larger Egyptian order awaited certificates of embarkation from the local prefect. Under Bourgès' orders, the prefect, who was responsible to the Ministry of Interior, returned the tanks to Paris. When Foreign Minister Antoine Pinay strenuously objected to the Interior Ministry's actions, Prime Minister Edgar Faure (February 1955-February 1956), left it to his ministers to find a "just solution." With the collaboration of Minister of Defense General Pierre Koenig, Bourgès-Maunoury informed the Council of Ministers that, if Egypt was to be armed, arms would have to be sent to Israel as well. Faure acquiesced, finding this solution "relatively just."[6]

Israel, 1947-1963 (Bridge over the Mediterranean. France-Israel Relations, 1947-1963; Tel-Aviv: 'Am ha-Sefer, 1964), p. 65.

[5] Tsur, *Prélude à Suez*, pp. 195, 210ff.

[6] Abel Thomas, then Deputy Director of the cabinet of Interior Minister Bourgès-Maunoury, interviewed in Paris, July 3, 1969.

In fact, France was already manifesting increasing reluctance to complete the proposed Egyptian arms deal. French relations with Egypt deteriorated rapidly in the face of daily vituperative anti-French broadcasts of Radio Cairo which were caused in part by the Egyptian belief that Israeli reprisals were French-inspired.[7]

There is some evidence that certain members of the French government found increasingly attractive the idea that France might support an Israeli strike against Gamal 'Abd al-Nasir. Israeli intelligence services were well informed on events in Algeria even before 1953 and had begun to work very closely with the French services in 1954. They supplied the French with convincing proof about the origins of the Algerian rebellion, its financing—often through illicit counterfeiting operations—Egyptian arms supplies and European arms purchases destined for the FLN (National Liberation Front).[8] There is little doubt the Israelis purposely fanned French fears of 'Abd al-Nasir's involvement in Algeria and stressed his ambitions elsewhere in the Middle East and sub-Saharan Africa in order to increase French willingness to cooperate with Israel.

See also Tsur, *Prélude à Suez*, pp. 210ff. For another version, see Kennett Love, *Suez: The Twice-Fought War. A History* (N.Y.: McGraw Hill, 1969), p. 98.

[7] See 'Abd al-Nasir in Peter Calvocoressi et al., *Suez Ten Years After. Broadcasts from the BBC Third Programme* (London & Frome: Butler & Tanner, 1967), p. 38; and Henri Azeau, *Le Piège de Suez (5 novembre 1956)* (Paris: Laffont, 1964), p. 91.

[8] General Paul Grossin, attached to Prime Minister Guy Mollet (1956-1957); Director-General of the *Service de documentation extérieure et de contre-espionnage* (SDECE) (1957-1962); member of the Superior War Council (1957), interviewed in Paris, June 25, 1969; and Zvi Dar of the Israel Defense Ministry, interviewed in New York City, May 2, 1969.

The opinion of Robert Lacoste, who later supported the Suez invasion with the comment that "One French division in Egypt is worth four divisions in North Africa," was typical of French governing circles.[9] It is possible that anti-Nasir rhetoric was merely a means of rallying domestic support for the government and to excuse the failure of the military to quell the rebellion. Egypt, as a matter of fact, ranked only seventh or eighth in amount of aid to Algeria. Although more arms were being supplied the rebels via Spanish Morocco and Libya than via Cairo, no one suggested invading these territories.[10] Whatever 'Abd al-Nasir's actual role, government officials saw him as their nemesis and suspected his influence whenever the Middle East erupted, whether in Libya, Lebanon, Jordan, or Iraq.

Additional pressure was provided by reports of Soviet intentions to furnish Egypt with a large quantity of arms. Such reports had appeared in the Hebrew-language press as early as August 28, 1955. It is quite possible that Israeli intelligence knew of 'Abd al-Nasir's negotiations with the Russians shortly after they were initiated in February, and had probably passed this information on to the French soon after.[11] 'Abd al-Nasir later claimed that intercepted documents detailing the 1954 France-Israel arms agreement caused him to initiate arms negotiations with "Czechoslavakia" in June 1955.[12]

[9] Merry & Serge Bromberger, *Les Secrets de l'expédition d'Egypte* (Paris: Aymon, 1957), p. 69.

[10] See Azeau, *Le Piège de Suez,* p. 160; and *New York Times,* March 6, 1956.

[11] See *Ha-Arets* and *Ma'ariv,* August 28-31, 1955; and Simha Flapan, "Swords Across the Sea," *Atlas,* vol. 8 (Sept. 1964), p. 87.

[12] 'Abd al-Nasir's secret document was in effect the May 1955 issue of the *Bulletin* of the *Centre d'Information du Proche*

On July 20, Israel requested 24 Mystère IVs, instead of the Mystère IIs ordered earlier, and contracted for more Ouragans, tanks, and cannon.[13] "Informed but unofficial quarters" cited in the *New York Times* on August 3, 1955, denied that the planes would be delivered since the Mystères had been a bone of contention between Paris and London for more than a year. However, there was little doubt among the French leaders at this juncture that France should supply Israel with more arms and at a faster pace, despite some disagreement as to the actual degree of threat to Israel implied in the Soviet arms agreement.

The decisive proportions of the Soviet deliveries to Egypt disturbed Israel, just as its source worried France. Apart from the sheer qualitative and quantitative upsurge in the arms race, 'Abd al-Nasir might have been tempted to dump his obsolete equipment in Algeria.[14] After the signing of a military alliance between Egypt

---

Orient, written by Edouard Sablier. According to *Le Monde,* October 11, 1955, the semi-official account reported only twenty tanks sold as replacements and fifty-five Sherman tanks sold to an unnamed French firm and reexported to Israel. See p. 39 above. This story loses credibility when compared with an interview 'Abd al-Nasir gave *Life* magazine, vol. 39, no. 20 (Nov. 14, 1955), pp. 127-130. His list matched details which were generally admitted after Suez and is similar to Michael Bar-Zohar's semi-official account in *Gesher,* p. 66: 70 Mystères, 100 tanks, 100 heavy 155 mm. guns, 150 high velocity 75 mm. tank guns. On the alleged documents, see E. B. Childers, *The Road to Suez: A Study of Western-Arab Relations* (London: MacGibbon & Kee, 1959), pp. 133-135; *New York Times,* Oct. 6, 1966; *Times* (London), Oct. 5, 6, 1955.

[13] Bar-Zohar, *Gesher,* p. 87; confirmed by Benjamin Kagan, *Combat Secret pour Israël* (Paris: Hachette, 1963), p. 262.

[14] See Nadav Safran, *From War to War. The Arab-Israeli Confrontation, 1948-1967* (N.Y.: Pegasus, 1967), pp. 50-51.

and Syria on October 19, 1955, Israel was menaced with Soviet arms both in the north and in the south. These developments enabled Peres and Sharett to bring their efforts to a successful conclusion in October.[15]

Following Peres' first meeting with Interior Minister Maurice Bourgès-Maunoury in October, the recently appointed Minister of Defense General Pierre Billotte offered to sell Israel at cost the tanks, artillery, and Mystère IVs needed to maintain Middle East "equilibrium." Billotte later explained that he, Foreign Minister Antoine Pinay, and Prime Minister Edgar Faure, the key members of the cabinet, had been able to overcome Quai d'Orsay resistance to the sale by pointing out that the matériel was being sold for much-needed convertible currency. They were aided by the acquiescence of Deputy Minister of Defense Jean Crouzier, who was in charge of arms sales, and military officers who might otherwise have been reluctant to share their new equipment. Moreover, as Billotte argued, there was no intention of rearming Israel, merely a desire to guard the status quo.[16]

General Dayan reports that on October 22, 1955, he was recalled from a vacation in France and instructed to plan a campaign against Egypt to capture the Strait of Tiran, Sharm al-Shaykh, Ras Nasrani, and the islands of Tiran and Sanafir. The objective was to break the Egyptian blockade and guarantee Israel free navigation in the Gulf of 'Aqabah. Ben Gurion failed to receive

[15] David Ben Gurion, "Israel's Security and Her International Position. Before and After the Sinai Campaign," *State of Israel Government Yearbook 5720 (1959/1960)*, p. 25. See also Moshe Dayan, *Diary of the Sinai Campaign* (N.Y.: Harper & Row, 1965), p. 4; and Kagan, *Combat Secret pour Israël*, pp. 264ff.

[16] General Pierre Billotte, interviewed in Paris, May 29, 1969. See also *Davar ha-Shavuah*, April 19, 1961, pp. 12-13.

cabinet approval for the plan, however, despite Dayan's evaluation that immediate action was imperative since delay would enable Egypt to absorb its new Soviet equipment.[17] From the little evidence available, it seems that the French military establishment, while not actually involved in these early strategic moves, was nonetheless kept informed as Israeli planning evolved.

On November 3, Ben Gurion resumed the premiership and launched a raid to secure the al-'Awja triangle, strategically located on the invasion routes to Egypt across the Sinai Peninsula.[18] The fact that these reprisal raids coincided with Foreign Minister Moshe Sharett's arms missions to Paris and Washington riled the Quai d'Orsay and was acutely embarrassing to Sharett. The lack of coordination between the Defense and Foreign Ministries was clear. Sharett's reluctance to countenance the policy of preemptive war toward which Israel was obviously moving led to his eventual replacement as Foreign Minister by Golda Meir in mid-June 1956.

A contract was signed on November 12, 1955, for the delivery of twelve Ouragans, but the fall of the Faure government on the 29th and subsequent cabinet changes delayed formalization of the October agreement until

[17] Dayan, *Diary,* pp. 13-15. Note also Menahem Begin's call for preventive war, State of Israel, *Divrei ha-Kneset,* 3rd Kneset, 1st sess., 19th mtg., Nov. 2, 1955, pp. 235-236.

[18] Childers argues that this proves Israel's expansionist aims in Sinai but overstates his case, relying too heavily on the "Meinertzhagen memo" of November 2, 1955. See Colonel Richard Meinertzhagen, *Middle East Diary 1917-1956* (London: Cresset, 1959), pp. 277-278, a biased pro-Israel account by an English non-Jew, who makes little attempt to disguise his intolerance for the Arabs. See also Terence Robertson, *Crisis. The Inside Story of the Suez Conspiracy* (N.Y.: Atheneum, 1965), pp. 8, 12.

the beginning of 1956. Actual delivery was further stalled by the Quai d'Orsay's reluctance to implement the sale. The latter reportedly had promised arms to 'Abd al-Nasir if Cairo's Voice of the Arabs ceased attacking French policy in Algeria.[19] The Quai was particularly irritated at Israel's indiscrete publicizing of earlier French arms sales, which had compounded French difficulties in the Arab world. France, they said, had always "scrupulously" obeyed the terms of the 1950 Tripartite Declaration.[20] The Quai was also intensely annoyed at Israel's propaganda program in the fall of 1955 which encouraged Jewish emigration from the soon-to-be independent North African territories. This contradicted French efforts to have the Jewish population remain as a stabilizing and pro-French element.[21]

Finally, there was the question of United States approval. Since the Mystère was being manufactured for NATO under offshore procurement agreements, France would theoretically not be free to sell it elsewhere until July 1956, when NATO production was scheduled for completion.[22] Until then, the negotiations were apparently stymied without United States approval. Moreover, the Mystère could not reach Israel surreptitiously, for the granting of landing rights en route was subject to American pressure. General Billotte claims to have offered to intercede with John Foster Dulles, but, he

[19] Hugh Thomas, *The Suez Affair* (Liverpool: Weidenfeld & Nicolson, 1967), pp. 16-17; Michael Bar-Zohar, *The Armed Prophet; A Biography of Ben Gurion,* trans. by Len Ortzen (London: Barker, 1967), pp. 204-205; and *Daily Telegraph,* Nov. 12, 1955.

[20] *Le Monde,* Oct. 11, 1955.

[21] *Ibid.,* Sept. 15, 1955.

[22] See Tsur, *Prélude à Suez,* pp. 271-282; 302-303.

said, the Israelis convinced him that it was futile to depend upon official American channels.[23]

Guy Mollet's government came into power in February 1956 with widespread support for a new policy of conciliation in Algeria. But on February 6, while in Algeria to install the new, liberal Resident Minister General Georges Catroux, Mollet saw his hopes for conciliation dashed when an enraged mob of *colons* demonstrated against his policies. He replaced Catroux with Robert Lacoste, a tough, independent proponent of *Algérie Française,* and committed himself to a military solution of France's Middle East problems.

In one of his first statements on the Middle East on January 31, 1956, Mollet had declared that he was opposed to any territorial concessions by Israel and intended to continue arms deliveries in order to ensure regional equilibrium. While no definite timetable for joint action against 'Abd al-Nasir had yet been established, the French defense establishment demonstrated its willingness to modernize the Israel armed forces as rapidly as possible.[24] Bourgès-Maunoury, the new Defense Minister, and Foreign Minister Christian Pineau met with Shim'on Peres at the end of January. As a result of that meeting, during the February tripartite sessions in Washington, Pineau tried to obtain American agreement for the transfer to Israel of twenty-four

[23] Billotte, interview cited. See also André Fontaine, "Il y a dix ans la Guerre de Suez," *Le Monde,* Oct. 30-31, Nov. 1, 1966.

[24] There is no evidence to substantiate the claim of *Akhbar al-Yawm* on March 11, 1956, cited in *Le Monde,* Oct. 30-31, 1966, that Eden, Mollet, and Ben Gurion had planned to attack Egypt but delayed in order to modernize Israeli forces. The idea of acting in concert did not crystalize for several months. See below, pp. 66ff.

Mystères manufactured under the offshore procurement financing arrangements.[25]

On March 7, 1956, the *New York Times* reported that Israel had ordered Nord anti-tank guided missiles from France, in addition to some two hundred radio-guidance devices for anti-tank shells.[26] Meanwhile, Pineau, in Cairo, continued to press 'Abd al-Nasir for some moderate reassurances. Unless Pineau was totally unaware of the Defense Ministry's growing commitment to Israel, his actions can only be interpreted as a final attempt at conciliation.[27] Any hopes for moderation were soon dispelled, however, when violent anti-French outbursts from Egypt attended the arrival in Israel on April 11, 1956, of the first eight Mystère IVs, which had been sold with Washington's approval. Four more were expected shortly. In May, at the Paris NATO Council meeting, the Americans approved the further diversion of Mystères from NATO production and urged Canada to accede to Israel's arms requests. Israel was simultaneously negotiating for forty jets and thirty Centurion tanks from Great Britain. Throughout the spring there were several secret meetings among Dayan, Peres, Thomas, Mangin, and Bourgès. Thomas laughingly recalls that, despite extremely complex security precautions to guard the complete secrecy of the meetings, news of Dayan's presence in Paris was leaked by the press. It seems there was another one-eyed man in the

[25] See Robertson, *Crisis,* p. 49; see also *Le Monde,* March 1, 1956; and Bar-Zohar, *Gesher,* p. 97.

[26] See also *New York Herald Tribune,* May 14, 1957; Bromberger, *Les Secrets,* p. 99.

[27] See *Journal Officiel de la République Française. Débats Parlementaires. Assemblée Nationale. Compte Rendu,* Aug. 3, 1956, p. 2869.

city who inconveniently sported a black patch identical to Dayan's.[28]

Shim'on Peres recalls that he first learned of the "serious possibility" of joint Anglo-French action in May.[29] According to Thomas and Louis Mangin, in June the idea began to crystallize within the French government that France should not only arm but act in concert with Israel. On the 17th, Dayan, Peres, General Gaston Lavaud, Mangin, and members of the secret service met, later informing Guy Mollet and Christian Pineau of the discussions. Louis Mangin has described the Israelis' reaction to the news that France was now disposed to provide them with whatever they needed.

> I wish . . . to note that at no point during the period when M. Bourgès-Maunoury was involved, did the Franco-Israeli relations take on the form of a "give and take." During the meetings of June 1956, after the problems of arms and matériel requested were regulated by the Israelis, Moshe Dayan turned to us and asked, "What do you want from us in exchange?" We replied to him that there was nothing. He could not hide a certain astonishment.[30]

The negotiations and commitments which preceded the Suez invasion and Sinai campaign present real difficulties to any interpreter. Many of the published first-hand accounts are incomplete and conflicting, since the French negotiations with Britain and Israel were pursued independently of each other. Much of the litera-

[28] Abel Thomas, Director of the cabinet of Defense Minister Bourgès-Maunoury (1956-1957), interview cited.
[29] See Shim'on Peres, *David's Sling. The Arming of Israel* (London: Weidenfeld & Nicolson, 1970), pp. 185ff.
[30] Louis Mangin, member of the cabinet of the Minister of Defense (1956-1960), correspondence with the author, July 2, 1969.

ture is often apologetic in nature, given to moralizing on the issue of collusion or, in the case of Israeli publications, subject to military censorship. David Ben Gurion reportedly has one of three leather-bound sets containing documents relating to the Suez expedition which will only be published after Anthony Eden (Lord Avon) dies. Supposedly Mollet and Eden were in possession of the other two sets. In the meantime, the former Israel Premier has been reluctant to discuss the Suez agreements beyond saying of Eden,

> He didn't keep his word. He was supposed to send me a very important letter—but didn't. He only sent it to French Premier Mollet, but Mollet is decent and gave me a photostat. After the affair Eden insisted that Paris have all the original documents destroyed— but when he found I had copies he became friendly.[31]

According to Anthony Nutting, no notes were taken of British decisions, nor was a record kept of the October 1956 meeting at Sèvres. Among the British leaders concerned, only Nutting has revealed anything about the negotiations. Other accounts of the Suez affair that have relied heavily on private correspondence and conversations with Pineau contain inaccuracies. Despite his claim to have been one of the architects of the Suez collusion, Pineau was ignorant of the earlier direct contacts between the Israel and France defense establishments. In preparing the report that follows I have relied on the personal recollections of individuals involved in the Suez planning to supplement the written record.

By nationalizing the canal company on July 26, 1956, 'Abd al-Nasir conveniently supplied the excuse for intervention long sought by the French. Mollet tele-

---

[31] Cited by C. L. Sulzberger, in *New York Times*, July 31, 1968.

phoned Eden on the 27th to suggest that the Egyptian threat to Israel security might be the pretext for military action against 'Abd al-Nasir that both nations had sought. He insisted on Israeli collaboration, partly to prevent Britain from uniting the "good Arabs" against France and thereby winning a monopoly of influence in the Middle East.[32] Peres flew to Paris on the 28th to argue that Israel was in imminent danger from Egyptian expansionism. He asked for French help in the event of an Egyptian attack and particularly for a French aerial umbrella to protect Israel's cities. The French cautioned him not to act hastily, but did not disclose to him the nature of their negotiations with the British.[33] Abel Thomas, Chief of Staff General Paul Ely, President of the Committee of Chiefs of Staff (interviewed in Paris, June 5, 1969), and Air Force General André Martin (interviewed in Paris, June 12, 1969) supplied most of the details of the events that followed.

French defense officials began formal contingency planning with Israel on July 29, independent of the British operations.[34] Only some ten French officers, the Ministers of Foreign Affairs and Defense, and the Prime Minister were involved. These meetings were kept secret from the foreign services of both countries. In

[32] See Thomas, *The Suez Affair*, p. 86; Bromberger, *Les Secrets,* pp. 11, 29, 39; Randolph S. Churchill, *The Rise and Fall of Sir Anthony Eden* (London: MacGibbon & Kee, 1959), pp. 243-244; Azeau, *Le Piège de Suez,* pp. 122-125; 128-129; and Robertson, *Crisis,* p. 76.

[33] Thomas, interview cited.

[34] Bar-Zohar seems unaware of the nature of the July talks, for he says they dealt only with speeding arms deliveries. See *The Armed Prophet,* p. 211. See also Bromberger, *Les Secrets,* p. 64; Thomas, *The Suez Affair,* pp. 86, 92; and Azeau, *Le Piège de Suez,* p. 125.

France, for example, the interministerial committee which was set up during the summer to study the Suez crisis, and which in theory could have included members up to ministerial rank, was so organized as to include only partisans of military action and to exclude its opponents from the Quai d'Orsay.

French military strategists were particularly anxious to secure bases in Israel in order to solve some of the tactical difficulties facing the Anglo-French forces. This move would also foreclose the possibility of 'Abd al-Nasir's sending troops to aid the rebel forces in Algeria. After a military commission reported that Israel would be the likely victor in an armed clash, Bourgès is reported to have sent for Peres on August 7. Recognizing at last the need for force, Bourgès and high-ranking officers planned the joint attack with Israel on the canal.

Several sources have reported that a secret arms agreement was signed which, under unusual security conditions, provided weapons in greater volume than that accepted by the Americans in the spring.[35] In referring to the agreement, however, Abel Thomas claimed that it was not so much a new accord, but a decision to accelerate deliveries of matériel promised in earlier agreements.[36] Sales receipts were said to have been falsified

---

[35] For the varied accounts, see Bar-Zohar, *The Armed Prophet,* p. 221; *Gesher,* pp. 116-119; Childers, *The Road to Suez,* pp. 174, 184; Calvocoressi et al., *Suez Ten Years After,* p. 68; *Le Monde,* Nov. 4, 1966; Robertson, *Crisis,* p. 135; Ben Gurion, "Israel's Security," p. 26; Herman Finer, *Dulles over Suez. The Theory and Practice of His Diplomacy* (Chicago: Quadrangle, 1964), p. 331; J.-R. Tournoux, *Secrets d'état* (Paris; Plon, 1960), p. 155.

[36] Thomas, interview cited. It is difficult to determine exactly how many planes were sent Israel at this time. Only sixteen Mystères were operational during the Sinai Campaign, leading

for planes from Marcel Dassault's factories, where no one checked them closely, and the same receipt was used several times.

From August 1956 on contacts increased. Each department of the Ministry of Defense was in direct liaison with its Israeli counterpart. The air and naval forces exchanged personnel, while Israeli pilots underwent intensified training on French aircraft. At this point, according to General of the Air Force Maurice Challe, Chief of Staff of the Armed Forces (1955-1958), Prime Minister Mollet gave his general support for the plans under consideration, and the Quai d'Orsay was notified.[37] General Martin has stated that during the August meetings, although the Israelis apprised France of their army's capabilities and overall strategy, French projects being prepared by the common headquarters in London were not discussed.[38] However, Peres has written that he was made aware of London's hesitations during the August meetings.[39] Until September, Abel Thomas has insisted, France kept the United States informed, and the Americans even provided replacement parts "should force be needed." Thomas recalls General Gruenther's query, upon handing over special airplane fuel tanks, whether they would be used for

---

us to believe that these sixteen were delivered earlier in the spring. See Dayan, *Diary*, Appendix 4. Washington had at first approved the delivery of nine Mystères, according to Abel Thomas, but he admits that more than nine were shipped. Thomas, Bourgès, and Mollet "interpreted" American acquiescence to mean "nine planes at a time" and, when Washington began to show curiosity over the comings and goings, explained that these were the same nine planes traveling back and forth.

[37] Interviewed in Paris, June 2, 1969.
[38] Interview cited.
[39] Peres, *David's Sling*, p. 185.

any "wicked purposes." Thomas replied, "That's what they are generally used for." [40] Only in September did Dulles make it evident that Washington opposed the use of force.

The French leaders expressed their bitterness at being let down by the Americans who, they argued, were too concerned with protecting their oil-producing clients and overly fearful that any decisions made at Suez might hurt their status in the Panama Canal Zone. The French were particularly incensed because they felt 'Abd al-Nasir had been able to achieve his position within Egypt and the Arab world only because of the initial support he had received from Washington.

On September 20, 1956, Ben Gurion informed the Mapai Central Committee that Israel would soon have a "true ally." [41] Meanwhile French and Israeli ministers and staff officers were meeting again in Paris and in Israel to discuss air and naval support for Israel. Foreign Minister Golda Meir, *Ahdut ha-'Avodah's* (the Unity of Labor) Minister of Transportation Moshe Carmel, Dayan, and Peres began to confer with Pineau, Bourgès, Thomas, and Challe on September 30.[42] Dayan and Peres were told that Israel would be able to act alone at a time of its choosing and could count on France for technical assistance and personnel as well as air support. On October 1, Dayan met with Chief of Staff Paul Ely at the home of Louis Mangin. They exchanged intelligence on the strength of Egyptian forces. Dayan, who had brought along a list of the most urgent and essen-

[40] Interview cited. American foreknowledge was also confirmed by Martin and Challe, interviews cited.

[41] *Jerusalem Post,* Sept. 24, 30, 1956; see also Azeau, *Le Piège de Suez,* p. 216; Churchill, *Eden,* pp. 264-265; and Bar-Zohar, *The Armed Prophet,* p. 221.

[42] Peres, *loc. cit.*

tial items needed for the campaign, recalls that Ely, "anxious to be helpful," was moderately generous, promising trucks and tanks. But despite the fact that a joint France-Israel staff headquarters had been set up in Paris, when Dayan tried to get Ely to discuss the Franco-British operation, Ely "was not disposed to talk about French plans for the Suez Canal. My efforts to get him to discuss those plans proved fruitless." [43] General Ely has explained that he was particularly reluctant to undertake the Suez action without British cooperation.[44] Since Christian Pineau had only requested a British commitment to air support for Israel on September 26, no agreement had been reached by the time of Dayan's visit.[45]

Generals Challe and Martin and Colonel Simon were dispatched to Israel to assess the situation. Their positive judgment facilitated French arguments, though there was still some hesitation on the part of Premier Guy Mollet and the British. As planning progressed, Max Lejeune, Robert Lacoste, and Jacques Chaban-Delmas were given certain details to pass on to General de Gaulle, whose plane was used to ferry the Israelis back and forth to Paris. According to Hugh Thomas, General de Gaulle was very unhappy that the allied command was integrated under the British, even though the French were contributing the greater share of manpower and equipment.[46]

Israeli Operations Planning Order No. 1, dated October 5, 1956, indicates that Israel had reevaluated its

[43] Dayan, *Diary,* pp. 30-34.

[44] Interview cited.

[45] See Robertson, *Crisis,* pp. 134-135, who contradicts Childers' account.

[46] P. 66.

original objectives in the planned strike against Egypt and, in contrast to the 1955 plans centering on the Strait of Tiran at the entrance to the Gulf of 'Aqabah, now proposed to enter Sinai and strike at the Suez Canal in support of French aims.[47] Since without air support the Israel Air Force would have been limited in its ability to protect Israel's skies and to cover troop movements at the same time, Egyptian planes would have to be destroyed while on the ground. The entire peninsula, moreover, had to be captured quickly to avoid outside intervention, including the possible arrival of Communist "volunteers." On October 10, Shim'on Peres and Abel Thomas reached an agreement on these points, with France promising Israel air cover, further arms deliveries, the participation of French soldiers as "volunteers," planes and repair services, naval protection, and air drops from the forces that had reached Cyprus in August. Finally, France promised to exercise its veto in the Security Council to protect Israel against any Russian threat.[48]

Meanwhile, relations between Britain and Israel could only be described as chilly. From the earliest days of the state, Israel had hardly felt warm toward the British and was particularly anxious to avoid a clash with the Royal Air Force over Jordan.[49] The September 1956 Israeli reprisal raid against Qalqilya in Jordan was probably therefore only an attempt to mask Israeli intentions toward the real enemy—Egypt. When Iraqi troops entered Jordan on October 14, concerned Israeli

[47] For the Operations Order, see Dayan, *Diary*, Appendix, p. 209.

[48] See *Davar*, Oct. 21, 1956; *Jerusalem Post*, Oct. 31, 1956; and Bar-Zohar, *Gesher*, pp. 123-124.

[49] See Dayan, *Diary*, pp. 20-21, 28.

leaders were tempted to consider the matter a *casus belli,* despite the small number of soldiers involved. Britain had warned Israel of its intention to use force against Israel, if Jordan invoked its defense pact. The French, trying to prevent their English allies from complicating matters and producing a three-way war, reported to the Israelis that the British initiative for an Iraqi presence in Jordan aimed at forestalling disturbances during the Jordanian elections.[50] Albert Gazier, a junior minister and confidant of Mollet who was ignorant of the military plans, reports that he and General Challe flew to London on the 14th to obtain some guarantee for Israel.[51] Eden and Lloyd then flew to Paris to see Mollet and Pineau on the 16th. According to the latter,

> We had to also examine the problems which are not always without a more or less indirect relation with the Suez Canal affair, the relations between Israel, Jordan and Iraq, problems which are, at the moment, rather preoccupying and on which it is truly more indispensable than ever that the British and French take a common position.[52]

[50] *Ibid.,* pp. 52-53, 58-59. Azeau gives a rather Machiavellian account, *Le Piège de Suez,* pp. 231-235. Bar-Zohar, *Gesher,* pp. 127-128, says Eden asked for French mediation to allow entry of Iraqi troops but gave up the idea on October 6. He seems to base his argument on Childers' theories. Childers also argues that Israel and Iraq were going to dismember Jordan in co-operation with each other; p. 189. Anthony Nutting, *No End of A Lesson. The Story of Suez* (London: Constable, 1967) p. 103, is in error when he states that the entrance of Iraqi troops was merely an Israeli intelligence rumor. Cf. Pineau's comments, note 52 below.

[51] Albert Gazier, Minister of Social Affairs (1956-1957), interviewed in Paris, July 2, 1969.

[52] *Journal Officiel,* Oct. 16, 1956, 2nd sess., p. 4154. Cf. Robertson, *Crisis,* p. 224; Ben Gurion, "Israel's Security," p. 116; and

Convinced that Israel would act against Egypt with or without them, the British finally agreed to cooperate.

Ben Gurion had announced to the Kneset on October 15 that Israel's real enemy was Egypt, not Jordan. But he was deeply concerned about British intentions, the timing of the attack against Egypt, and the need to protect Israel's exposed cities.[53] At the request of Challe and Mangin, Ben Gurion flew to Paris on October 22. Together with Dayan, Peres, and Nehemia Argov, he expressed his worries and tried to exact more concrete proof of French-Israeli cooperation. He was joined at Sèvres in the next two days by Selwyn Lloyd and Patrick Dean of the British Foreign Office, who finally agreed to sign what has been described as either a formal "declaration of intent" or a treaty outlining the undertaking.

Essentially the Sèvres document reconfirmed the October 10 agreement between Abel Thomas and Shim'on Peres, although the British were never completely informed about the full extent of French aid to Israel— partly as a result of their own insistence on not being informed.[54] Anglo-French operations were to begin on October 31. Dayan has emphasized that

> . . . the moment chosen by Israel and the nature of the military operations which we undertook were subordinated to the Franco-English projects . . . . That is to say that the Sinai Campaign could never have taken place if the French and the English had not offered us the occasion. Personally, I would not have taken the risks that I took if I hadn't known in

Anthony Eden, *The Memoirs of Anthony Eden: Full Circle* (Boston: Houghton-Mifflin, 1960), p. 569.

[53] Thomas, *The Suez Affair*, p. 87. On Ben Gurion's fears the British might bomb Israeli troops, see Bar-Zohar, *The Armed Prophet*, p. 225; Robertson, *Crisis*, p. 147; and Pineau in *Le Monde*, Nov. 14, 1966.

[54] Bar-Zohar, *The Armed Prophet*, pp. 230-231.

advance that the Egyptian airfields would be destroyed by our allies of the moment, thus greatly facilitating our task. If Israel had acted alone the plan of our operations would have been very different.[55]

As reflected in the October 25 Operations Order, the Israelis would provide the pretext for Anglo-French intervention by threatening the canal,

and only after that come the basic purposes of the campaign—capture of the Straits of Tiran (Sharm e-Sheikh and the islands of Tiran and Sanapir) and the defeat of the Egyptian forces.[56]

According to Abel Thomas, the French hoped that the result would find "the Israelis at the canal, in Sinai and in the Gulf of 'Aqabah, with a cordon of Anglo-French troops strategically emplaced to enforce freedom of passage through Suez." [57]

[55] Dayan, cited in *Le Monde,* May 12-18, 1966.
[56] Dayan, *Diary,* p. 61; for text, see p. 210.
[57] Interview cited.

IV

The Suez War and Its Consequences

FROM October 22 to 27, 1956, French matériel was rushed to Israel in preparation for the Sinai Campaign and the Suez invasion. Much of the equipment was lent for the duration of the campaign without an inventory having been taken, according to General Ely. Some equipment was an outright gift, while some was paid for at commercial rates.[1] Some twenty-four or twenty-five additional Mystères, two French NATO Mystère squadrons and one of Sabrejets, under General Raymond Brohon, brought to over one hundred the total number of planes either sold or loaned to Israel in the months prior to Sinai.[2] On October 27,

[1] Chief of Staff General Paul Ely, President of the Committee of Chiefs of Staff, interviewed in Paris, June 5, 1969.

[2] General Raymond Brohon, interviewed in Paris, June 26, 1969. Nadav Safran, *From War to War. The Arab-Israeli Confrontation, 1948-1967* (N.Y.: Pegasus, 1967), p. 223, note 14, bases his figure of 60 planes on President Dwight D. Eisenhower's count—obtained from high-altitude reconnaissance planes. But this does not consider the possibility of underground hangars. Safran cites General Moshe Dayan's statement that Israel could put five jet squadrons into the air during the campaign, including 37 Mystères. Five squadrons would be approximately 120 planes; Safran is probably not including the three French squadrons in his tally, although since the size of Israeli squadrons varies, the confusion is understandable.

  37 Mystères (16 operational, including 12 sent in the spring; the rest probably flown by French pilots)
  48 Dijon squadron Mystères
  24 F-86 Sabrejets
  ―――
  109

77

two hundred 6×6 trucks with front-wheel drive arrived and, as Dayan has asserted, "saved the situation." [3] General Ely recalls that two hundred tanks were also shipped.[4] Meanwhile, members of the French secret service were stationed in Israel to oversee security arrangements. The French vessels *Surcouf, Kersaint,* and *Bouvet* steamed to the coasts of Israel, operating independently of the integrated Anglo-French command. On the morning of the 31st, the *Kersaint* assisted the Israeli navy in the capture of the *Ibrahim al-Awwal,* underway to shell Haifa. The *Georges-Leygues* took up its position "off the coast of Alexandria," where it later shelled Egyptian positions at Rafah.[5]

On October 28, Ben Gurion and Dayan formally presented to the cabinet plans for an offensive whose main aim was to secure freedom of navigation through Suez. It was understood that Israeli forces would limit their operations to Sinai, without crossing the canal.

The remainder were probably Ouragans and Meteors approved by Eden for sale in the spring; see Hugh Thomas, *The Suez Affair* (Liverpool: Weidenfeld & Nicolson, 1966), p. 20. According to Abel Thomas, Director of the cabinet of Defense Minister Bourgès-Maunoury (1956-1957), interviewed in Paris, July 3, 1969, some two hundred planes were sent, a few at a time. However, this figure seems high. Note also that Safran misjudges the timing of French arms sales, pp. 50-51.

[3] Moshe Dayan, *Diary of the Sinai Campaign* (N.Y.: Harper & Row, 1965), p. 68.

[4] Interview cited.

[5] See "Remise de la Médaille commémorative du Moyen Orient," *La Revue Maritime,* no. 137 (Oct. 1957), pp. 1271-1273; Thomas, *The Suez Affair,* p. 129; J.-R. Tournoux, *Secrets d'état* (Paris: Plon, 1960), p. 158; and Merry & Serge Bromberger, *Les Secrets de l'expédition d'Egypte* (Paris: Aymon, 1957), pp. 7-8, 27.

Only a few ministers from Mapai and Ahdut ha 'Avodah had known of the plans before this time. Neither Ambassador Ya'akov Tsur in Paris nor Abba Eban in the United States was aware that invasion was imminent, and, apart from Golda Meir, few members of the Foreign Office staff had been informed.[6] The discussion was purely formal since Ben Gurion had contacted each cabinet member separately the day before. Two ministers who opposed the operation were nonetheless willing to support the government decision. In the French cabinet, all government parties were informed. According to Hugh Thomas, the sole criticism came from the Right, on the grounds that action was proceeding too slowly, and from one or two radicals who opposed Mollet's decision in principle.[7]

Israel launched its attack on the 29th. French planes from Cyprus dropped supplies to the advancing troops, while General Brohon's command bombed the airfields at Luxor. Other French aircraft based in Israel, immediately began patrolling the skies and engaging the Egyptian Migs in combat. According to the original timetable, the landing of Anglo-French airborne units had been scheduled for November 6. Continued allied bombing of Egyptian airfields was to have preceded the landings and should have begun within twelve hours after the expiration of an Anglo-French ultimatum to Egypt and Israel to cease hostilities and withdraw—the Israelis "to a distance of 10 miles east of the Canal" and

[6] See David Ben Gurion, "Israel's Security and Her International Position. Before and After the Sinai Campaign," *State of Israel Government Yearbook 5720 (1959/1960)*, pp. 31-32; Michael Bar-Zohar, *Gesher 'al ha-Yam ha-Tikhon. Yahasei Tsarfat-Israel, 1947-1963* (Bridge over the Mediterranean. France-Israel Relations, 1947-1963; Tel-Aviv: 'Am ha-Sefer, 1964), p. 141.

[7] Pp. 69, 74.

Egyptians from its "neighborhood."[8] Israel, as planned, agreed to the terms while Egypt refused, but the two allies waited twenty-five hours, beginning to bomb only on the 31st.

British commanders, overestimating the strength of Egyptian forces and particularly anxious to prevent 'Abd al-Nasir from blocking the canal, had argued for a cumbersome and complicated plan of action with ten to fourteen days of air raids to precede the landings.[9] The French military attaché's office reported to Dayan that the British obstinately refused to move forward the landing date despite the speed with which Israeli forces had advanced. The French wanted to proceed without them. Matters were complicated by a United Nations resolution of November 2, demanding a cease fire. Israel was reluctant to acquiesce, since another day or two was needed to capture Sharm al-Shaykh. But Ben Gurion doubted whether his British and French allies would resist increasing international pressure and would carry out the invasion as planned. He also wanted to remain aloof from the struggle for control over Suez. "I see no point in joining a coalition on an issue which is opposed by the entire world," he is quoted as saying.[10] For these reasons, Israel decided to accept the cease-fire on November 3, with the proviso that Egypt do the same. However, as Dayan noted in his diary, a cease-fire would have removed Britain's elaborately structured justification for intervention.

> Britain therefore asked France to use the full weight of her influence to persuade us to retract our announce-

[8] For text, see Thomas, *The Suez Affair*, Appendix VIII, pp. 193-194.

[9] See Anthony Eden, *The Memoirs of Anthony Eden: Full Circle* (Boston: Houghton-Mifflin, 1960), pp. 596ff.

[10] Dayan, *Diary*, p. 159.

ment. . . . France has done this, begging us to do nothing which might shake the tottering foundations underlying Eden's position on Suez. As our friends, the French, explained it, if we did not accede to Britain's request, Eden would be compelled to abandon completely his military plan on Suez.[11]

Submitting to French entreaties, Israel stalled for time, qualifying its acceptance of the cease-fire by posing five questions. Having thus cooperated with the allies, however, Ben Gurion was enraged and embarrassed by a subsequent Anglo-French note to the United Nations which proposed an international force to secure the canal and included a phrase calling for "prompt withdrawal of the Israeli forces." [12] To Ben Gurion this formula, although later modified by France, meant that France had sacrified Israeli interests in hopes of ending further British hesitation.

By November 5 the Israel army had achieved its war aims; ground fighting ended just as the first allied paratroops dropped into the Canal Zone. Seaborne forces from Malta finally arrived on the 6th, the day Eden, under pressure from the United States and from within his own government, decided to abandon the Suez war. Mollet acquiesced in the British decision despite fierce opposition from Bourgès-Maunoury, Pineau, Lejeune, and others in his government who wanted to continue hostilities with Israeli assistance.[13]

Immediately after the Sinai Campaign and Suez in-

[11] *Ibid.*, p. 181; cf. Eden, *Memoirs,* p. 617.

[12] Letters from representatives of France and United Kingdom to Secretary General, UN Docs. A/3268 and A/3269, Nov. 3, 1956. See also Michael Bar-Zohar, *The Armed Prophet; A Biography of Ben Gurion,* trans. by Len Ortzen (London: Barker, 1967), p. 246; for text of telegrams to the French in response to notes, see pp. 182-184.

[13] Pineau, cited in *Le Monde,* Nov. 4, 1966.

vasion, French support for Israel was no longer an almost clandestine arrangement between the two defense ministries, but shifted instead to the public arena as official government policy. In a state of euphoria, the Israel press optimistically hailed its new champion. Often minute developments in tone and emphasis were headlined and token gestures of normal diplomatic courtesy were sometimes magnified out of all proportion to any concrete political meaning they may have had. France and French activities received daily coverage in the *Jerusalem Post, Ha-Arets,* and *Ma'ariv* far more often than did Israel in *Le Monde* or *Le Figaro*.[14] Israel did not always distinguish between internally oriented and externally oriented information, and the "disclosures" that followed the course of the France-Israel relationship were probably directed at a local audience, to convince the Israeli public—and perhaps the French as well—that the new rapprochement would endure.

In France despite some conservative hesitation and condemnation by seventeen Socialists, the Suez expedition had been backed by a united cabinet and received wide public acclaim. Lack of support for Israel came only from the extreme Left, which couched its opposition in terms of anti-colonialism. Although French collusion with Israel had been generally suspected, it became public knowledge in spring 1957 with the publication of *Les Secrets de l'expédition d'Egypte* by Merry and Serge Bromberger.[15] There were some recriminations, especially by the army, which was angered by

[14] On the attitudes toward Israel displayed in the French press, see Jean-William Lapierre, *L'Information sur l'Etat d'Israël dans les grands quotidiens français en 1958* (Paris: Centre National de la Recherche Scientifique, 1968).

[15] For Israeli reactions, see *Jerusalem Post,* April 8, 15, 1957.

what was regarded as a military defeat inflicted by the politicians, and there was opposition from those civilians who felt that parliament should have been consulted. There was also some dismay at the diminution of French prestige and cultural influence in the Arab world. Others regretted the financial losses caused by the sequestration of French property and loss of French investments in Egypt.[16]

A few deputies called for the reaffirmation of traditional French policies centered on Syria and Lebanon. Syria, so the argument went, had been alienated only after France began to arm Israel and so could still be recovered. Such a policy would forestall the East/West polarization which would otherwise be the inevitable outcome of France's ouster from the area, particularly if defense pacts were the only evidence of western presence.[17] Others, including some Gaullists, expressed cautious sympathy for Israel, but preferred to seek an East/West detente by serving as an independent buffer between the blocs and as the leader of the smaller nations. Israel, they argued, had, after all, been conceived by the United Kingdom and nurtured by the United States. Yet these countries had prudently and shrewdly managed to preserve their ties with the Arabs while French relations were now severed. Moreover, an Arab-Islamic policy orientation was imperative for France because of French links to Africa and the Sahara. There-

---

[16] See interpellation by Jacques Isorni, *Journal Officiel da la République Française. Débats Parlementaires. Assemblée Nationale. Compte Rendu,* Dec. 18, 1956, 2nd sess., p. 6092; statement by Emile Hugues, p. 6095; and by Pierre Mendès-France, p. 6110. See also Paul Reynaud, "De Sarajevo à Amman," *La Revue de Paris,* 64th yr. (June 1957), pp. 3-13.

[17] Jean de Lipkowski, *Journal Officiel,* Dec. 19, 1956, 1st sess., p. 6149.

fore, France should avoid any alliance or community of interest with Israel and concentrate on Lebanon, pursuing the principle of tripartite consultation for Middle East policies. In that way France could also serve as a mediator between Israel and the Arab world.[18]

The Mollet government continued to stress the Soviet threat in the Middle East, pointing to Russian-made booty taken from the Egyptians in Sinai and alluding to the participation of Russian soldiers, whose conversations were allegedly overheard emanating from Egyptian tanks during the campaign. The growing Soviet presence in Syria added to the sense of danger.[19] Having lost confidence in the Atlantic alliance, the French were convinced that the Russian foothold in the Middle East could cripple Europe's defenses and threaten the supply of Middle East oil upon which Europe depended.[20]

This was one area in which Israel aroused particular French concern. Even before the Suez invasion, France had been interested in Israeli plans to build an oil pipeline from Eilat to Ashkelon or Haifa. With the blockage of the Suez Canal, France feared a major economic crisis. Not only was it cut off from export markets (and those in the Middle East were worth 51 billion francs annually), but between 30 and 35 percent of its oil supply

---

[18] See François de Menthon, *idib.*, Dec. 18, 1956, 2nd sess., pp. 6097-6098; and General Georges Catroux, "La Méditerranée orientale, Foyer des Tensions Internationales," *Etudes Mediterranéennes* (Autumn 1958), pp. 27-35. For a variation on these themes, see Jacques Feron, *Journal Officiel*, Dec. 19, 1956, 1st sess., p. 6146; and Pierre Cot, March 27, 1957, 1st sess., p. 1894.

[19] See *Journal Officiel*, Dec. 18, 1956, 2nd sess., pp. 6092-6093, 6095-6096.

[20] See Marshal Juin & Henri Massis, *The Choice before Europe* (London: Eyre & Spottiswoode, 1958).

was automatically stopped. Many enterprises were completely closed; the fragile auto industry was suffering and workers in other fields were being laid off by the thousands.[21] There was no reason why Iranian oil could not reach France, since Iran had remained favorable to unobtrusive but close relations with Israel; the Gulf of 'Aqabah was now open, and a pipeline could be built from Eilat to the Mediterranean coast.

France had begun to seek United States approval for the project in November 1956, and hoped that Washington would guarantee the sea path, oil fields, and operation of the line. Italy and Belgium agreed to participate, and the United Kingdom was reported ready to support the project. French and American oil companies reacted negatively, however, the latter holding out with the British for a line across Turkey. After meetings among Levi Eshkol, Mollet, Pineau, and Bourgès, official French backing for the pipe was announced.[22] France would contribute $15 million and buy one-half of the 16-inch line's five to eight million ton annual capacity.[23] Some $24 million was invested in a 413 kilometer 16-inch pipeline, begun early in 1959 to replace the 8-inch link finished in 1956.[24] French investment, via the Rothschild Group's Swiss interests, accounted for only one-third, while the United States and Israel provided a third each.[25] In the end, although Greece and Italy used some of the oil, most of it went

[21] The foregoing is based on debates in *Journal Officiel,* Dec. 18, 1956, 2nd sess., pp. 6095, 6106-6113; Dec. 19, 1956, 1st sess., pp. 6142-6149, 6163; Dec. 20, 1956, p. 6176.

[22] *Ibid.,* March 27, 1957, 1st sess., p. 1901.

[23] *Jerusalem Post,* April 5, 7, 1957.

[24] *Ibid.,* Aug. 21, 1959; Aug. 2, 1960.

[25] François Perreire of the Rothschild Bank, Chairman of the Eilat Oil Pipeline Company, interviewed in Paris, July 3, 1969.

for local consumption and official French interest diminished with the reopening of the canal. Israel was ultimately allowed to purchase the pipeline from the concessionaires in 1967, although not without some ill-will over the price and manner.[26]

With collective responsibility for the defense of western interests in the Middle East at an end, Israel was the logical and only means by which France could preserve some influence in the area. At the same time, Israel was the "most certain and most solid bastion of the West in the Near East, except perhaps for Turkey."[27] Moreover, France felt frustration at the role of the United Nations, where control seemed to have passed to powerless "nonstates," whose weakness and inaction had failed Hungary and ruined the Suez plan. Although these states had been quick to condemn France in the world forum, they had been unable and unwilling to protect Israel. France, guarding its traditional image as protector of the weak, considered it a moral responsibility to place Israel under its wing.[28] It is in this context that one must consider French claims after Suez that the Mollet government had acted to save Israel. Bulganin's threat to wipe Israel off the map added to the sense of menace.[29]

Mollet did not deny a link between Algeria and the Suez invasion, but argued that his primary cause for action had been an "anti-Munich reflex" provoked by the obvious encirclement of Israel: ". . . if we had, for

[26] *Idem.;* and Baron Edmond de Rothschild, interviewed in Paris, July 1, 1969.

[27] Jean Gottmann, *Etudes sur l'Etat d'Israël et le Moyen Orient* (Paris: Colin, 1959), p. 171.

[28] See, for example, Edouard Bonnefous, *Journal Officiel,* Dec. 18, 1956, 2nd sess., p. 6104.

[29] See Christian Pineau, *ibid.,* Dec. 19, 1956, 1st sess., p. 6154.

our part, allowed Israel to be crushed by a coalition mounted against us, with what reproaches would we berate ourselves today." The government would be pro-Israel as "none of the preceding governments had been." [30] France sought an Arab-Israel peace treaty, "notably between Egypt and Israel," the demilitarization of Gaza, and guarantees for Israel of freedom of navigation in the Gulf of 'Aqabah and the Suez Canal.[31]

Former Premier Edgar Faure admitted that concern for Israel's use of the canal was a major and welcome change in French policy. ". . . *battons tous notre culpe;* it must be recognized that, until these most recent events, this question did not interest world opinion very much." [32] A goverment motion, passed December 20, 1956, by a solid majority, called for "The bringing about of a general peace settlement in the Middle East and the establishment of a system of international control for the Suez Canal or any other system giving all the users the same guarantees." [33] This motion was not as strong in support of Israel as the MRP (Mouvement Républicain Populaire) *ordre du jour,* which had been withdrawn in favor of the government's proposal, nor did it go as far as the position championed by Mendès-France, who hoped that by constructive action France could force the two superpowers responsible for world peace to deal with it on the major issues. Mendès-France called for (1) settlement of the Jordan River problem; (2) cultural and scientific cooperation, which had "already begun most efficaciously" in the atomic field; (3) support for free passage in the canal and Gulf

[30] *Ibid.,* Dec. 20, 1956, pp. 6175, 6185.
[31] Pineau, *ibid.,* p. 6156.
[32] *Ibid.,* Dec. 20, 1956, p. 6182; see also p. 6185.
[33] *Ibid.,* pp. 6179, 6186, 6195.

of 'Aqabah; (4) action to assure the security of Israel especially by neutralizing a band of territory in Sinai; (5) reciprocal disarmament in the Middle East; and (6) cessation of arms shipments.[34]

The final foreign policy debate of the Mollet government in March 1957 reaffirmed French support for a security guarantee for Israel and its borders, free navigation through the canal and in the Gulf of 'Aqabah, and regularization of the canal affair according to the principles of the London Conference. France generally approved of the United Nations Emergency Force (UNEF), but agreed with Israel that provisions would have to be made to prevent Gaza from ever again becoming the staging area for *fidaiyun* raids. France, however, rejected the Secretary General's interpretation that the UNEF's presence depended upon Egyptian sufferance.[35]

During Mollet's tenure (January 1956-May 1957), France did appear to uphold Israel's interests in discreet negotiations, and often voted along with Israel as a minority of two in the General Assembly. However, despite the warmth and integrity of Socialist intentions, Mollet was severely hampered by the relative impotence of France. Militarily and economically, there was simply very little France could actually do for Israel. Diplomacy was just about the only avenue open for effective action. On those issues which were raised in the United Nations as a direct result of the Suez invasion, France did speak in Israel's behalf and it may even be said that a political alliance operated, at least throughout the first half of

[34] *Ibid.*, pp. 6179, 6114, respectively.
[35] Arthur Conte, *ibid.*, March 26, 1957, 2nd sess., p. 1869. For Pineau's statement, see *ibid.*, March 27, 1957, 1st sess., pp. 1901-1902.

1957. But where other Israeli interests were concerned, such as freedom of passage through the Suez Canal or NATO guarantees, Mollet and his successors were limited to offering good offices and lukewarm support.

As soon as the Suez issue was placed before the United Nations, France honored its commitment to protect Israel—at the emergency session, in votes on the establishment of the Emergency Force, and later resolutions in January and February 1957 calling for Israeli withdrawal from Sinai, Gaza, and Sharm al-Shaykh.[36] France and Israel were among the nineteen nations abstaining in the November 3, 1956, vote of the first emergency special session, in which fifty-seven nations called for the establishment of UNEF.[37] France later voted for the November 26, 1956, resolution establishing UNEF and allocating contributions, while Israel abstained (52:9: 13).[38] France was assessed 5.7 percent for 1957, and its contributions to UNEF from 1957 to 1962 totaled $400,000.[39]

Despite Soviet support for Egyptian opposition, France and the United Kingdom had demanded the effective functioning of UNEF along the canal pending

[36] SC Resolution 119 (1956), Oct. 31, 1956, in accordance with GA Resolution 377 A (V), Nov. 3, 1950; see also GA Resolutions 1120 (XI), Nov. 24, 1956; 1121 (XI), Nov. 24, 1956; 1123 (XI), Jan. 19, 1957; 1124 (XI), Feb. 2, 1957; 1125 (XI), Feb. 2, 1957; 1126 (XI), Feb. 22, 1957.

[37] *United Nations General Assembly Official Records* (UNG-AOR), 563rd mtg., p. 71.

[38] Resolution 1122(XI). See UNGAOR, 596th mtg., Nov. 26, 1956, p. 343, para. 228.

[39] See "On Financing the Force," Gabriella Rosner, *The United Nations Emergency Force* (N.Y.: Columbia, 1963), pp. 158-185; and G. F. Hudson, "The United Nations Emergency Force: A Notable Precedent," *Current History*, vol. 38 (June 1960), pp. 327-331.

settlement of the Suez problem as a precondition for withdrawal. The first United Nations contingents entered Egypt November 15 and Port Sa'id on the 21st, and by mid-December they were in the canal area. Anglo-French troops left the canal on December 22. While Quai d'Orsay spokesmen were calling for internationalization of Gaza in January, many Frenchmen, especially in the army and defense establishment, were initially sympathetic to Israel's retention of both Sinai and the Gaza strip. Ultimately, however, there was little alternative to Israeli withdrawal. In reply to queries about aid to Israel in case of Russian intervention, Pineau had said, "France will share all she has with Israel. But our combined means are not sufficient against the Soviet menace." [40] Even though Israel had not received any guarantees, Sinai was evacuated by January 22. French troops, however, sympathetically protected Zahal's stalling operations in Sinai while captured arms and equipment were spirited from the peninsula to within Israel's borders.

General de Gaulle had told Menahem Begin of Israel's Herut Party, "Don't let go of Gaza. It is a sector essential for your security." [41] Ben Gurion determined not to move without some concrete assurances not only on Gaza but on 'Aqabah and Tiran as well.[42] In this he was supported by the French delegate to the

[40] Cited by Bar-Zohar, *The Armed Prophet*, p. 251. Cf. Thomas, *The Suez Affair*, p. 145.

[41] Cited by Eric Rouleau, "Au Moyen-Orient, diversification des amitiés dans la sauvegarde des intérêts nationaux," *Le Monde Diplomatique*, Jan. 1968, p. 8. See Terence Robertson, *Crisis: The Inside Story of the Suez Conspiracy* (N.Y.: Atheneum, 1964), pp. 296-297; and *Jerusalem Post*, Jan. 6, 1957.

[42] For the Israeli position, see UNGAOR, 11th sess., 638th plen. mtg., Jan. 17, 1957 (Vol. II-III), pp. 890ff.

United Nations, Guillaume Georges-Picot, who argued that the General Assembly was not a tribunal whose members could reestablish the status quo ante, but a political body "whose primary responsibility is to preserve peace." However, while Georges-Picot referred to reopening the canal, he did not mention Israel's right of passage.[43] Israel and France both voted against the resolution of January 19, 1957, on Israeli withdrawal, and negotiations reached an impasse.[44] The resolution of February 2 stated that "withdrawal by Israel must be followed by action which would assure progress towards the creation of peaceful conditions"; UNEF forces were to be placed on the armistice demarcation lines at Sharm al-Shaykh and Gaza.[45] Israel and France were among the twenty-two nations abstaining (56:0:22).

By the end of February, the French let it be known that they were willing to participate in an international action to secure freedom of navigation for Israel in the Gulf of 'Aqabah.[46] Guy Mollet and Christian Pineau flew to Washington to obtain some form of guarantee for Israel. According to Pineau, the United States at first wanted to send a squadron to Eilat to establish the Gulf of 'Aqabah as an international waterway. Israel argued, however, that, while Egypt might let American ships pass, there was no way to prevent 'Abd al-Nasir from later halting Israeli vessels. Therefore, France suggested, and it was agreed, that Israel could resort to

[43] *Ibid.*, 642nd plen. mtg., Jan. 19, 1957, pp. 947-948, paras. 23-37.

[44] Resolution 1123 (XI); see also Resolution 1124 (XI), Feb. 2, 1957, which Israel and France opposed.

[45] Resolution 1125 (XI). For discussion and vote, see UNGAOR, 11th sess., 639-642, 644-646, 649-652, 659-661, 664-668 plen. mtgs., Jan.-Feb. 1957.

[46] *Jerusalem Post*, Feb. 21, 1957.

action on the grounds of legitimate self-defense under Article 51 of the United Nations Charter if its shipping were barred from the gulf.[47] According to information supplied by Abel Thomas and Pierre Gilbert, this proposal was evidently embodied in an exchange of letters between the French and Israeli governments, and contained an implied or definite commitment which was, at the very least, a moral engagement on the part of France and, at the most, an alliance for Israel's defense.[48] As for Gaza, military occupation and administration were to continue until such time as a peace treaty was signed, but UNEF forces would not be allowed on Israeli soil. Pineau admitted the limitations of this formula for Israel's security. That is why "France did not exert the least pressure on the Israel government so that the latter would accept or refuse the compromise in question." [49]

[47] Article 51 states: "Nothing in the present Charter shall impair the inherent right of individual or collective self-defense if an armed attack occurs against a Member of the United Nations, until the Security Council has taken the measures necessary to maintain international peace and security. Measures taken by Members in the exercise of this right of self-defense shall be immediately reported to the Security Council and shall not in any way affect the authority and responsibility of the Security Council under the present Charter to take at any time such action as it deems necessary in order to maintain or restore international peace and security."

[48] Thomas, interview cited; and Pierre Gilbert, Ambassador to Israel (1953-1959), interviewed in Paris, June 11, 1969.

[49] *Journal Officiel*, March 27, 1957, 1st sess., p. 1901. See also *Jerusalem Post*, March 22, 29, 1957; for denial of French pressure by Madame Meir, see *ibid.*, April 2, 1957. For brief mention of the French role in these negotiations, see also Herman Finer, *Dulles over Suez. The Theory and Practice of His Diplomacy* (Chicago: Quadrangle, 1964), p. 487; and on French and Canadian support, Ben Gurion, *"Israel's Security,"* p. 51. Cf. Bar-Zohar,

On March 1, 1957, Foreign Minister Golda Meir announced in the United Nations that Israel would withdraw from Sharm al-Shaykh and Gaza. She referred to the February 11, 1957, memo from the United States Secretary of State to the Israeli ambassador confirming the support of the maritime powers for the French formula.[50] After her statement, Henry Cabot Lodge rose to speak for the United States. To the great consternation of Israel, he ignored the agreed formula in his remarks. Leaving open the question of the return of Egyptian forces to Gaza, Lodge called for immediate Israeli withdrawal and United Nations consideration of any incidents arising therefrom, without alluding to the recognition of Israel's right to self-defense under Article 51. Georges-Picot, by contrast, stuck to the agreed text, claiming that the Gulf of 'Aqabah was an international waterway, assuring Israel the right to self-defense under Article 51, and announcing that, as no state of war existed, Israel's position was in accordance with international law. UNEF's task would be to remain until a settlement was reached by the parties or until international agreement and, in the French view, UNEF contingents should not be withdrawn without first considering the proposal. The French delegate then

---

The Armed Prophet, p. 253, where the description of the French role ignores the subtle distinction that the French suggested the form in which the guarantees would be couched. The emplacement of UNEF had already been embodied in the resolution of February 2, cited above.

[50] UNGAOR, 11th sess., 666th plen. mtg., March 1, 1957, pp. 1275-1276, paras. 1-24. On the aide-memoire, see Ben Gurion, "Israel's Security," pp. 47-48, and Department of State, *United States Policy in the Middle East, September 1956-June 1957, Documents* (Washington, GPO, 1957), pp. 290-292.

concluded with a call for a Middle East peace settlement.[51]

While Ben Gurion hesitated at the apparent American double-cross, awaiting reassurance and explanation from Eisenhower, Pineau sent the following telegram to the Israeli Prime Minister.

> If it is true that the solution proposed for the agreement of the Government of Israel is the result of a formula of French inspiration, the form given this solution by the American government is too far from that which we had initially proposed, and which is that which had been exposed in the United Nations by M. Georges-Picot, in order for us to give it our endorsement.

Admitting that France was limited in the concrete assistance it could offer Israel, Pineau added,

> We cannot recommend the adoption of a solution of which we will be incapable of guaranteeing the execution, maintenance and final issue.

While there was to be no military alliance with Israel, Pineau promised that France would work with the United States on the problems of Gaza, Tiran, and 'Aqabah in an attempt to internationalize them. If Israel were forced to defend itself against Egyptian forces in Gaza, he concluded, "France, in that case, will not only not associate itself with any sanctions, but would continue to aid Israel in seeking a just solution to the problem." [52] Israel evacuated Gaza, and UNEF began functioning there on March 7, 1957.

[51] UNGAOR, 11th sess., 666th plen. mtg., March 1, 1957, pp. 1277-1278, 1280, paras. 25-44, 57-67.

[52] *Journal Officiel*, March 27, 1957, 1st sess., pp. 1901-1902. Evidently American reassurance took the form of a special letter from President Eisenhower to Ben Gurion. See Shim'on Peres,

While United States' "friendly persuasion" as well as a hazily defined "commitment" was a major factor in Israel's retreat, it must be recognized that France had the primary role. The American economic pressure that many observers thought could be brought to bear was limited. From 1948 to 1956, official government aid to Israel amounted to less than sixteen percent of the total net capital imports from the United States, and most of this came from contributions of the Jewish community. Washington was unlikely for political reasons to repeal the tax exemptions for donations to Israeli causes or to prohibit the sale of Israel Bonds. These factors reduced the ability of the State Department to apply economic pressure on the Israel government. Nor was Israel exclusively dependent on American trade.[53] It was undoubtedly the French formula, which recognized Israel's right to self-defense, that prompted Israeli withdrawal. Israel's delegate to the United Nations Abba Eban on March 8 expressed his thanks to "The eminent leaders and representatives of the Government of France [who] played a decisive role in solving this deadlock. . . ."[54]

Israel's expectation that its withdrawal would be followed by a United Nations administration in the Gaza strip proved illusory when the Egyptian army reentered the strip. The UNEF remained in Gaza, however, and at Sharm al-Shaykh. According to a semi-official Israeli source, Bourgès-Maunoury had promised Golda Meir French aid in the event of a "second round."

David's Sling. The Arming of Israel (London: Weidenfeld & Nicolson, 1970), pp. 16, 214. While Peres' book has apparently been censored by Israel authorities, it does offer occasional useful confirmation of events.

[53] See *The Economist*, vol. 186 (Feb. 1, 1958), pp. 415-416.

[54] UNGAOR, 11th sess., 668th plen. mtg., March 8, 1957, p. 1325, para. 256.

Yet on June 11, 1957, in reply to a Soviet note of April 19, 1957, France explicitly denied having promised economic or military aid to Israel in the event of an Egyptian attack.[55]

While it is not quite certain just what commitments were made and what Israel might reasonably have expected, France, the United States, and other maritime powers had unquestionably assumed a strong moral commitment to support Israel's right of innocent passage through the Strait of Tiran and to prevent Gaza from being again used as a base for guerrilla attacks against Israel. The right of passage for Israeli ships through the Suez Canal remained unresolved, however. Israel delayed dispatching a test ship through the canal pending the outcome of international pressure on Egypt and perhaps in hopes that France would take the issue to the United Nations. In May a French naval squadron was reported hovering around the Red Sea approaches to the canal as protective cover for an Israeli test ship, to prevent its being stopped, as the *Bat Galim* had been, while still south of the canal's southern entrance.[56] Nothing more was heard of the matter. As Israeli goods on non-Israeli ships were generally allowed to pass through the canal in 1957 and 1958, it is reasonable to assume that international and possibly French pressure made itself felt in Israel's favor during those years.

French diplomacy, moreover, did serve Israel's interests at the NATO Council of Ministers meeting in December 1957. Ben Gurion, supported by Reuven Shiloah of the Foreign Ministry and Shim'on Peres, had

[55] See Bar-Zohar, *Gesher*, p. 180; and Walter Eytan, *The First Ten Years: A Diplomatic History of Israel* (London: Weidenfeld & Nicolson, 1958), p. 171.

[56] See *Jerusalem Post*, April 7, May 15, 17, 19, 1957.

made it one of his foreign policy aims for 1957 to carve a military alliance or to obtain security guarantees from the United States and NATO. Ya'akov Tsur recalls that Israel's European ambassadors were generally pessimistic about his chances for success since Turkey and Greece were likely to resist Israel's inclusion in NATO, while the Scandinavians were generally unenthusiastic about new responsibilities.[57] Even France was not wholeheartedly in favor of the idea. "Not wishing to disappoint our Israeli friends," French Foreign Minister Christian Pineau says he presented the Israeli request to the Council of Ministers fully expecting its rejection.[58] A series of moves and countermoves ensued, which saw Turkey, as spokesman for the Muslim Baghdad Pact members, appeal for Israel's return to its 1947 borders, primarily in order to forestall the extension of NATO guarantees to Israel.[59] The French pressed Israel to establish individual ties with Atlantic pact nations. France was, of course, more than willing to give a moral guarantee, declaring its resolute hostility "to any modification of frontiers, notably of Israel's frontiers," and categorical opposition to any return to the 1947 demarcation lines.[60]

[57] Ya'akov Tsur, Israel Ambassador to France (1953-1959), interviewed in Jerusalem, August 13, 1969.

[58] Cited by Bar-Zohar, *Gesher*, p. 182; and *The Armed Prophet*, p. 258.

[59] See Paul Giniewski, *Israël devant l'Afrique et l'Asie* (Paris: Durlacher, 1958), pp. 8off; and *Le Monde*, Dec. 27, 1957.

[60] Pineau, cited in *Jerusalem Post*, Jan. 23, 1958; see also Dec. 15, 16, 18-20, 1957.

V

Broadening the Alliance

IMMEDIATELY after the Socialists' defeat in France on May 22, 1957, the overt political and diplomatic alliance with Israel seemed to wither. In Israel, the unwritten alliance was now rarely mentioned in the press, while, in France, the political instability which followed the demise of the Mollet government was bound to increase the freedom with which the Quai d'Orsay's traditionally pro-Arab diplomats discharged day-to-day foreign policy. Support for Israel was confined to relatively ineffectual pro-Israel pressure groups such as the *Alliance France-Israël*, which had been organized in November 1956 under the presidency of Jacques Soustelle. Many prominent political figures were included among its approximately one hundred members.[1]

Within the National Assembly, supporters of Israel formed a parliamentary group led by Edouard Depreux. The membership represented a wide range of political

---

[1] For example, Pierre André; Arthur Conte, Alfred Coste-Floret; former Defense Minister Jean Crouzier; Michel Debré; Georges Duhamel; André Marie; Maurice Faure, Secretary of State for Foreign Affairs; Maurice Schumann, Chairman of the Foreign Affairs Committee; Pierre Montel, Chairman of the National Defense Committee; François Mitterand; Edmond Michelet; Emile Roche; Generals Billotte, Catroux and Laurent; Jacques Piette; Pierre Lazareff, Managing Director of *France-Soir;* Guy Desson, Chairman of the Press Committee; Guy Oupfer, Chairman of the Committee on Justice; and Jules Ninine, Chairman of the Committee on Overseas Territories.

loyalties and by 1958 numbered over one hundred deputies, at least fifty senators, and five ministers of the Félix Gaillard government. Their only real contribution was the publication in January 1958 of a manifesto calling for a guarantee of Israel's borders. The manifesto was signed by fifty deputies, including former Premiers André Morice, Joseph Laniel, and Félix Gouin.

It is obvious that Jacques Soustelle had his own views of how a formal alliance with Israel might be useful to France. For Soustelle, only the existence of Israel prevented Syrian volunteers from marching into Algeria.[2] He suggested that a tripartite alliance between France, Israel, and the world Jewish community would enable "Jewish influences" to be brought to bear in support of pro-*Algérie Française* policies.[3] Going to great pains to deny that Israel Premier Ben Gurion was lukewarm toward a pact, Soustelle said,

> If and when French foreign policy rises superior to certain besetting weaknesses . . . then the question of an alliance between our two countries will be officially raised.
>
> We believe that, given the influence which not only Israel but above all the Jewish communities throughout the world exert on international opinion, this alliance would produce happy results for us.[4]

The importance of both the *Alliance* and the parliamentary group was generally exaggerated by the Israeli press, which tended to place too much importance on

[2] *Jerusalem Post,* Aug. 12, 1957.

[3] Jacques Soustelle, Gaullist Deputy, Fourth Republic; President of the *Alliance France-Israël,* interviewed in Paris, May 27, 1969.

[4] Cited in *Jerusalem Post,* Feb. 14, 1958.

the stream of public and private figures who visited Israel—generally by invitation—and who voiced support for a formal association between the two states. These were at best amorphous groupings of limited effectiveness and influence, unlike pro-Israel and Jewish organizations in the United States which can exert influence on both houses of Congress. The absence in France of any crystallized Jewish vote was partly responsible for their ineffectuality, but the nature and locus of the Fourth Republic decision-making process, it must be remembered, left great power to the bureaucracy while denying it to parliament. Moreover, no substantive discussion of Middle East foreign policy took place in the National Assembly during Bourgès-Maunoury's tenure as Prime Minister from June through September 1957, and in the only two brief interpellations on Middle East policy in January 1958, no mention was made of Israel. The French were preoccupied with the financial crisis, the Algerian question, and the related dispute over the bombings of Tunisian villages in retaliation for aid given FLN rebels, together with the rapid succession of governments and growing fears for the survival of the Republic.

On the international level, apart from those issues resulting from Suez, there were few official manifestations of Israel's amity with France during the last two years of the Fourth Republic. Israel, for example, never gave France unequivocal support in United Nations debates on the issue that concerned it most—North Africa. Indeed, Israel rarely spoke on the Algerian question and, while accepting the French contention that it was a domestic issue, nonetheless voted for resolutions of concern that called for negotiations.[5] Yet Israel was apparently guided by its relationship with France in other areas, particularly with regard to Germany and the decision to opt for a European orientation in foreign affairs.

As early as 1957, Jean Monnet had privately suggested to Shim'on Peres that he contact the Germans. The principal partisan of reconciliation with Germany, Peres convinced Ben Gurion that,

> . . . if it is imperative that we should develop our relations with France—and this no one doubts in Israel, except the Communists—, we must develop our relations with France's friends: with Italy, in so far as it depends on us, and no less, with Germany.[6]

Both Pierre Maillard and Pierre Gilbert have denied that France played any concrete diplomatic role in Israel's rapprochement with West Germany.[7] As *Le Monde* put it, France merely followed Israeli efforts "with greatest amity" and was kept informed of the developments.[8] By the end of 1958—after a cabinet crisis

[5] See *United Nations General Assembly Official Records* (UNGAOR), 11th sess., 654th plen. mtg., Feb. 15, 1957; Resolution 1012 (XI), Feb. 15, 1957; 12th sess., 1st ctte., 921st mtg., Dec. 4, 1957, pp. 311-312, paras. 63-75; 726th plen. mtg., Dec. 10, 1957; Resolution 1184 (XII), Dec. 10, 1957.

[6] David Ben Gurion, "Israel's Security and Her International Position. Before and After the Sinai Campaign," *State of Israel Government Yearbook 5720 (1959/1960)*, p. 81.

[7] Interviews in Paris with Maillard, chief of the Levant desk at the Quai d'Orsay, 1954-1959; Deputy Counsellor to the Secretariat General of the President (1959-1964), June 24, 1969; Gilbert, Ambassador to Israel (1953-1959), June 11, 1969.

[8] Dec. 27, 1957, referring to West German sale of light-tonnage submarines to Israel.

—Israel was selling machine guns, munitions, and shells to the Germans, and, in turn, Germany shipped Israel vast quantities of armaments. General of the Air Force André Martin recalls that the French army actively assisted in delivering the arms to Israel.[9]

Maillard, Gilbert, and Peres have hinted that in dealing with the Arab world Israel was guided by an understanding that it was to avoid conflict with Syria and Lebanon, which might prejudice French attempts to reestablish influence there. At the same time, France apparently served Israel as a go-between with Lebanon, presumably until 1967.[10] Paris had been consulted before a diplomatic offensive in Africa was launched in 1957 by visits to that continent of Ambassador Ya'akov Tsur and Foreign Minister Golda Meir. Apart from a few isolated instances, French colonial authorities at the local level were rarely cooperative and generally hostile to Israel's plans. French residents in Djibouti asked the French government to veto an Israeli presence there, fearing that complications with the Muslim population would follow. While France-Israel cooperation on African affairs was much more intimate at the central government level, throughout the late 1950s, the Quai d'Orsay delayed in granting Israel permission to open consulates in French territories.[11] This was particularly onerous to Israel in view of increasing Arab efforts south of the Sahara. No doubt France was reluctant to see Arabs and

[9] Interviewed in Paris, June 12, 1969.

[10] Interviews cited with Maillard and Gilbert; and Shim'on Peres, Director-General of the Ministry of Defense until 1959; interviewed in Tel-Aviv, July 31, 1969.

[11] The above is based on interviews cited with Gilbert and Martin; and with General Pierre Billotte, in Paris, May 29, 1969.

Israelis compete for influence in its overseas territories, but France's role as a Muslim power, commercial rivalry, and local jealousies also contributed to its hesitations. Such France-Israel cooperation as did exist in Africa tapered off in the early 1960s, once Israel's program of technical cooperation with developing nations was underway. By then Israel had established its own representatives in almost every major African capital and had less need of France's good offices.[12]

While overt political cooperation was limited and problematical, the tacit relationship continued unabated in those quasi-governmental spheres controlled by the defense establishment. Friendship for Israel was expressed primarily through the sale of arms and aircraft, direct collaboration between the armed forces of the two states (including the shadowy areas of intelligence), and cooperation on atomic research. In part this was possible because the authors of the tacit alliance still held key posts in the Defense and Interior Ministries, despite rapid changes of government. Ten of Bourgès' fourteen cabinet ministers had served in the Mollet government; Lacoste and Pineau had remained in office, while André Morice took over the defense portfolio until the government fell and Bourgès returned to the Interior Ministry. Under Félix Gaillard (November 1957-April 1958), Chaban-Delmas was Defense Minister.

In anticipation of an eventual third round between Israel and the Arabs, joint strategic planning continued after Suez with a view to the protection of mutual interests in the Arab world, the Mediterranean basin,

[12] The above is based on a conversation in Jerusalem with Yoel Sher, Department for International Cooperation, Israel Ministry for Foreign Affairs, July 15, 1969.

and the Red Sea.[13] All branches of the French armed forces considered Israel as the strategic key to Middle East stability. Military planners were particularly interested in Israel's location with regard to the Sinai Peninsula and as a protection for the fifty-three percent of France's oil supplies which came from the Middle East. The air force considered the possibility of using Israel as an air platform because of its location vis-à-vis the Red Sea, Djibouti, Réunion, and Madagascar, where French interests were based; and the navy, also thinking of potential bases, wanted to develop a common strategy for the Red Sea.[14] Reasoning that, as long as the Algerian war continued, Israel had the same enemies and same friends as France, military planners could see no problems arising between the two in the Mediterrean or other regional waters.

In addition to joint exercises involving the debarkation of commando forces, the French navy invited Israel in January 1958 to participate in joint maneuvers, during which the French taught their Israeli counterparts anti-submarine warfare techniques recently evolved. The Israeli destroyers were the "first foreign warships let in on the secrets by the French." [15] It was also the

[13] The following is based on interviews in Paris with Generals Billotte and Martin, cited above; a confidential source who served under General Paul Ely (1957-1958), June 14, 1969; General of the Air Force Maurice Challe, June 2, 1969; General Gaston Jean Lavaud, attached to the Ministry of Defense, June 12, 1969; and Admiral Maurice Amman, Director of the cabinet of the naval General Staff (1955-1959), June 26, 1969.

[14] On naval strategy, see Capitaine de Corvette H. Labrousse, "Les Menaces sur les Territoires Français et Anglais du Moyen-Orient," *Revue de Défense Nationale,* vol. 14 (June 1958), pp. 934-944.

[15] *Jerusalem Post,* Jan. 3, 1958. For confirmation of naval cooperation including the training of Israeli seamen, see com-

first time Israel's navy had participated in joint maneuvers as an integral part of a foreign task force. In order to appreciate the timing of these exercises, it should be noted that Egypt had just previously acquired Russianmade submarines, and a Soviet note to the tripartite powers on September 4, 1957, had protested against the "essentially military" Israeli alliance with France.[16]

On the basis of information supplied by Generals Ely, Grossin, and Jacquier, Jacques Piette, Ya'akov Tsur, and Louis Mangin, it is possible to confirm the general outlines of military cooperation.[17] The air forces exchanged information and shared equipment as well as new ideas for battle tactics. Israeli pilots continued to be trained by the French Air Force despite the expenses involved. Israeli officers and technicians attended French military academies and specialists' schools while French observers were sent to Israel, and regular exchanges of personnel were organized.

Although technology usually passed from France to Israel, in several instances French ground forces' equip-

---

ments by Admiral Georges Abanier, Chief of Staff of the French Navy (1960-1968), in *The Israel Digest,* vol. 24, June 11, 1971.

[16] *Le Monde,* Sept. 6, 1957. See also Walter Eytan, *The First Ten Years: A Diplomatic History of Israel* (London: Weidenfeld & Nicolson, 1958), p. 174.

[17] Interviews in Paris with General Paul Ely, Chief of Staff and President of the Committee of Chiefs of Staff (1954-1956, 1958-1961), June 5, 1969; Jacques Piette, a confidant of Guy Mollet, June 6, 1969; General Paul Grossin, Director-General of the *Service de documentation extérieure et de contre-espionnage* (SDECE) (1957-1962), June 25, 1969; General Paul Jacquier, Director-General of SDECE (1962-1966), June 25, 1969; Israel Ambassador to France Ya'akov Tsur (1953-1959), interviewed in Jerusalem, August 13, 1969; some of the details were confirmed by Louis Mangin of the French Ministry of Defense, correspondence with the author July 2, 1969.

ment was modified on the basis of Israeli suggestions. For example, tanks and particularly oil circulation circuits were adapted to desert conditions using an Israeli technique. In Algeria the French also adopted a method of convoy bombing that they had learned from Zahal at Suez.

Although airplane sales were negotiated bilaterally with the industry, the French military facilitated the sale of arms to Israel in every way possible, making available the latest developments in their arsenal such as cannon possessing sufficient range to hit Egyptian targets. Requests for arms went directly from one Defense Ministry to the other, bypassing the Israel Foreign Office and the ambassador in Paris. The French Chief of Staff could decide what arms should be delivered and would report only the general lines of his activities to the Premier, often leaving the latter in ignorance as to details. The Defense Minister had the credits at his disposal and therefore the final say, but he usually followed the inclination of the Chief of Staff.

In several other spheres, cooperation was very close. The intelligence services of the two countries had been working closely for years, and there was widespread suspicion at the time that the French were involved in the Israeli spy ring uncovered in Egypt in 1954. Two of the accused spies held French citizenship, and several of them had received training in France, according to Egyptian Interior Minister Zakariah Mohieddin.[18] Since the French service was not involved in "actions" until 1957, the earlier contacts consisted mostly of an exchange of information and documents, usually in Paris. General

---

[18] Mohieddin was interviewed by Kennett Love on August 19, 1954. See *Suez: The Twice-Fought War. A History* (N.Y.: McGraw Hill, 1969), p. 76.

Ely confirmed that the Chiefs of Staff also met at least twice a year after Suez, once in Paris and once in Tel-Aviv, to exchange intelligence data, primarily on the Arab world and occasionally on the USSR. The two services cooperated closely in Africa, particularly in East Africa, according to several knowledgeable sources, and Israeli contacts there were utilized by the French. The French secret services also assisted Israel with recruiting and supplied false papers to facilitate Jewish emigration from Morocco and Rumania.[19]

Algeria was another arena for cooperative effort in the last years of the Fourth Republic. Many French officers felt they could learn new techniques of psychological warfare from the Israelis. According to General Maurice Challe, the Israelis were "consummate artists" at dealing with the Arabs. General Challe hoped, moreover, to use the Israeli *qibbutz* as a model for his pacification program in Algeria, but his plans never materialized before independence.[20] As part of this friendly collaboration among professionals, Israeli study missions were welcomed in Algeria, where they expressed particular interest in the French use of helicopters to fight the guerrillas. Through the efforts of officials in the Resident General's personal cabinet, a handful of Israeli civilians were surreptitiously permitted to aid the Algerian Jewish population in emigrating to Israel and in organizing the *"auto-défense"* of their villages.[21]

The Israeli Foreign Ministry generally objected to the wide-ranging activities of the defense establishment and its encroachment on other aspects of Israeli economic,

[19] See note 17.

[20] Challe, interview cited.

[21] Confidential source in the Resident General's cabinet, interviewed several times during May and June 1969, in Paris.

political, and diplomatic ties with France. According to Ben Gurion's biographer, Foreign Minister Golda Meir repeatedly threatened to resign, protesting Shim'on Peres' independent foreign policy on the grounds that the lack of coordination between the ministries was detrimental to the whole fabric of Israel's foreign relations.[22]

On at least one occasion in 1958, the lack of coordination between the two ministries almost wrecked good relations with France. The Israeli Defense Ministry had shipped a planeload of arms abroad. When the plane landed mysteriously at Bône, Algeria, French officials there suspected that the arms were either for the rebel FLN, the *ultras,* or alternatively for the Moroccan rebellion against Spain. The Quai d'Orsay was furious, and the issue was brought before both the Kneset and the National Assembly. Ultimately, the French reluctantly accepted the Israeli explanation that the arms were for the Dominican Republic (which had aided Israel in 1948). Press reports at the time indicated that the Israeli defense authorities in contact with their French counterparts had received permission to fly by way of Algeria, but had neglected to inform the proper local authorities. In Israel the press demanded an end to independent action by defense officials, calling for Foreign Ministry control over the sale of arms abroad. However, the Defense Ministry would agree only to closer liaison between the two ministries in the future.[23]

[22] Michael Bar-Zohar, *The Armed Prophet; A Biography of Ben Gurion,* trans. by Len Ortzen (London: Barker, 1967), p. 277; and *Gesher 'al ha-Yam ha-Tikhon. Yahasei Tsarfat-Israel, 1947-1963* (Bridge over the Mediterranean. France-Israel Relations, 1947-1963; Tel-Aviv: 'Am ha-Sefer, 1964), pp. 191-199.

[23] On the above incident, see *Jerusalem Post,* March 2, 5, 7, 13, 1958; *Le Monde,* March 1, 2-4, 6, 1958; and *France-Soir,* March 2, 1958.

Israel's preemptive strike against Egypt in 1956 had been aimed at eliminating—at least temporarily—the danger imposed by 'Abd al-Nasir's massing of weapons along the Sinai frontier. That and the securing of free navigation in the Gulf of 'Aqabah were the major achievements of Suez from the Israeli point of view. But even more important for its long-range security, arms supplies had ceased finally and utterly to be conditional upon prior agreement among the three major powers. For the first time, Israel could plan for long-range arms purchases, particularly of jet aircraft. Zahal was thus able to reevaluate its strategic priorities. Both Air Force chief Dan Tolkovsky and Shim'on Peres pushed for the development of Israel's air arm, whose potential had been previously underestimated by General Moshe Dayan.[24] This was not due to any lack of strategic foresight on Dayan's part, but was probably a direct result of the difficulties Israel had theretofore faced in purchasing modern equipment. When the French government agreed to sell twenty-four Super Mystère B-2s, for delivery in 1959, Israel acquired the first truly supersonic airplane in its arsenal. With the signing during the final months of the Fourth Republic of the preliminary accord in principle for the sale of the Mirage III-C, Israel superiority in the air seemed assured, for the Mirage was considered a response to both the Mig 21 and the Sukhoi 7.

It is important to put into perspective the kind of relationship Israel offered the French air industry at this stage. Israel could contribute little in terms of advanced technology or research and development skills. However, a symbiosis had begun to emerge in 1956. As soon as Israel began to receive and use French warplanes

[24] See Ben Porat and Uri Dan, *Mirage Contre Mig* (Paris: Laffont, 1967), pp. 56-57.

in quantity, it was inevitable that widened bilateral contacts with the air industry would follow. Any manufacturer has to keep in mind the special requirements of his prime customer in designing his product, and the air industry viewed Israel in just that light. As a matter of fact, Israel was the first country to develop an operational theory for the Mystère, and Ya'akov Tsur confirms that Israeli demands had been already incorporated into the planning stage of the Super-Mystère.[25]

As Israel continued to utilize French products, there was a constant flow of information on modifications, specifications, and ameliorations. Such technical feedback was vital to the air industry and helped to create an unusually amicable relationship between client and supplier. General Paltiel Makleff notes that, during the Suez-Sinai war, Israel had made improvements in the Mystère in parts and methods, reducing the time and number of techniques needed to make the plane combat-ready. Turn-around time was cut in half, while an engine change was completed in about one hour and a half to two hours, instead of the twelve originally envisaged.[26] Moreover, as use by Israel exceeded by several years the supposed life-expectancy of the planes in service (900 hours for the Mystère IV, for example), new techniques for maintenance and parts replacement were developed.

After Suez, the Chiefs of Staff also exchanged ideas on improvements and simplifications and on the con-

[25] Interview cited.

[26] General Paltiel Makleff, Director of Elta Electronics Industries, interviewed at Israel Aircraft Industry near Lydda, Israel, August 14, 1969; see also Porat and Dan, *Mirage Contre Mig,* pp. 28-29, 80.

ception of planes still on the drawing-boards. Neither organized nor continuous, these exchanges were nonetheless frequent and mutually beneficial. Israeli influence on strategic planning at this level was considerable. For example, General Makleff recalls Israel's role in deciding whether it would be cheaper or more advantageous to design the Mirage for ground-to-air or interceptor air-to-air missions.[27] In another instance, Israel insisted on transforming the original Mirage design so that two 30 mm. cannon could be added. When the plane was first proposed to Israel, it was to be equipped solely with Matra missiles. Although Marcel Chassagny affirms that the missiles added at least twenty percent to the price of the aircraft, cost was not the prime factor in Israel's preference of armament.[28] Israel's defense needs differed from those of France. Considering the performance and effectiveness of air-to-air and air-to-ground missiles at high and low-level flight, Israel argued that cannon were needed for low-level defense.[29] By accepting the Israeli point of view, France widened the appeal of the aircraft for Switzerland, South Africa, and Australia, which bought the Mirage on Israeli advice.[30]

In addition to these exchanges, the Israel Aircraft

[27] Presumably this took place in late 1957-1958. Production began in 1960; deliveries started in 1963. Makleff, interview cited.

[28] Marcel Chassagny, President and Director-General of *Société des Engins Matra* since 1937, interviewed in Paris, June 16, 1969. Cf. Porat and Dan, *Mirage Contre Mig*, p. 30, who disagree with the author's conclusion.

[29] General Aharon Nahshon, Director-General Bet Shemesh Engines, Ltd., interviewed in Bet Shemesh, Israel, July 18, 1969.

[30] See *Aviation Week and Space Technology* (AWST), vol. 86 (May 29, 1967), pp. 84-91.

Industry (IAI) began to widen its contacts with French firms. IAI had worked closely with France almost from its inception in 1950, undertaking maintenance, overhaul, and modifications for Air France and the French Air Force, while overhaul agreements were signed with Hispano-Suiza, Turboméca, and Snecma. By repairing the engines of its French-built planes at home, Israel saved approximately $6,000 per repair job. In 1955, IAI, with French cooperation, made major modifications on the C-46 Commando, giving it a new lease on life and better payload. Auxiliary jet pods added under each wing increased maximum take-off weight. Turboméca Marboré-2 turbojets podded under the wings were not tested in France, however, but in the United States.[31]

On July 24, 1957, after six months of negotiations, IAI and Air Fouga (Etablissements Henry Potez) signed a licensing arrangement which permitted Israel to build the Fouga Magister CM-170, a twin-jet trainer and close support fighter, from domestically manufactured parts. Six months after signing the agreement, IAI began production.[32] According to Georges Volland of Potez-Fouga, Israel was sold one prototype, assembly packages for three planes, and some small parts.[33] It cost Israel the price of the original materials given, plus five percent royalties on the value of the airplane cell for the right of reproduction. Volland emphasized that this was not a completely private contract between IAI and Potez, since the French government had paid for the prototype and therefore had to approve the licensing

[31] Charles W. Cain, "Israel's International Air Line," *Aeroplane,* vol. 88 (March 4, 1955), pp. 279-282.

[32] The first Fouga left the assembly line in June 1960. A total of 48 were produced by June 1967. See *Ha-Arets,* July 7, 1960.

[33] Interviewed in Paris, June 17, 1969.

arrangements. Royalties on foreign payments were paid to the state. By approving the deal, the French government was essentially agreeing that Israel would not only train its own jet pilots but, even more important, take the first steps toward an independent air industry. Israel, in return, demonstrated the Fouga's operational versatility by modifying the plane for ground attack. Two machine guns were fitted in the nose and under each wing the plane could carry sixteen unguided air-to-ground rockets, one napalm package or one one-hundred pound bomb. Moreover, Israeli modifications extended the time between overhauls by fifty percent.

According to General Maurice Perdrizet, from 1957 and until about 1961-1962 France "gave Peres Dakotas to overhaul" in order to "recompense a good client," while radio and radar parts were manufactured under license in Israel for French sale abroad. This boost to the Israeli air industry was "a direct result of the good relations existing between the two Defense Ministries." [34] There were still problems, however, with the Quai d'Orsay's occasional diplomatic interventions, as in late 1957-early 1958 during a period of governmental instability. General Perdrizet told of one instance following the arrival of the twenty-four Vautours sold to Israel. They were grounded for some three months until "the difficulties were resolved" and Israel received permission to fly them.[35] The Vautour, a light twin-jet reconnaissance and tactical bomber manufactured by Sud Aviation, was Israel's most important delivery system at the time. Considered a response to the IL-28 in

[34] General Maurice Perdrizet, former representative in Israel of *L'Office Français d'Exportation de Matériel Aéronautique* (L'OFEMA); interviewed in Paris, June 18, 1969.
[35] *Idem.*

the Egyptian inventory, it could carry a 6,000-8,000 pound bomb load and had a sufficient combat radius to threaten most Egyptian targets.

Cooperation between France and Israel on nuclear research had first been publicized by French delegate to the United Nations Jules Moch in 1954, when he enthusiastically described an Israeli process for the production of heavy water which France had received.[36] The *Israel Government Yearbook* for 1955 states:

> Especially close contact between scientific institutions in both countries was reached in the field of nuclear research. France was enabled to make use of the process discovered in Israel for the extraction of heavy water, while young Israel scientists are doing post-graduate work in French laboratories.[37]

Pierre Mendès-France was the first officially to acknowledge earlier, discreet collaboration when he addressed the National Assembly in the post-Suez period.[38] François Bénard, former Minister of Atomic Affairs and a member of a parliamentary delegation which visited Israel in 1958, admitted in an interview with the *Jerusalem Post* that France was supplying uranium to Israel, which in turn made its advances in peaceful uses of atomic energy available to France.[39] Apart from these isolated statements, however, public officials have declined to elaborate on the existing connections.

In 1949, Israeli leaders had decided "at the highest political level" to look to France for assistance on

[36] Moch, interviewed in Paris, June 2, 1969.

[37] P. 190.

[38] *Journal Officiel de la République Française. Débats Parlementaires, Assemblée Nationale. Compte Rendu,* Dec. 18, 1956, 2nd sess., p. 6114.

[39] Feb. 4, 1958.

nuclear research. Professor Ernst Bergmann explained, "We felt that Israel could not develop such a program on its own, but needed to collaborate with a country close to its own technical level. First it was important to train Israeli experts. Then we would decide exactly what sort of collaboration to seek and what kind of contribution could be made in a joint endeavor, considering Israel's capacities and resources. Every effort was to be made to keep cooperation from being entirely one-directional." [40]

Since a large number of French atomic scientists in the postward period were Jewish, numerous unofficial contacts were easily established over the years. Many Leftist-leaning French scientists had close associations with leading members of the Socialist party and with Léon Blum who, in turn, had close ties with Israel. Others, like Fréderic Joliot-Curie, the High Commissioner, had played an important role in the Résistance, where many of the French connections with Israel were forged. French physicist Bertrand Goldschmidt confirms that friendly relations existed between the French and Israel Atomic Energy Commissions in the early 1950s, and that from 1953 on there were "technical exchanges with the Israeli Atomic Energy Commission for the study of heavy water production and for the treatment of low grade ores." [41] The Weizmann Insti-

---

[40] Professor Ernst Bergmann, Chairman of the National Committee for Space Research; former head of the Defense Ministry's Scientific Department and in charge of Israel's atomic energy program; interviewed in Jerusalem July 29, 1969.

[41] Bertrand Goldschmidt, *L'Aventure Atomique. Ses Aspects Politiques et Techniques* (Paris: Fayard, 1962), p. 100; see also p. 252; and his article, "The French Atomic Energy Program," *Bulletin of the Atomic Scientists,* vol. 18 (Sept. 1962), pp. 40, 47-48. See also Bar-Zohar, *Gesher,* p. 247.

tute of Science in Israel, a major source of heavy oxygen
for scientific research, had developed a cheap method for
producing heavy water without electrical power. At the
time, the only other sources of heavy water were the
United States and Norway, and American policy restricted access to fissionable materials.[42] Jean Renou of
the French Commissariat for Atomic Energy (CEA) confirms that two agreements on atomic research were
signed with the Weizmann Institute—one for the exchange of information to develop a process for extracting
uranium from Dead Sea low-grade phosphate ores, and
the other a ten-year research contract for the production of heavy water.[43] The first process was important at
the time because France had no other source of uranium.
But, according to Renou, the process was never used
because an alternative supply of uranium became available. The second accord, which was later renewed, was
widened in 1955 to include British participation in
mutual exploitation of the patent rights. Although the
importance of these accords has, at times, been over-
stated by analysts as well as journalists, at a minimum
they did constitute an essential bond between the nuclear programs of both countries at a critical stage in

[42] See William B. Bader, *The United States and the Spread of
Nuclear Weapons* (N.Y.: Pegasus, for the Center of International
Studies, Princeton, 1968), pp. 12, 23, 27-31; and *Jerusalem Post,*
July 6, 1961. See also Bar-Zohar, *Gesher,* p. 61; and Ruth
Mehrtens, "Israel's Burgeoning Science-Based Industries. Business
Around the Globe. Report from Tel-Aviv," *Fortune,* vol. 77
(April 1968), pp. 61, 64.

[43] Jean Renou, since 1959 head of the Department of Foreign
Relations (Interior and Public Relations) of the French Commissariat for Atomic Energy; interviewed in Paris, June 16, 1969;
see also *Ha-Arets,* Dec. 21, 1960.

their development.[44] In addition, Israeli scientists were admitted to the Institute of Nuclear Science and Techniques at Saclay, near Paris, to work on nonmilitary research and were also allowed at the Marcoule reactor.[45]

From the establishment of the CEA on October 8, 1945, the top levels of command remained fairly stable despite continual changes of government. Nuclear policy was effectively removed from political control and left in the hands of the Administrator General, the High Commissioner, and the CEA. Early efforts to develop an atomic program were taken without any actual decision at the cabinet level. In 1951, the military phase began with a decision in November to construct two high-power plutonium reactors. The CEA was reorganized, and the balance of control over atomic policies passed from the scientists to government administrators and, in particular, to the Administrator-

[44] Ann Williams, for example, argues that the aircraft and arms subsequently delivered by France to Israel, as well as the 1954 visit of Dayan, were in direct return for the Israeli processes. There is no evidence of immediate cause and effect to back this assumption. It is important to keep in mind the timing of the arms negotiations, which began in 1950, as well as the larger political factors favoring the weapons sales. Furthermore, one must be careful in evaluating the importance of Israel's contributions to the French nuclear program at a time when France had not yet decided upon a military option. See Ann Williams, *Britain and France in the Middle East and North Africa, 1914-1967* (N.Y.: St. Martins, 1968), p. 119.

[45] Jean Daniel, "Prophet of the Arab World? De Gaulle and the Jews," *Atlas*, vol. 15 (Feb. 1968), p. 23; Goldschmidt, "The French Atomic Energy Program," vol. 18 (Oct. 1962), p. 46; John Walsh, "France: First the Bomb, Then the 'Plan Calcul,'" *Science*, vol. 156 (May 12, 1967), p. 768.

General Pierre Guillaumat.[46] A *Polytechnicien*, like Bourgès and Abel Thomas, he served until 1958, when he became Minister for Atomic Energy Affairs. Guillaumat was to prove a consistent supporter of Israel, and his appointment seems to have opened new possibilities for formal cooperation.

In October 1954, Premier Pierre Mendès-France (June 1954-January 1955), generally considered a critic of nuclear force, merely acquiesced in the face of earlier events when a nuclear weapons planning unit, the Committee on Nuclear Explosives, was established within the CEA. In December a study of atom bomb production was undertaken, and in 1955 a secret protocol was drawn up between the CEA and the national defense establishment on a joint program for 1955-1957 which was signed by Minister for Atomic Planning Gaston Palewski and by Defense Minister General Pierre Koenig.[47] On December 5, 1956, the Committee for the Military Application of Atomic Energy was created. Plutonium was refined on January 7, 1957, and in July a decision was taken to build an enriched uranium plant at Pierrelatte.

---

[46] See Lawrence Scheinman, *Atomic Energy Policy in France under the Fourth Republic* (Princeton: Princeton, 1965), p. 22. See also Robert Gilpin, Jr., *France in the Age of the Scientific State* (Princeton: Princeton, for the Center of International Studies, 1968); Wilfrid L. Kohl, "The French Nuclear Force and Alliance Diplomacy, 1958-1967," unpublished Ph.D. dissertation, Columbia University, 1968; and "Atomic Energy Development in France During 1946-50," *Nature,* vol. 165 (March 11, 1950), pp. 382-383.

[47] George A. Kelly, "The Political Background of the French A-Bomb," *Orbis,* vol. 4, no. 3 (1960), p. 290; Kohl, "French Nuclear Force," p. 15; and *Le Monde,* April 8, 1954.

While atomic policy had become a "real controversy" in French politics by the middle of 1955, most military authorities remained uninterested in nuclear weapons.[48] The atomic program was guided and developed by a relatively small group within the CEA, the government, and the military, well situated in authority but operating largely through informal channels outside the mainstream of political activity. Only a small group of officers in the Ministry of Defense had favored an atomic policy ever since the defeat in Indochina. Many were survivors of Dienbienphu who had also been involved in the Suez invasion and the North African campaigns. Having come to see Israel as a natural ally in the Middle East, from 1955 to 1958, by various devices, they complied with Israeli arms requests. Among them were Admiral Lepotier and the Generals Gallois, Beaufre, Challe, and Ely. Since a March 1954 debate, they had been supported within the government by Maurice Bourgès-Maunoury, Félix Gaillard, Maurice Faure, Christian Pineau, Pierre Koenig, André François-Monteil, Max Lejeune, and Jacques Soustelle.[49] At the heart of their position was the conviction that France could not rely on allied support to preserve purely French interests. As Lawrence Scheinman observed, they concluded that "the respect of the French Community and the emergent Afro-Asian nations turned on whether

[48] Ciro Zoppo, "France as a Nuclear Power," *The Dispersion of Nuclear Weapons. Strategy and Politics,* R. N. Rosecrance, ed. (N.Y.: Columbia, 1964), p. 119.

[49] This analysis is based on interviews in Paris with General Paul Ely, cited above, and with Jacques Soustelle, Minister for Atomic Affairs (1959-1960), May 27, 1969. See also Kohl, "French Nuclear Force," pp. 16-17; Kelly, "Political Background," pp. 292-294.

the mother country was endowed with a nuclear weapons capability." [50]

Increasingly independent of governmental control, by early 1958 the French army and the Ministry of Defense had complete responsibility for the conduct of the war in Algeria. As the officers and officials of the defense establishment intervened more and more directly in political life within metropolitan France, they pressed for an independent nuclear deterrent. It is conceivable that these men encouraged scientific cooperation with Israel to reinforce a military nuclear policy not formally approved, but one they considered essential to the survival of the non-Communist world. In view of the military group's larger world strategy, Israel was extremely important not only for its scientific capacity which might, in a small way, compensate for American refusals to share information, but as a trusted ally, and thus an ideal partner for sharing the tasks of nuclear research.

In 1956 negotiations were begun for a new and important agreement between Israel and France in the field of nuclear research. The official CEA version offered by Renou claims that private French industry contracted to help Israel construct a nuclear reactor at Dimona, with "government approval," in order to gain experience and enhance French prestige. However, Abel Thomas insists that the agreement—signed by Louis Joxe and Ya'akov Tsur during the premiership of Bourgès-Maunoury (June-September 1957)—was a political decision designed to enable Israel to protect itself independently of the vagaries of foreign aid. [51] According to J. C. Hurewitz, the probable cost of the

---

[50] Scheinman, *Atomic Energy Policy*, p. 21; see also pp. 95-98.
[51] Interviews cited.

reactor reached somewhere near $75 million, which is high for a research project.[52] It is reasonably safe to assume, therefore, that the reactor was designed to offer Israel a military option. The only evidence that France may have hoped for some mutual technological benefit has come from Bourgès-Maunoury, who admitted the possibility of gaining from "Israel's strength in pure and theoretical science."[53]

[52] *Middle East Politics: The Military Dimension* (N.Y.: Praeger, 1969), pp. 476-477.

[53] Conversation with the author in Paris, June 23, 1969.

VI

A Return to Orthodox Diplomacy

WITH the fall of the Mollet government in May 1957, the almost complete identification of interests that had characterized French relations with Israel during the Socialists' government ceased to exist. It became apparent that French political and diplomatic support for Israel would henceforth be confined to a few narrow areas. The continuation of earlier patterns of governmental behavior, however, enabled the defense establishments of France and Israel independently to broaden their contacts in the fields of military technology and atomic research as long as the architects of the tacit alliance remained in power in the armed forces and the Defense Ministry. However, these were the same individuals who helped bring down the Fourth Republic. They installed—and then rejected—Charles de Gaulle, and finally they in turn were ejected by the new system under the Fifth Republic. Their exit from the scene and the ensuing tensions between the civilian and military institutions in France were bound to have a profound—and adverse—effect on French relations with Israel.

From 1958 to 1962, far-reaching constitutional changes designed to consolidate de Gaulle's power were initiated. Administrative and political developments creating a powerful crisis executive permitted de Gaulle to curb the rebellious, resentful military establishment while he deliberately and cautiously proceeded to end the Algerian war, move toward a position of neutrality, and restore normal relations with the Arab world. The evolution of international and domestic politics in the Fifth Republic and the style of government developed by General de Gaulle altered the content and operation and contributed to the decline of the special relationship with Israel.

In the period of agony which accompanied the fall of the Fourth Republic and the appearance of the Fifth, French foreign and defense policies became increasingly vulnerable to internal political developments. Because Rightist, pro-*Algérie Française* politicians and high army officers had permitted de Gaulle to come to power, only a thin line divided foreign from domestic policy until the question of Algeria was settled. While de Gaulle's foreign policy rarely questioned any of the fundamental decisions of the Fourth Republic—even those taken in opposition to him—there was an essential difference in tone, style, ideological inspiration, and, most of all, in the mechanisms of decision-making.[1]

A strict reading of the French Constitution promulgated on October 4, 1958, limits the President of the Republic in foreign affairs. Under Article 52, he "shall negotiate and ratify treaties. He shall be informed of all negotiations leading to the conclusion of an international agreement not subject to ratification." In practice, however, General de Gaulle interpreted this article, and the role of arbitrator and "guarantor of national independence" ascribed to him under Article 5, to mean direct responsibility for decisions on foreign policy. His broadcasts and public pronouncements left no doubt

[1] Alfred Grosser, *La Politique Extérieure de la Ve République* (Paris: Seuil, 1965), pp. 25-26.

that he placed foreign policy within a reserved, presidential domain.

According to Dorothy Pickles, foreign affairs, the French Community, Algeria, and defense were within that domain.[2] Pierre Maillard confirms that it was the General who determined policy on major United Nations votes, relations with Germany, Eastern Europe, and the superpowers, or decisions in principle on arms sales.[3] On other matters, where de Gaulle fixed only the outer limits of policy, it is difficult to ascertain exactly how much latitude of action he permitted his Foreign Minister.

Obviously, the President could not give his attention to every detail. Unfortunately for Israel, as Ambassador Gilbert has explained, Middle East problems usually fell in the category of secondary issues except in times of crisis such as April-May 1967.[4] More often than not, they were left to the Quai d'Orsay, where "traditionalist" Maurice Couve de Murville and his staff consistently displayed a pro-Arab tendency, often interfering with the execution of decisions favorable to Israel. Since de Gaulle was generally thought to be pro-Israel, Israeli diplomats tried to bring important matters to the attention of the Elysée, rather than have them dealt with at the Quai d'Orsay.[5]

---

[2] *The Fifth French Republic. Institutions and Politics,* 3rd ed. (N.Y.: Praeger, 1966), pp. 75, 140.

[3] Pierre Maillard, Deputy Councillor in the Secretariat General of the Presidency (1959-1964) and Assistant Secretary of National Defense (May 1964-November 1968), interviewed in Paris, June 24, 1969.

[4] Pierre Gilbert, French Ambassador to Israel (1953-1959), interviewed in Paris, June 11, 1969.

[5] David Catarivas, Israel Ministry for Foreign Affairs, interviewed in Jerusalem, July 16, 1969.

Prestigious individuals could be used as intermediaries to reach the President, but General Pierre Koenig recalled that it grew increasingly difficult to gain admission to the Elysée when it became known he was coming to plead Israel's cause.[6] This was particularly true after September 1959, once the General's decision to opt for self-determination in Algeria was made known. Thereafter, de Gaulle's relations with these Fourth Republic Gaullists and ex-Résistance fighters who had supported close ties with Israel were hardly characterized by mutual trust. The Right, which had brought de Gaulle to power, openly challenged him, while among those who were reported to be in sympathy with the January 1960 Algiers revolt were his own premier, Michel Debré, André Morice, Léon Delbecque, Jacques Chaban-Delmas, Roger Frey, Edmond Michelet, and Raymond Triboulet, all of whom were members of the *Alliance France-Israël* or the pro-Israel parliamentary group.[7] Other friends of Israel, among them Generals Jouhaud, Salan, Challe, and Minister for Atomic Affairs Jacques Soustelle (1959 to February 1960), were led to treason as they disavowed Gaullist policies.

If these developments altered the nature of ties with Israel, so also did changes in the Assembly's role. While most of the politics of the tacit alliance had been conducted in secret, in the past the parliamentary foreign affairs or defense committees could, in principle at

[6] Interviewed in Paris, June 16, 1969.

[7] See *Le Monde*, May 18-19, 1958; *Jerusalem Post,* Jan. 25, 1959; Jan. 20, May 24, 1963; Dec. 20, 1964; and Alexander Werth, *The De Gaulle Revolution* (London: Hale, 1960), pp. 2, 40-41. See also Philip M. Williams, *The French Parliament (1958-1967)* (London: Allen and Unwin, 1968), p. 99.

least, criticize administration and policy, in addition to drafting legislation. These committees, Philip M. Williams has pointed out, were now limited in duration, scope, and effectiveness as "another object of Gaullist suspicion." [8] From 1958 to 1962, parliamentary life was reduced to a rudimentary level. The government nearly always denied the Assembly an opportunity to vote on its own declarations of policy and, while Debré was Prime Minister, often refused to permit debate. Although fewer declarations were made and more debate was allowed after the Algerian settlement and Pompidou's accession to the premiership in April 1962, the minority was often frustrated and unable to use the Assembly effectively to appeal to public opinion. Senator André Monteil noted that any concessions by the government were made in private, usually as a result of the influence deputies could occasionally exercise on budget matters by calling ministers for questioning before commissions and by threatening adverse votes. [9]

As a result of the constitutional provision making ministerial office incompatible with membership in parliament, many of the key posts in the first government of the Fifth Republic passed to nonpolitical technicians and bureaucrats who lacked the feelings for Israel that had characterized the Fourth Republic politician-ministers. When politicians were appointed by Pompidou, they were relegated to obscurity, while the power of the technocrats to make policy on the operational level increased. [10]

A number of inter-Ministerial Committees were set up,

[8] *Ibid.*, p. 50; see also pp. 19, 52, 55, 102.
[9] Interviewed in Paris, June 20, 1969.
[10] Pickles, *The Fifth French Republic,* pp. 121-123; see also p. 102, note 3.

in which, under General de Gaulle's Presidency, policy was formulated on Algerian affairs, foreign affairs and defense. Ministers were frustrated by technical committees, by-passed by the President's personal advisers, confused by the duplication of Ministerial departments and others under the control of the Elysée or of the Hôtel Matignon, reduced to the status of executants of a policy in whose formulation they took less and less part.[11]

The trend was toward decision-making at the top, rather than the fragmented multilevel decision-making of the Fourth Republic which had served Israel's interests. Thus Israel could no longer benefit as it had in the Fourth Republic, from independent-minded bureaucrats, influential deputies, highly placed ministers or their cabinets. Israeli diplomacy was forced into more shadowy, often less respectable arenas in order to reach the ear of the President. David Catarivas recalls seeking out a friendly priest-confessor here, a mistress there, or an official open to "other sorts of persuasion." [12]

That de Gaulle faced the challenge of a generally hostile army explains the domestic and much of the foreign policy of the Fifth Republic. The military could exert pressure on de Gaulle in the early stages of the Fifth Republic because of its key role in the demise of the Fourth Republic. A high-ranking general states that when Pflimlin formed his government in May 1958, he had asked the army chiefs for reassurance that they would support the government in the event of

[11] The Hôtel Matignon is the premier's official residence. *Ibid.*, p. 140. See also Gaston Jean Lavaud, "La Délégation Ministérielle pour l'Armement," *Revue Militaire Générale* (Dec. 1961), p. 617; (Jan. 1962), pp. 103-114.

[12] Interview cited.

national disorder. The resignation, first of General Ely and then of General Guy Grout de Beaufort, permitted the Fifth Republic to come into being.[13] However, as many of the officers who served under de Gaulle's presidency came to disapprove of the General's policies they were effectively removed from office. During the succeeding power struggle and open rebellion, de Gaulle took measures to curb the military, inevitably affecting the functioning if not the very substance of the tacit relationship with Israel. While he may not have deliberately forced a disengagement at any time before 1967, his actions gradually restricted the autonomy previously enjoyed by the military establishment. Although it is open to question just how effectively this reorganization reduced independent contacts between the French and Israeli defense establishments, it did place cooperation between the two countries along more orthodox lines.

Article 21 of the Constitution of October 4, 1958, reinforced by the Ordinance of January 7, 1959, concentrated responsibility for defense in the hands of the President, who formally presided over the Superior Council of Defense.[14] The council functioned as the major planning group, while the smaller Defense Committee, which could be activated by the Premier, had

[13] Interview with confidential source attached to the military staff of General de Gaulle (January 1959-April 1960); served under General Ely (1957-1958), in Paris, June 14, 1969.

[14] For the 1959 regulations, see Bernard Chantebout, *L'Organisation Générale de la Défense Nationale en France Depuis la fin de la Seconde Guerre Mondiale* (Paris: Bibliothèque Constitutionnelle et de Science Politique, 1967), pp. 183-194; and on Debré's role, pp. 205-206; see also Edgar S. Furniss, Jr., *De Gaulle and the French Army. A Crisis in Civil-Military Relations* (N.Y.: Twentieth Century Fund, 1964), p. 131.

only secondary importance. It was at this level that influence could be exerted in behalf of Israel. General André Martin reports that council meetings were generally attended by the Prime Minister, Chiefs of Staff, and Ministers of the Armed Forces, Interior and Defense, as well as a delegate responsible for armaments.[15] De Gaulle himself defined the broad lines of policy, while Michel Debré executed them. The creation by Debré of a General Staff for National Defense to coordinate the activities of various ministries and actually direct the armed forces, relegated the Chief of Staff and the Minister of the Armed Forces to a relatively low position in the administrative hierarchy. As a result, when Pierre Guillaumat was Minister of the Armed Forces from January 8, 1959, to February 5, 1960, he suffered from bad relations with and lack of control over the armed forces. His successor, Pierre Messmer, managed to reduce overt conflict, but his power was tenuous at best. Thus neither was able to attend to the problems of Israel, despite their close connections with the state and presumable willingness to do so.[16]

As part of de Gaulle's administrative reorganization of the national defense structure in the decrees of April 5 and December 2, 1961, authority was centralized in a Chairman of the Ministerial Committee for Armaments. This eliminated the supervisory responsibility previously enjoyed by the Minister of State and the Ministerial Committee for Air, both of which had tended to be sympathetic to Israel's arms needs under the

---

[15] General André Martin, Chief of General Staff under Minister of the Armed Forces Guillaumat (1958-1959), interviewed in Paris, June 12, 1969.

[16] *Idem.*

Fourth Republic.[17] Paralleling similar reforms elsewhere in the French government, the 1961 measures improved general coordination among various departments, but also reduced ease of access for Israel.

Additional restructuring of defense under the July 18, 1962, reform further reinforced the President's power and increased that of the Armed Forces Minister at the expense of the Premier.[18] After the November 1962 elections, the virtual elimination of the Right from the Assembly, and the Algerian settlement, de Gaulle was in undisputed control. He held the army in check through administrative measures and by dangling the atomic *force de frappe* in front of their eyes. Ballistic missile research and development were placed under an autonomous branch, and Gaston Palewski as Minister of State for Scientific Research and Atomic and Space Questions became a key figure, especially because of the wide economic powers at his disposal. Martin recalls that neither Palewski nor General Charles Ailleret, a key spokesman for French atomic independence who became Chief of Staff in 1961, was particularly inclined to support Israel.[19]

Gradually the military manifested less strategic interest in Israel and the eastern Mediterranean. Israel was no longer so important as a base or air platform for a fully modernized French army as it had been for a colonial one. However, it was still favored by the air arm because of Israeli purchases of French aircraft. Moreover, the French delivery system was based on the Mirage series, which required aerial refueling in order

[17] For regulations, see Chantebout, *L'Organisation Générale,* pp. 216ff., pp. 291ff.

[18] *Idem.*

[19] Interview cited.

to reach distant targets, and Israel was strategically located for that purpose. As the high-level officers who enjoyed the closest ties with the Israel defense establishment gradually retired or resigned from the French forces, however, leadership passed to a generation which had known neither Suez, Algeria, nor Israel. Even if the Suez and Algerian experiences impregnated their spirits, their commitment to the preservation of Israel could only be less strong.[20]

Hoping that cultural cooperation would reinforce ties between the two countries, given the Gaullist vision of France's cultural mission, Israel in 1958 had begun to press for the conclusion of a cultural agreement. As a result of the large-scale immigration to Israel of French-speaking Jews from North Africa and Rumania, there was increased interest in French language and culture, which was fostered by the *Centres de Culture Française* and *L'Information,* a French-language daily newspaper which had begun publication in 1957.

French culture, however, could never have the same prestige in Israel that it had enjoyed among the educated Arab elite for in Israel the revival of the Hebrew language and the teaching of national Hebrew culture go hand-in-hand with citizenship training. Moreover, while Israel book imports per head were the second highest in the world, French literature could not really compete with English. Not only were there more scientific, technological, and general works written in English, but French books were expensive. While Israel, as a gesture to the Fourth Republic, had permitted importers of French books to pay in local cur-

[20] This view is shared by General Gaston Jean Lavaud, Chief of Staff of the Army (February 1959); Ministerial Delegate for Armament (1961-1963), interviewed in Paris, June 12, 1969.

rency into a special bank account used by the Embassy to cover expenses, there was no corresponding action by France designed to lessen their cost. On the other hand, France might have looked askance at Israel's overriding interest in seeing an expansion of the teaching of Hebrew within France as opening the door to the dissemination of Zionist ideology and the encouragement of emigration.[21] David Catarivas recalls the endless French delays before November 30, 1959, when Israel became the thirty-sixth state to sign a cultural agreement with France. Presidential pressure from the Elysée had to be brought to bear to bring about its signature and, Catarivas asserts, only perfunctory formalities were elicited from the Quai d'Orsay officials.[22]

Rather than producing closer ties, however, the cultural agreement seemed to cause disharmony.[23] The French were dissatisfied at the rate with which French was introduced into the Israeli school system, while Israel was disappointed to find that, instead of the wide study of Hebrew that had been envisioned, only the universities of Montpellier and Toulouse would establish chairs in Hebrew.

While economic relations were of only marginal importance to the tacit alliance, they were nonetheless a barometer measuring its development and decline, espe-

---

[21] See Levi Eshkol's complaint that fewer Jews than non-Jews had chosen to study Hebrew in France. State of Israel, *Divrei ha-Kneset*, 5th Kneset, vol. 40, 384th sess., July 15, 1964, p. 2363.

[22] Catarivas, interview cited.

[23] For further details on the agreement and the Joint Committee for its application, see *The Middle East Record*, vol. 1, 1960, p. 296; *Jerusalem Post*, Oct. 27, 1966; State of Israel, Ministry for Foreign Affairs Information Division, *Facts About Israel* (Jerusalem: Jerusalem Post, 1967), pp. 140-141; *State of Israel Government Yearbook 5726 (1965/1966)*, p. 103.

cially since Israel's constant security threat made it impossible to divide issues neatly into political or economic spheres. Ambassador Ya'akov Tsur observed that the France-Israel accord was "based on different but parallel interests" and would always "bow before considerations of vital national self-interest." [24] When France displayed an increasingly narrow conception of those interests in the economic sphere, however, Israeli officials began to have serious doubts about the durability of the special relationship.

In October 1959, the French automobile manufacturer Renault, without cabinet knowledge but evidently with the concurrence of the Quai d'Orsay, decided to terminate its three-year association with Kaiser-Ilin of Israel for the assembly of Dauphine automobiles. Renault was motivated mostly by a Tunisian and Moroccan decision to adhere to the Arab boycott at a time when increased Volkswagen competition was hurting Renault's export sales. When Israel complained, Couve de Murville openly expressed annoyance at "false interpretations" which made a political issue out of essentially economic decisions.[25] Since Renault is a nationalized concern, however, it was futile for him to assert that the issue was not political or that "The Quai d'Orsay cannot intervene in Renault export trade policy." [26] In fact, the government could have invoked several measures to influence the company, such as offering to protect Renault against the loss of investments due to noncommercial causes. It is significant that,

[24] Cited in *Jerusalem Post,* Jan. 18, 1960.

[25] *Journal Officiel de la République Française. Débats Parlementaires. Assemblée Nationale. Compte Rendu,* Oct. 30, 1959, pp. 2123-2124.

[26] Citation from *Jerusalem Post,* Oct. 21, 1959.

when difficulties had arisen over the renewal of the original agreement in 1958, both the French Ambassador and the government intervened in Israel's favor. Moreover, the government did not in the end allow Renault to invoke a 1958 clause which would have absolved the company of all damages.[27]

The Renault decision was probably partly in retaliation for Israel's actions in 1958, when a French company had been outbid by $200,000 for a IL 30 million Haifa dockyard contract by a Dutch firm. Both the Israeli defense establishment and French Ambassador Pierre Gilbert had warned that loss of the contract would alienate powerful interest groups in France. They objected to Finance Minister Levi Eshkol's insistence that only economic factors should guide Israel's decision.[28] Air France's cancellation of a proposed agreement for cooperation with El Al Israel Airlines might not have caused such a flurry had it not coincided with the Renault affair. Once again, France reacted negatively to "irresponsible Israel journalism" which imputed the basest motives to France.[29]

During the Suez period, French policy was dictated by the desire to aid Israel and ease its economic problems. Long-term credits were granted for the purchase of industrial equipment, including a $10 million credit for

[27] *Ibid.*, Oct. 18-26, 1959; and Maillard, interview cited. For the dénouement of the affair and attempts to resume relations, see *Jerusalem Post*, Nov. 5, 1963; Jan. 29, 31, Feb. 12, May 7, 1964.

[28] *Jewish Observer and Middle East Review* (JOMER), vol. 8 (Oct. 30, 1959), pp. 5-6; *Jerusalem Post*, April 22, 1959.

[29] *Ibid.*, Jan. 1, 5, 13, 1960; JOMER, vol. 9 (Jan. 8, 1960), pp. 4-5; *L'Année Politique 1959*, pp. 400-401; and Ya-akov Tsur, Ambassador to France (1953-1959), interviewed in Jerusalem, August 13, 1969.

chemical and chocolate factories. Repayment was guaranteed by the French government's foreign credits insurance scheme. In July 1957, a $30 million credit agreement was signed granting Israel short-term credits on goods for which France expended dollars, and longer-term credit of two to eight years for others. Israel was to spend $5 million on cereals and African produce (coffee, cocoa), $5 million on semi-finished goods, $20 million on capital goods.[30] A second $15 million loan was granted under easier terms for development projects to be carried out with French technical assistance.[31] Private French interests had earlier presented tenders exceeding $100 million for the construction of the Haifa Carmelite (subway), a Beer-Sheva-Eilat railroad, the ports of Eilat and Ashod, a Haifa shipyard, and a central water supply and sewerage system for Tel-Aviv.[32]

Once political factors no longer determined economic relations between the two countries, the imbalance in trade illuminated the harsh fact that the two economies were in no way complementary. As one Israeli analyst noted,

> In any case, the prevalent notion that political cooperation must needs be followed by commercial exchange (and vice versa) is borne out neither by facts nor by common sense. . . . France-Israel trade relations will be largely influenced by factors quite distinct from mutual sympathy and common stand against Pan-Arab conspiracies.[33]

The decisive factors determining trade relations were the extension of French credits—the amount and terms

[30] *Jerusalem Post,* April 2, July 5, 1957.
[31] *Ibid.,* July 8, 1957; see also July 14, 1957; Jan. 26, 1958.
[32] *Ibid.,* May 17, 1956.
[33] Moshe Atar in *Jerusalem Post,* July 14, 1957 supplement.

offered—and the effect of anti-inflationary policies adopted by the French government, including the impact of import cuts on Israel exports. Even given the most favorable conditions, there was little scope for future growth.

Although the first trade agreement with France was signed in 1953, Israel purchased little from France. French prices were high, and, since official and unofficial dollar aid came primarily from the United States and German reparations payments, most Israeli purchases were made in those countries. When political and military interests drew France and Israel together after 1955, the rise in the level of trade was largely accounted for by Israel's importation of great quantities of military equipment. The sixfold increase in French importation of Israeli products from 1954 to 1955, largely in the agricultural sector, and the twofold increase from 1955 to 1956, reflected in part a French political decision to help ease Israel's negative balance of payments.[34] The Israel government found it increasingly difficult to pay. While imports from France totaled $22.7 million in 1959, rising to $25.4 million in 1960 and $46.8 million in 1961, exports reached only $4.2 million, $4.5 million, and $4.7 million, respectively.[35] In 1958 France ranked seventh in imports from Israel, behind the United Kingdom, the United States, West Germany, Switzerland, Belgium, and Yugoslavia. Industrial products accounted for only $750,000; the remainder was agricultural goods,

[34] For trade statistics, see the *Yearbook of International Trade Statistics,* UN Sales Pub. Nos. 1955.XVII.9; 1957.XVII.6.Vol. 1; 1959.XVII.2.Vol. 1; 1961.XVII.9.

[35] *The Middle East Record,* vol. 1, 1960, p. 57; vol. 2, 1961, pp. 82-85. For comparisons with French trade with other Middle East states, see also *Middle East Affairs,* vol. 12, no. 7 (1962), pp. 199-207.

which faced stiff competition from other Mediterranean exporters.[36] Although France reduced customs duties on Israel citrus and other agricultural products by ten percent, possibilities for growth in trade were limited. High French production costs, aggravated by the devaluation of the franc, meant that French prices could be undercut elsewhere in Europe, while France had little need for Israel's high quality specialty products. Moreover, certain economic interests in the oil and textile industries were actually opposed to closer ties with Israel.

Trade talks were stalled throughout 1959 as Israel sought liberalized quotas along the lines of privileges granted to Common Market members. After prolonged negotiations, on January 21, 1960, a commercial agreement was signed which abolished some quotas, left nominal ones on certain categories, and continued to restrict imports of eggs, vegetables, orange juice, textiles, and other items.[37] Payment for the unfavorable 1959 $2 million trade balance was to be arranged for by loan. Israel continued to apply pressure, planning to lodge a complaint with GATT against France and Italy for their quantitative restrictions and discriminatory practices against Israeli industrial products.[38] The 1962 trade protocol was a major breakthrough, for the first time freeing Israel to sell industrial products in France (and vice versa), without restrictions. Quotas remained fixed, however, on Israeli citrus and agricultural exports.

As the French Ministry for Foreign Affairs prepared for the normalized relations with the Arab world which

[36] JOMER, vol. 8 (Oct. 30, 1959), pp. 5-6; *Jerusalem Post,* Jan. 18, 1959.

[37] For details, see *Jerusalem Post,* Jan. 21, 22, 1960.

[38] *Ibid.,* March 12, 1961.

would accompany a peace settlement in Algeria, it found its freedom of diplomatic action—especially in Cairo—complicated by Israel's conduct of diplomacy by rhetoric.[39] Partly out of a sense of isolation and partly out of a certain measure of parochialism, the Hebrew press fostered the notion that a "little entente" or un-written alliance existed between France and Israel.[40] At every new development in French politics, headlines would nervously question whether the alliance remained intact, while Israel sources—usually in Paris—would trumpet a reassuring "yes." To some degree this may have been a form of pressure on France to formalize the illicit affair by a treaty, but internal Israel politics were also at play, with each party outdoing the other in a desire to appear pro-French. The opposition Herut Party, which made slight gains in 1959, seemed at times to be conducting its electoral campaign in Paris.[41]

Shortly after coming to power, General de Gaulle began discreetly to disengage France from the close ties with Israel which had characterized the Suez period. In the future there would be fewer mutual declarations of identity of outlook and community of purpose. The French would be less publicly committed to Israel and the Israelis not expected to underwrite every French action. While de Gaulle directed that Israel's vital in-terests were not to be harmed, pledging his support in case Israel was menaced, "needless demonstrations of friendship, which could be misconstrued," were to be

[39] See French criticism in JOMER, vol. 9 (Oct. 14, 1960), p. 3.

[40] See *ibid.*, vol. 8 (Oct. 30, 1959), pp. 5-6; for a typical example, see Golda Meir's remarks, cited by Eric Rouleau, "Au Moyen Orient, diversification des amitiés dans la sauvegarde des intérêts nationaux," *Le Monde Diplomatique* (Jan. 1968), pp. 8-9.

[41] See *Jerusalem Post*, July 27, 1958; Feb. 5, July 3, 1959; and *Le Monde*, Feb. 5, 1959, for a critical editorial.

avoided.[42] The Jeanneney Commission's report, which reflected official thinking, argued that after seven years' absence from the area, "favorable conditions now made France more acceptable to the Arabs." The report cautioned France to maintain and increase its influence in the Middle East through benevolent neutrality—by avoiding involvement with "disruptive forces" or regional quarrels and by a "necessary revision" of certain marked attitudes of the last years. The Jeanneney Report urged that French aid be centered upon Iran and Lebanon, and widened to include Syria and Jordan.[43] Credits were, in fact, ultimately extended to Iran, Syria, Turkey, the UAR, and Iraq. By 1967, 21,153 French teachers and 5,577 technicians were in the Arab world—the majority in North Africa—while in Israel there were only thirty-three French teachers and no French technicians.[44] The change in the French relationship with Israel was further underscored by the recall of Pierre Gilbert as Ambassador to Israel and his replacement by J. A. A. Bourdeillette in December 1959 and when Walter Eytan replaced the popular Ya'akov Tsur in February 1960.

[42] *Jerusalem Post,* May 17, 1959; J.-R. Tournoux, *Secrets d'état* (Paris: Plon, 1960), p. 177. See also *Jerusalem Post,* March 7, 1960; and JOMER, vol. 9 (June 17, 1960), p. 4, on French anger at leakages concerning the sale of Mirages.

[43] For abbreviated French version, see *Rapport Jeanneney. La Politique de Coopération avec les pays en voie de développement,* No. spécial 201 (Paris: La Documentation Française, 1964). See also JOMER, vol. 13 (Feb. 28, 1964), p. 18; Pierre Rondot, "Politique Occidentale dans l'Orient Arabe," *Etudes* (June 1962), pp. 369-380; "Vers un Orient sans Liens?" *L'Afrique et l'Asie,* no. 4 (1963), pp. 41-46.

[44] See *Middle East Economic Digest* (London), Oct. 12, 1967, p. 696; *The Middle East Journal* chronologies, 1962-1969; and *Jerusalem Post,* Oct. 4, Dec. 12, 1967.

Suddenly in 1961 and 1962, a rash of newspaper reports condemned Jewish support for and alleged Israeli involvement with the ultra-Rightist terrorist organization in Algeria, the rebel OAS. Claims that Jacques Soustelle had received support from Ben Gurion and that Israeli intelligence agents or extreme Rightists were directly involved in OAS activities were based on a germ of truth: Soustelle's Committee of Democratic Defense did include Duhamel, Koenig, André Speri, and Solomon Friedrich-Formaset, who represented the Rightwing Herut in France.[45] Soustelle's friendship with wealthy American Jews and the financial support he allegedly received from them during his exile fanned suspicions of Israeli involvement.[46] In March 1961, an Algerian Jew and suspected OAS leader, Jean Ghenassia, was arrested and charged with being in touch with Israeli agents who had supposedly been smuggled into Algeria by submarine in late December 1960 with the aid of the secret service and the Etzel or Stern Gang (a terrorist faction during Israel's pre-independence struggle for statehood, associated with the Herut Party).[47] The *Jerusalem Post* on January 11, 1962, re-

[45] *Ibid.*, Oct. 7, 17, 1960; and see Jean Daniel, "Prophet of the Arab World? De Gaulle and the Jews," *Atlas*, vol. 15 (Feb. 1968), p. 23.

[46] I am indebted to Nicholas Wahl for bringing to my attention the question of Soustelle's relationship with such individuals as Abe Spanel, former head of *International Latex*. Spanel published an anti-de Gaulle, pro-Israel French newsletter in New York during the period of Soustelle's OAS activities. Wahl reported the "whispered view" that Soustelle was being financed in his exile by the Israeli secret service and by wealthy contributors to Israeli causes.

[47] *Jerusalem Post*, March 23, 26, May 16, 18, 1961; *Le Monde* and *L'Express*, May 15, 1961; and JOMER, vol. 11 (Feb. 2, 1962), p. 6.

ported an unsubstantiated but widespread belief that Jewish commandos in Oran were inspired by an Israel government policy which sought partition of Algeria. According to the article, the commandos were supposed to have the support of Maurice Schumann and Raymond Schmittlein within the French government. Matters were further complicated by General Salan's mobilization order and threats to kill any non-Muslims leaving Algeria. This had a devastating effect on those Algerian Jews who wanted to emigrate to Israel, particularly after one of the highest-ranking Jews in the French police was murdered by extremists in Algeria. According to reports he was executed because his involvement in Jewish emigration "weaned the youth away" from extremist local politics.[48]

Israel's role in the Algerian developments was probably exaggerated by the reports and rumors that circulated in the press and by word-of-mouth; nevertheless, it is difficult to ascertain to what degree they were based on fact. At his treason trial after the abortive Algiers coup of 1961, General André Zeller gave fuel to the allegations of Israeli involvement by testifying that the rebels expected support from "Portugal, South Africa, South America and perhaps Israel." [49] However, General Challe has emphatically denied any Israeli in-

---

[48] *Ibid.* (March 2, 1962), p. 4; and *Jerusalem Post,* Sept. 24, 1961; see also Jan. 27, 1961. On relations between the Jews, the FLN, and Israel, and the problem of Jewish citizenship in Algeria, see *Le Monde,* Dec. 28, 1960. On emigration, see *Jerusalem Post,* July 13, March 30, 1961. Note that the formation of the Israel Committee for Free Algeria was considered sufficiently interesting to be reported in *L'Année Politique 1961,* p. 734.

[49] *Le procès des généraux Challe et Zeller: textes complets des débats réquisitoires-plaidoiries, annèxes* (Paris: Latines, 1961), pp. 95, 98-99, 101, 226.

terest in the coup, saying that Zeller's testimony was "badly phrased," although he admitted the rebels would undoubtedly have exploited their contacts abroad—including those in Israel—had the coup been successful.[50] General Billotte has said that de Gaulle was "truly unaffected by the revolt and didn't even notice the imbeciles involved." [51] Yet he could hardly have accepted a situation in which foreign policy and the issue of support for Israel threatened to become enmeshed with domestic politics. Whether or not the General believed the reports of Jewish or Israeli participation, as he tightened his control over the armed forces in the wake of the revolt, his ministers, according to André Monteil, were required to sever their ties with the *Alliance France-Israël.*[52]

After the upheavals in Lebanon, Iraq, and Jordan in 1958 and 1959, there was a fundamental difference in the French and Israeli interpretations of events in the Arab world. The Israelis, fearing Arab encirclement, called for the construction of a defensive line to contain Nasirism, to be drawn from Ethiopia and the Sudan through Libya, Israel, Turkey, and Iran. De Gaulle's preference for a multilateral approach to Middle East problems was strengthened by Nikita Khrushchev's call in July 1958 for a summit meeting. But when an East/

[50] General Maurice Challe, Commander-in-Chief in Algeria (December 1958-April 1960), participated in the Algiers coup of April 21-25, 1961; interviewed in Paris, June 2, 1969. Suspicions of Israeli involvement were revived when after his pardon and subsequent release from prison, General Challe was employed by ZIM, Israel's shipping line, in an executive capacity.

[51] General Pierre Billotte, Vice President of the UNR group in the National Assembly (1962-1966), interviewed in Paris, May 29, 1969.

[52] Interview cited.

West detente failed to materialize, Ben Gurion in 1959 began once again to sound out western capitals on the long-standing issue of freedom of passage through the Suez Canal. He had little success, for from 1959 to 1961 'Abd al-Nasir was involved in a bitterly polemical anti-Soviet press and radio campaign. Thus the western powers were reluctant to provoke him. Besides, the Soviet government was unlikely to cooperate with any western action. Instead, de Gaulle urged Israel to rely on the personal intervention of the Secretary General of the United Nations, which came to nought.[53]

From 1959 on, confiscation at the Canal of cargoes destined for Israel became the rule, although it was at first not followed consistently. In 1960, however, the Danish *Inge Toft* and the Greek *Astypalae* bound for Haifa were forced to unload their cargoes. In September 1959, French naval forces in the Red Sea and the air force at Djibouti had taken precautions to prevent Egyptian interference with Israel shipping in the Gulf of 'Aqabah as well. But thereafter, General Martin claims, de Gaulle opposed suggestions to develop a common Red Sea strategy with Israel.[54]

That both countries were keeping their diplomatic distance seemed particularly evident at the United Nations. While the Israeli cabinet decided to vote with France on the question of Algeria, it abstained in the dispute over the French base at Bizerta, Tunisia. On two issues of interest to France—disarmament and nuclear test bans—Israel voted independently.[55] While

---

[53] *L'Anneé Politique 1959*, p. 361; *Jerusalem Post,* Oct. 1, Dec. 22, 23, 1959.

[54] Interview cited. See also JOMER, vol. 8 (Sept. 11, 1959), p. 5.

[55] See *Jerusalem Post,* Sept. 7, 13, 1960; and *Ha-Arets,* July 14, 23, 24, Aug. 28, 1961, for the Israeli view on Bizerta.

it stood with France on General Assembly Resolution 1379 (XIV) of November 20, 1959, it abstained on paragraphs (a) and (b) of Resolution 1652 (XVI), of November 24, 1961, which called upon member states to refrain from nuclear tests in Africa. On paragraph (c), concerning respect of Africa as a denuclearized neutral zone, Israel voted in favor, while France, supported by the United States, abstained. Israel also favored a test ban treaty, while France abstained, though the former echoed the latter's concern that such a treaty might prejudice general disarmament negotiations.[56] On the November 27, 1963, Resolution 1909 (XVIII), calling for a test ban conference, France, the United Kingdom, and the United States were among those opposed; Israel abstained.[57]

On all issues in the fifteenth General Assembly session of 1960, out of 145 votes, Israel voted 92 times with the United States, 74 times with the United Kingdom, and 58 times with France. In the sixteenth session (1961), out of 125 votes, Israel voted 74 times with the United States, 77 times with the United Kingdom, and 56 times with France. On Cold War issues, the breakdown is nearly identical, with Israel voting more often with the United States than with France. The same holds true of disarmament, with the greatest divergence from

[56] General Assembly Resolution 1649 (XVI), Nov. 8, 1961. The United States was in favor. See also Resolution 1648 (XVI), Nov. 6, 1961, urging states to refrain from further test explosions, with Israel in favor; France, the United Kingdom, the United States and the USSR opposed. See also *United Nations General Assembly Official Records* (UNGAOR), 17th sess., Annexes, Agenda Item 77, Resolution 1762 (XVII), Nov. 6, 1962. Cf. replies by France and Israel, *ibid.*, Agenda Item 26, Dec. A/5174, Annex II, pp. 9, 10.

[57] See also Resolution 1910 (XVIII), Nov. 27, 1963.

France appearing in votes on colonialism and the Congo crisis. On the Arab-Israel question, Israel voted with France and the United States on six out of eight votes in the fifteenth session, but only on five out of nine votes in the sixteenth session.[58]

French votes were apparently predicated on hopes of conciliating between Arabs and Jews, with France judging each issue on its merits. French diplomat Pierre Maillard admitted, however, that "objectivity often demanded a pro-Israel vote." [59] France voted for the December 1959 General Assembly resolution on the refugee question, although Israel had requested its abstention. *L'Année Politique* gave the following explanation:

> Despite all its desire not to appear to be moving away from solidarity with Israel, it was difficult for France as a member of the Palestine Conciliation Commission with the United States and Turkey, to separate itself from these two powers in the vote.[60]

In 1961 and 1962, France did not support an African initiative calling for direct negotiations between the Arabs and Israelis. In part this was the result of pressure from the United States, which felt that such initiatives should come from the Palestine Conciliation Commission.[61] But in the seventeenth and eighteenth sessions (1962-1963), France continued to stress its impartiality and friendship for all countries in the Middle East, although, by supporting a formula that called for the reintegration of the refugees with resettlement as an

---

[58] *The Middle East Record,* vol. 2, 1961, pp. 5, 8-13, 14-42.
[59] Interview cited.
[60] *L'Année Politique 1959,* p. 583.
[61] *Jerusalem Post,* Dec. 15, 1961; Sept. 12, 1962.

alternative to repatriation, it gave tacit support to Israel and forestalled a harsher resolution insisting on repatriation.[62] The French representative was quick to note that one "could not ignore the political considerations in which the exodus of the refugees and their exile had had their origins." [63] And, in voting for continued efforts by the Conciliation Commission, he made it clear that no United Nations custodian could intervene in the domestic affairs of Israel.[64]

France followed the same course of action when the Security Council dealt with complaints of border violations by Israel or Syria. After the bloody 1962 action in which Israel troops stormed Nukeib in retaliation for repeated Syrian shellings, France took the position that wrongs had been committed on both sides. This was a crucial time in the Evian negotiations for an Algerian peace settlement, but, instead of courting Arab favor, France reaffirmed its impartiality. French ties to both parties existed, and it believed "that these ties are not, and should not be, mutually exclusive." [65] A particularly harsh resolution was passed 10:0:1, reaffirming the post-Suez Security Council Resolution III of January 19, 1956. Paragraph 2 condemned Israeli military action "whether or not undertaken by way of retaliation." Paragraph 3 "Determines that the Israel attack of 16-17 March 1962 constitutes a flagrant violation of that resolution, and calls upon Israel scrupulously to refrain

[62] See, for example, UNGAOR, 18th sess., Special Political Committee, 414th mtg., Nov. 21, 1963 (A/SPC/SR.414), paras. 32-34; General Assembly Resolution 1956 (XVIII), Dec. 20, 1963.

[63] UNGAOR, 17th sess., Special Political Committee, 374th mtg., Dec. 17, 1962 (A/SPC/SR.374), paras. 6-13.

[64] *Ibid.*, 375th mtg., Dec. 18, 1962 (A/SPC/SR.375), para. 1.

[65] *United Nations Security Council Official Records* (UNSCOR), 17th yr., 1002nd mtg., April 5, 1962, p. 2, para. 6.

from such action in the future." [66] France abstained on the grounds that the resolution did not "justly apportion the responsibilities involved and is in some respects not entirely objective." [67]

Acting on an Israeli complaint against Syria in 1963, France again spoke in a conciliatory manner of the "old-established close relations which France has had and wishes to develop further with the two countries in question." [68] No resolution was adopted due to a Soviet veto. During the debate, however, France called for an exchange of prisoners between Syria and Israel, and a handful of Israeli prisoners held by Syria was eventually released.[69] After the Israeli aerial bombardment of Syria in 1964, the pattern was repeated, with France trying to find a formula acceptable to all parties, but no resolution was adopted.

General de Gaulle's policies followed his dictum that "no nation worthy of the name has friends—only interests," while alliances are only temporary.[70] However, he received David Ben Gurion, first in June 1960 and again in 1961, with the words, "We insist on assuring you of our solidarity, of our friendship, and I raise my glass to Israel, our friend and ally." [71] Michael Bar Zohar reports that Ben Gurion's visit had finally come after two years of effort only because of pressure by the Israel Ministry of Defense and de Gaulle's military

[66] Resolution 171 (1962), April 9, 1962.

[67] UNSCOR, 17th yr., 1002nd mtg., April 5, 1962, p. 5, para. 23.

[68] *Ibid.*, 18th yr., 1060th mtg., Aug. 26, 1963, p. 2, para. 5.

[69] *Ibid.*, para. 15.

[70] Cited in *US News and World Report,* vol. 61 (Sept. 19, 1966), p. 46.

[71] Cited in *Le Monde,* June 8, 1961.

advisers.[72] The few available details indicate that Ben Gurion had first hoped to see the French General in March 1959, when he was planning a visit to the United States, and again during a vacation in France in August. He was put off again in March 1960, during an arms purchasing mission to the United States and Britain. Although his first visit, when finally arranged, lasted a week, only one day was given to an official state visit. Such effusiveness and commitment on the part of de Gaulle might, therefore, be considered as a polite diplomatic formula. Yet, as the authoritative *L'Année Politique 1961* observed, "This is the first time that public and official mention has been made of an alliance between France and Israel." [73] De Gaulle normally measured every word, and his statement would be heard not only in Jerusalem but in the Arab capitals as well. One might speculate that his remark was calculated to be as ambiguous as the *"Je vous ai compris,"* he delivered to the people of Algiers: Ben Gurion may have sought a military alliance with France, and, by publicly declaring that Israel was an ally, de Gaulle was able to obviate the necessity of formalizing or equalizing or even defining the relationship.

The General's reference to an alliance and his reported acceptance of the necessity for rectifying Israel's frontiers in a conversation with Ben Gurion in 1960

---

[72] *Gesher 'al ha-Yam ha-Tikhon. Yahasei Tsarfat-Israel, 1947-1963* (Tel-Aviv: 'Am ha-Sefer, 1964), pp. 221, 233-234; and *The Armed Prophet; A Biography of Ben Gurion,* trans. by Len Ortzen (London: Barker, 1967), p. 284; and pp. 268-270 for report of conversations. See also JOMER, vol. 9 (June 17, 1960), pp. 3-4; *The Economist,* vol. 194 (March 26, 1960), pp. 1200, 1203; *Ha-Arets,* June 13, 14-17, 1960; *Jerusalem Post,* June 12, 1960; *The Middle East Record,* vol. 2, 1961, p. 306.

[73] P. 479.

may also be understood in another light.[74] One cardinal principle General de Gaulle consistently followed was to support the Middle East status quo. Thus, if Israel's existence were threatened, he would offer a guarantee. De Gaulle would not support territorial aggrandizement, but, since he held the conviction that peace is only possible where there is a balance of power, some redrawing of the borders might be required. Ben Gurion, on the other hand, had always insisted that Israel sought not a formal commitment, but freedom to purchase weapons for self-defense. He asserts that the "unwritten" or "informal alliance" was indeed reaffirmed in his talks with the General, and France not only undertook to supply Israel with arms and aircraft, but also promised aid in the event of attack.[75]

While there is no evidence that the full potential of such an arrangement was ever realized, Israel may have hoped to exploit the General's interest in the third world by serving as a sort of broker for French interests in certain parts of Asia and Africa. With the rapid growth of Israel's program of cooperation with the developing countries, Israel might well have been a means by which France could retain its presence in newly independent countries without the risk of arousing fears of neo-imperialism.

Israel was anxious to convince France of its im-

---

[74] See "Ben Gurion and de Gaulle: An Exchange of Letters," trans. by Hillel Halkin, *Midstream*, vol. 14, no. 2 (1968), pp. 22-23. Ambassador Tsur quotes de Gaulle as having said in 1955, "I am sure that Israel must correct its frontiers, including that of Jerusalem and above all you must assure yourselves an access to the Red Sea, even if it costs you a war." See *Le Monde*, Nov. 30, 1967; and Erel Ginay, "De Gaulle and Israel," *New Outlook*, vol. 11, no. 1 (1968), p. 17.

[75] David Ben Gurion, interviewed in Tel-Aviv, July 30, 1969.

portance as counselor in the third world and emphasized its unique abilities to demonstrate and adapt western techniques there. In his 1960 and 1961 talks with de Gaulle, Ben Gurion stressed that Israel's technological expertise could counter the influence of both 'Abd al-Nasir and the USSR in Africa.[76] Generally Israel had hoped that France and other European nations would participate financially in its programs, while Israel provided the expertise and facilities for training.[77] Ben Gurion received support for Israeli efforts from the Elysée and especially from Jacques Foccart, the President's special adviser on African affairs, despite initial suspicion of Israel's motives on the part of some individuals in the government.[78] Without French acquiescence, Israel would certainly have faced difficulties in former French dependencies, particularly where local French interests could hardly be expected to react favorably to an expansion of Israeli export trade with these territories. In fact, Israel was unable to benefit materially from its aid program, managing to export very little to French-speaking Africa.

David Catarivas emphasizes, moreover, that Israel did not compete with efforts in the spheres reserved to France—education and military training.[79] *Nahal* and *Gadna,* the fighting pioneer youth programs, were acceptable in Cameroon, the Central African Republic,

[76] JOMER, vol. 9 (June 10, 1960), p. 2; (June 17, 1960), pp. 3-4; *Jerusalem Post,* June 17, 19, 1960; *Le Monde,* June 15, 1960.

[77] The author recalls exploratory talks during 1961-1963 when she served as Assistant to the Director of Information, Department for International Cooperation, Israel Ministry for Foreign Affairs.

[78] Catarivas, Martin, and Maillard, interviews cited.

[79] Interview cited.

Dahomey, Niger, Togo, Upper Volta, and Senegal, only because they were presented as civilian youth organizations. In response to Israeli efforts, there was some French collaboration in Gabon and the Malagasy Republic, while, according to Leopold Laufer, a French subsidy of $160,000 financed the Ivory Coast *Service Civique Féminin* camp program, established in 1964.[80] But on the whole, French and Israeli sources concur that the Quai d'Orsay and especially Couve de Murville were hostile to the idea of joint projects.[81]

[80] *Israel and the Developing Countries: New Approaches to Cooperation* (N.Y.: Twentieth Century Fund, 1967), pp. 49, 119.

[81] Raymond Triboulet, Minister Delegate in Charge of Cooperation (1962-1965), interviewed in Paris, June 13, 1969; and Yehoshua' Almog, Department for International Cooperation, Israel Ministry for Foreign Affairs, interviewed in Jerusalem, July 28, 1969.

VII

Scientific and Technological Cooperation

WITH a return to orthodox diplomacy, the relationship between France and Israel was no longer based on sentiment but was transformed into a more commercial affair. The continued sale of arms and aircraft was thought necessary for the expansion of the French aerospace industry and the concomitant economic growth of France. On the one hand, de Gaulle was motivated by a desire to close the "technological gap" between France and the United States. He argued that a modern aerospace industry was essential to the technological advancement which would make France a major industrial power despite its lack of raw materials. Moreover, expansion of the aeronautics industry would not only serve as an accelerator of economic growth, but would help to modernize and restructure the economy by spurring the shift from small, archaic, economically marginal plants to integrated ones designed for a greatly expanded market.

With the General in power, the drive for increased markets abroad was intensified. By 1966 aerospace exports were eight times larger in dollar terms than imports and amounted to four percent of total exports; one-half of the dollar value was accounted for by the sale of airframes and aircraft.[1] At first most export

---

[1] For details on the development of the French air industry, see the following sources: *Interavia*, vol. 16 (May 1961), p. 596; vol. 17 (Sept. 1962), p. 1080; *Aviation Week and Space Tech-*

orders were for civilian equipment designed for the
American market. But after 1961, the emphasis shifted
to military aircraft and above all, the Mirage III.[2]
Missiles and drones accounted for thirteen percent of
export orders by 1963. Among them was the widely
used Nord Aviation SS-10 anti-tank missile which was
first employed by the Israel army against Egypt in the
1956 Suez war, and a two-stage anti-tank projectile, the
SS-11. Powered by a solid propellant, and simple to
operate, the SS-11 effectively doubled the performance
of the SS-10, extending its range to 3,000 meters. Israel
mounted the SS-11 on its Fouga Magisters and the
Alouette II and III.[3] By 1963, Nord was reported ready
to add a project for air-to-air missiles and a surface-to-
air system which Israel rejected in favor of the American
Hawk.[4]

As arms sales and joint research and development projects continued, a powerful industry-wide "lobby" found
itself with a vested interest in a pro-Israel policy for
France. General Gaston Lavaud recalls that, although
the Minister of Foreign Affairs consistently opposed the

---

nology (AWST), vol. 74 (June 5, 1961), p. 21; vol. 88 (June 17,
1968), pp. 18-19; Robert E. Farrell, "French Score in Drive to
Widen Market," *ibid.*, vol. 74 (March 13, 1961), pp. 280-281;
283-285; and "French Nuclear, Space Work Moves Toward
Major Goals," *ibid.*, vol. 80 (March 16, 1964), p. 270; J. F. Simon,
"France's Flourishing Exports," *The Aeroplane and Astronautics*,
vol. 101 (Dec. 14, 1961), pp. 763-764; and p. 763 for French aircraft exported as of October 1, 1961.

[2] AWST, vol. 86 (May 29, 1967), pp. 84-91.

[3] See *New York Herald Tribune*, May 14, 1957; *Interavia*,
vol. 14 (Jan. 1959), p. 56; and *Jerusalem Post*, April 25, 26, 1963.

[4] See Edgar S. Furniss, Jr., *De Gaulle and the French Army.
A Crisis in Civil-Military Relations* (N.Y.: Twentieth Century
Fund, 1964), p. 194.

sale of aircraft to Israel as threatening Middle East equilibrium, the defense establishment argued the reverse, supported by the air industry. In order to outmaneuver the Quai d'Orsay, Lavaud and other officers of the General Staff tried to have approval for arms contracts deliberated in the Superior Council of Defense. There, Lavaud asserts, decisions were normally reached by a "manifestation of majority opinion" rather than a formal vote, and the President—at least through 1965— could usually be counted on to side with the military in favor of arms sales to Israel.[5]

Thus, in 1959, when Shim'on Peres was informed that France would no longer make modern aircraft available to Israel because of Foreign Ministry opposition, the Chiefs of Staff—Ely, Zeller, Stehlin, Nomy, and de Beaufort—approached the General directly in the Superior Council of Defense. According to one of de Gaulle's counselors, sentiment weighed uppermost in the officers' minds, but they argued that the army was interested in the sale because of the technical advantages that would accrue and the economies of scale needed to gain domestic approval for weapons systems destined for the French arsenal.[6] The matter was decided in favor of Israel. Similarly, in 1961, the sale of the Mirage III-C reached the interministerial committee before de Gaulle approved the delivery of seventy-two planes.[7]

With the order of the Mirage III-C, instead of work-

[5] General Gaston Jean Lavaud, Army Chief of Staff (1959) and Ministerial Delegate for Armaments (1961), interviewed in Paris, June 12, 1969.

[6] Confidential source attached to General de Gaulle (January 1959-April 1960), interviewed in Paris, June 14, 1969.

[7] See Ben Porat and Uri Dan, *Mirage Contre Mig* (Paris: Laffont, 1967), p. 84. Israel bought 96 planes at a cost of $1 million each. *Jerusalem Post*, April 25, 26, 1963.

ing through the French defense establishment, Israel began to deal directly with the aviation industry and its principal supplier of warplanes, the Dassault aircraft company. This was consistent with de Gaulle's administrative reforms, which gradually restricted independent contacts between the two military establishments. In 1961-1962, Israel began to request some offsetting benefits as compensation for its extensive purchases. Previously the French Air Force had contracted for the repair of Mystère IVs and Dakotas in order to help Israel develop its air industry. Now, Dassault spokesmen confirm, it became a question of good business practice to ensure future Israeli purchases by lessening the disequilibrium in the balance of payments between the two countries. Israel was allowed to produce material for maintenance requiring "medium-level technical ability" and manufactured drop or jettisonable tanks for France under the quality control of an OFEMA (*L'Office Français d'Exportation de Matériel Aéronautique*) branch in Israel.[8]

Ties with the French air industry were further reinforced after the first major combat between Egyptian and Israeli planes on May 30, 1960, when the Super-Mystère made its fighting debut. Thereafter, as Israel's military policy became increasingly centered on active air defense, a technological symbiosis evolved. Israeli

[8] Roger Nordmann of the *Société des avions Marcel Dassault*, interviewed at St. Cloud, June 17, 1969; Pierre Gallois, General of the Air Force (ret.), commercial director of the *Société des avions Marcel Dassault* since 1958, interviewed in Paris, June 10, 1969; and General of the Air Force André Martin, Chief of the General Staff under Minister of the Armed Forces Pierre Guillaumat (1958-1959), Chief of the Interarmy General Staff (1961), and Inspector General of the Air Force (1963-1967), interviewed in Paris, June 12, 1969.

pilots sent continuous performance reports and flight photos to the Dassault company, and, as noted above, many of their recommendations—especially on radar, electronics and the use of 30 mm. cannon—were to find their way into the Mirage.[9]

Israel also rendered a unique service in interpreting and enlarging the missions for which French arms were originally planned. The Mirage, to cite one example, was initially conceived as an interceptor designed to penetrate a Soviet radar system based on the Sam missile. In response to Israel's needs it came to be utilized as a bomber. Israel was also particularly adept at developing maintenance procedures and was strong in practical, tactical areas, designing new bombing techniques and maneuvers to exploit the vulnerability of the Mig's fuel tanks or the Sam missile's weakness at low altitudes and against planes undertaking evasive maneuvers. This was to prove useful in June 1967, for while some electronic devices may have been used, it is generally believed that Israeli aircraft eluded the Russian-built Egyptian radar by a low altitude approach and slow speeds attained by lowering the planes' landing gear.

Israel continued to be a laboratory for French experimentation, especially after 1962, when it was the only country where French equipment was being tested in combat against Russian-made arms. On the basis of the Mirage III's encounters with Arab-piloted Migs, for example, Dassault decided to include a simple visual fire control system as a backup in new models designed for nonindustrial countries.[10] Israel also offered France a unique service as a showroom for French merchandise,

[9] See pp. 110-111 above; and Porat and Dan, *Mirage Contre Mig*, p. 95.

[10] AWST, vol. 86 (May 29, 1967), p. 263.

and arms purchasing agents from other nations often consulted their Israeli counterparts.

Shim'on Peres recalls that, although he anticipated the growing centralization of European arms industries and recognized the need to diversify Israel's arms purchases, France was nonetheless the only reliable source for a certain range of arms lying between less sophisticated weapons and advanced, long-range ballistic missiles.[11] The United States had refused their sale, and the United Kingdom had renounced their manufacture. Pierre Gallois of Dassault confirms that, as early as 1958-1959, Israel had begun to participate financially in research and development projects "of particular interest to Israel defense needs," with the "general approval" of the French government.[12] In his talks with de Gaulle in the summer of 1960, Ben Gurion admits that he was primarily interested in extending such scientific and technological cooperation to include joint efforts on aerospace research.[13] Although both parties have been understandably reticent as to the details, it is generally acknowledged that a decision was taken to permit private French industry to collaborate with Israel on missile development. Obviously, since the distinction between private and government controlled sectors of the French aerospace industry is quite cloudy, this is not very different from a government-to-government arrangement.[14]

[11] Shim'on Peres, Deputy Minister of Defense (1959-1965), interviewed in Tel-Aviv, July 31, 1969.

[12] Interview cited.

[13] David Ben Gurion, interviewed in Tel-Aviv, July 30, 1969.

[14] The government had the controlling interest in and provided most of the funds for the Company for the Study and Manufacture of Ballistic Missiles (SEREB), established in July

Although Dassault received authorization to work with Israel, it is interesting to note that the government had specifically barred the company from major participation in French missile developments in favor of the state-owned companies. De Gaulle may have allowed Dassault to cooperate with Israel as compensation for its exclusion from the French program, or, alternatively, one might speculate that Dassault was excluded from French efforts because the company was already researching missile technology in conjunction with a foreign power. This explanation gains credence from Marcel Chassagny's assertion that Matra, a leader in missile technology, was unable to erect a joint program with Israel, despite the reputed interest of both parties.[15]

While on some projects research in Israel and France was coordinated, Israel financed research and development in France for other weapons systems, such as several Matra missiles and the long-distance surface-to-

---

1959. SEREB was the prime contractor for missile research under the Ministry of the Armed Forces. Among the firms represented were Dassault, Breguet (now merged with Dassault), Matra, and SEPR (*Société d'Etudes de la Propulsion à Réaction*), as well as the nationalized concerns—Sud Aviation, Nord Aviation, and Snecma, the *Office National d'Etudes et de Recherches Aéronautiques* and the *Service des Poudres*. The National Space Research Center, established in 1961, is an executive organ under the Premier, directly responsible to the Minister of State for Scientific Research and for Atomic and Space Affairs.

[15] Marcel Chassagny, President and Director-General of the *Société des Engins Matra* since 1937, interviewed in Paris, June 16, 1969. The foregoing is also based on an interview in Jerusalem with Ernst Bergmann, until 1966 director of Israel's atomic energy program, former Chairman of the National Committee for Space Research and head of the Defense Ministry's Scientific Department, July 29, 1969; and *Dun's Review*, vol. 91 (April 1968), pp. 61-62.

surface Dassault MD 620.[16] Israel was reported to have paid approximately $100 million for the Dassault project, which was begun around 1963, with deliveries initially scheduled for 1968. Undoubtedly, Ben Gurion believed Israel's technological and scientific expertise would help revive a dying political alliance as well as further Israel's defense needs. France lagged behind the United Kingdom and the two superpowers in missile production, and "it was recognized that France was starting with little technological knowhow in this area and . . . the road would be a long one, unless foreign help could be enlisted." [17] However, since the United States had prohibited the export of high-performance computers which could have helped France bypass the liquid propellant generation, and in August 1960 refused its assistance, de Gaulle was not adverse to continuing cooperation with Israel. Considering Israel's theoretical contributions to space technology and French difficulties in developing a guidance system, the General no doubt

welcomed Israel investment of capital and scientific

[16] Gallois, interview cited. The MD 620 has also occasionally been designated in press reports as the MD 660. See Geoffrey Kemp, "Arms and Security: The Egypt-Israel Case," *Adelphi Papers,* no. 52 (London: Institute for Strategic Studies [ISS], 1960); and *New York Times,* April 24, 1968; July 18, 1970. Eleven of the missiles were tested in France, and 14 more reported shipped by 1970.

[17] Wilfrid L. Kohl, "The French Nuclear Force and Alliance Diplomacy, 1958-1967," unpublished Ph.D. dissertation, Columbia University, 1968, p. 38. See also Judith H. Young, "The French Strategic Missile Programme," *Adelphi Papers,* no. 38 (London: ISS, 1967); and Appendix for detailed description of Flight-Test Vehicles of the Basic Ballistic Studies Programme; see also pp. 11-13 for list of contractors. The first successful French launch took place on December 19, 1962.

skill and research and engineering for a mobile me-
dium-range-surface-to-surface missile. Israel's share in
the missile development project took the form of a
small advance order, with a reported delivery date
of 1970. As a carrier of high explosives that would
make up in guaranteed penetrability what it might
lose in accuracy, the French missile would, seemingly,
give Israel a psychological edge in the competition with
Egypt. It would also constitute an obvious delivery
system for an atomic bomb.[18]

The world first suspected collaboration on rocketry
research between France and Israel on July 5, 1961,
when the two-stage solid fuel meteorological sounding
rocket "Shavit Shtayim" was launched with a weight of
six hundred pounds and carried a sodium flare to an
altitude of fifty miles.[19] France had fired similar rockets
in the Sahara, when, according to General Ely, Israeli
observers were present. Thus, while the Israelis maintain that Shavit was a purely local product, they probably received some technical advice from France.[20]

Although this launching of Shavit was publicized,
successive efforts were not, which reinforces the assumption that continuing research was geared to military use.

[18] J. C. Hurewitz, *Middle East Politics: The Military Dimension* (N.Y.: Praeger, 1969), p. 476; and AWST, vol. 81 (July 6,
1964), pp. 264-267.

[19] A member of the General Staff had suggested calling the
rocket Shavit Shtayim (II) so 'Abd al-Nasir would worry about
what had happened to Shavit I. See *Jerusalem Post,* July 9, 1966;
Ha-Arets and *Le Monde,* July 7, 1961.

[20] Chief of Staff General Paul Ely, President of the General
Staff of National Defense (1959-1961), interviewed in Paris, June 5,
1969. See *The Economist,* vol. 200 (July 8, 1961), p. 120; and
Don E. Kash, *The Politics of Space Cooperation* (Lafayette:
Purdue, 1967), p. 34.

Although the construction and principles involved would be different on a military instrument, the solid fuel developed by the Scientific Department of the Israel Ministry of Defense could also be used for a weapons system. In this sphere, Professor Bergmann has testified, Israel was more advanced at an earlier date than France.[21] Up to 1966 the French had been having trouble developing a light-weight warhead for the medium-range Diamant, and this is another area in which joint research may have operated. Once the initial stages of research were over, however, and both countries had embarked on their individual rocket and missile programs, the immediate need for cooperation was bound to diminish. This is especially true in view of the increasing trend toward joint European projects which would offer an attraction for France, but which would necessarily exclude Israel.

In December 1960, the United States disclosed that Israel was building a twenty-four megawatt atomic reactor at Dimona with French help.[22] In the rash of newspaper reports that followed, nothing was written about the extent of French collaboration, the terms agreed to, or the costs—about which not even the Kneset was informed.[23] The spectacular fashion in which Washington released the news embarrassed the French. Within Israel there was a general feeling that the United States sought to end French-Israel collaboration on atomic research in part because Weizmann Insti-

[21] Bergmann, interview cited. Cf. Hurewitz, *Middle-East Politics,* pp. 474ff.

[22] See United States *Department of State Bulletin,* vol. 44 (Jan. 9, 1961), p. 45, for report on request for information from Israel Ambassador Avraham Harman, Dec. 9, 1960.

[23] *New York Times,* Aug. 1, 1962.

tute research was integrated with American science. A sizable proportion of the Institute's budget came from the National Institutes of Health, United States Air Force funds, and from West Germany's Ministry of Scientific Research. The Institute was also engaged in classified nuclear physics research for the United States Air Force and Navy.[24] It is also possible that the United States government was reacting to disclosures two months earlier that Egypt was building a reactor with the probable assistance of the USSR and was trying to forestall domestic pressures for similar aid to Israel.[25] Washington could argue that Israeli needs in the nuclear field were already amply supplied by France. There might also have been some degree of pique, since, in response to American queries, the Israelis had called the Dimona reactor everything from a pumping station to a textile plant.

There were very real fears in Washington that the secrecy surrounding the project obscured a weapons program. From its inception, Israel's atomic program had been closely allied with the defense establishment. The first discoveries of uranium in Negev bitumen limestone and phosphates, in 1948, were made by a scientific unit of the defense forces. The Negev reactor was not placed under the IAEA, but under the jurisdiction of the army; HEMED, the scientific branch of the Israel army—which succeeded in developing a light armaments and munitions industry—also had the

[24] *Ha-Arets*, Dec. 21, 1960; *Times* (London), Dec. 20, 1960; Gid'on Gottlieb, "Israel and the A-Bomb," *Commentary*, vol. 31 (Feb. 1961), p. 94; and Victor K. McElheny, "Fundamental Biology at the Weizmann Institute," *Science*, vol. 148 (April 30, 1965), pp. 614-618.

[25] Gottlieb, "Israel and the A-Bomb," p. 96.

high-explosive experts needed for detonating atomic bombs.

The small Nahal Soreq enriched uranium research reactor was under American safeguards and could be ignored for weapons purposes, except insofar as nuclear technicians received invaluable experience. However, the United States was alarmed by announcements in 1960 of a cheap German technique for separating fissionable material with a gas centrifuge. While not necessarily suitable for the needs of large countries, the technique could have caused a glut on the uranium market and made it possible for the smallest states— such as Israel—to produce enough fissile material each year for one or two bombs. Moreover, a centrifuge could more easily be hidden than a gaseous diffusion plant, and the process could already be known to Israel; Germany had already exported one centrifuge to Brazil and one to the United States before American pressure had it classified as secret.[26]

France was quick to call "canard" the suggestion that military aid was involved, insisting that the Dimona reactor would be used for research, to produce heavy water and natural uranium. Spokesmen pointed to open and often publicized exchanges of information and personnel between Israel and France dating from 1956, maintaining that France was interested in arid zone research and wanted to adapt the Israel-developed Zarchin desalination process for use in the Sahara. Moreover, they argued that Washington's disclosures were designed to place France at a competitive disad-

[26] Alastair Buchan, ed., *A World of Nuclear Powers?* (Englewood Cliffs: Prentice-Hall, 1966), p. 14; *Time*, vol. 76 (Oct. 24, 1960), p. 63; and vol. 77 (Jan. 2, 1961), pp. 15-17; *Times* (London), Oct. 13, 1960; and Gottlieb, "Israel and the A-Bomb," pp. 93-99.

vantage in the sale of atomic reactors to nonindustrial states.[27]

Israel, meanwhile, contended that the secrecy was intended only to deny the Arabs information on suppliers of materials, nationality of technicians or trainees, and international scientific connections of Israel's atomic researchers.[28] This secrecy, however, together with French reluctance to discuss nuclear aid to Israel, suggests that at the least France collaborated in helping Israel achieve an option to produce atomic weapons. Professor Ernst Bergmann, former director of Israel's atomic energy program, supports this view with his cogent statement, "It's very important to understand that by developing atomic energy for peaceful uses, you reach the nuclear option; there are no two atomic energies."[29]

Leonard Beaton has reported that France exercised no apparent controls over the use of Israel's reactor, nor did Israel seem to have undertaken any commitment with regard to France.[30] However, this policy may have changed, for the *Jerusalem Post* quoted a French spokesman in 1966 as saying that adequate steps ensured the reactor's exploitation for peaceful purposes. Admitting that nuclear cooperation instituted under the Fourth

[27] JOMER, vol. 9 (Dec. 23, 1960), pp. 3-4; *New York Times,* Oct. 12, 1967; Robert Gilpin, Jr., *France in the Age of the Scientific State* (Princeton: Princeton, 1968), p. 339; and see *Ha-Arets,* Dec. 20, 22, for Prime Minister Ben Gurion's remarks.

[28] JOMER, vol. 13 (May 1, 1964), p. 14.

[29] Interview cited; see also *New York Times,* May 14, 1966.

[30] *Must the Bomb Spread?* (Middlesex: Penguin for the ISS, 1966), p. 36; and with John Maddox, *The Spread of Nuclear Weapons* (N.Y.: Praeger, for the ISS, 1962), p. 43.

Republic had been more loosely organized, he said that "Inspection of peaceful utilization of such aid has since been considerably tightened up." [31]

Where did Israel obtain its fuel for the first charge of twenty-four tons (1,000 kilograms)? Ten tons were imported through the IAEA from South Africa—a country which, incidentally, also benefited from close relations with France. Home production from Dead Sea phosphates could equal ten tons a year while yielding fertilizers. There were plans to make Dimona self-sufficient by increasing home production to fifty tons a year. However, refining uranium from phosphates costs as much as ten times more per ton than does uranium on the world market. Since the market is flexible and subject to loopholes, it is likely that domestic medium grade ores in the Negev would be exploited only in an emergency.[32] Some fuel is known to have been supplied by France, the leading uranium producer in western Europe. In 1960, France produced 900 tons of pure uranium annually, with an expected rise to 1,200 tons by 1961 and 1,500 by 1962. Domestic use accounted for 110 tons annually; the rest was exported. It was suggested, particularly in the United States, that France needed the Dimona reactor as a source of plutonium for its weapons program, and that Israel would return the plutonium created through irradiation of natural

[31] *Jerusalem Post,* Jan. 9, 1966; see also "Sources of Conflict in the Middle East," *Adelphi Papers,* no. 26 (London: ISS, 1966), p. 43, note 36; and Buchan, *A World of Nuclear Powers?,* p. 21.

[32] Leonard Beaton, "Must the Bomb Spread? The Case of India, Egypt and Israel," JOMER, vol. 15 (Jan. 14, 1966), pp. 8-12; see also L. A. Frank, "Nasser's Missile Program," *Orbis,* vol. 11, no. 3 (1967), p. 748; and Bergmann, cited by *New York Times,* May 14, 1966.

uranium in the reactor core. The Israelis have denied this.[33]

The preferred fuel of the Israel Atomic Energy Commission is natural uranium with about three percent plutonium added. This is based on scientific considerations but creates a valuable technical position from which Israel has an option to produce atomic weapons. If operated at full capacity, the Dimona reactor could produce enough plutonium a year for several small nuclear bombs. In 1960, the Israel chemical engineering industry was not considered capable of separating plutonium, and there was little evidence of plans to build a plant. If Israel did not build a chemical separation plant, the military value of Dimona would be negligible, and Israel would be dependent upon France for separation.[34] Israel reportedly would have been able to achieve a prototype fission device, most likely of U-235 design, by 1969.[35]

France would gain useful experience from helping in the construction of an Israeli reactor, especially in the period before it achieved its first nuclear explosion in 1960. Moreover, in view of de Gaulle's overriding desire

[33] Beaton, JOMER, p. 12; *Jerusalem Post,* Dec. 26, 1960; and *New York Times,* Dec. 19, 1960. See also Beaton and Maddox, *The Spread of Nuclear Weapons,* p. 172. France supplements domestic uranium supplies with imports from Madagascar (Malagasy Republic) and Gabon, two countries which, parenthetically, have had excellent relations with Israel over the years. Argentina and Africa have been cited as Israel's sources of uranium oxide. See *New York Times,* July 18, 1970.

[34] See Beaton, JOMER, p. 12; *New York Times,* May 14, 1966; and *Must the Bomb Spread?,* p. 78.

[35] See *Jerusalem Post,* Jan. 17, 1966; and Frank, "Nasser's Missile Program," pp. 752-753.

to preserve national independence vis-à-vis the super-powers, aiding Israel to become an independent nuclear power would test his belief that world stability increases in direct proportion to the number of nuclear powers. Giving Israel a nuclear option permitted de Gaulle to counter both Russian and American influence in the Middle East; the trump card was in his own hand.

However, it is open to question just how far France continued to collaborate with Israel on atomic research. Shortly after coming to power, during Jacques Sous-telle's tenure as Minister for Atomic Affairs (1959-1960), de Gaulle seems to have put an end to certain phases of scientific collaboration with Israel as being "incompatible with the national sovereignty and interests of France." [36] The General, for example, opposed having Israeli scientists continue working at Saclay, where they had been the only foreign group admitted to the nuclear research center under the Fourth Republic.[37] Although Jean Renou of the Commissariat for Atomic Energy contends that French aid to Israel was ended shortly after the disclosure that France assisted in building the Dimona reactor, out of fear of the Arab boycott, the decline may have been more gradual.[38] Professor Bergmann maintains that, while a

[36] Eric Rouleau, "Au Moyen-Orient, diversification des amitiés dans la sauvegarde des intérêts nationaux," *Le Monde Diplomatique* (Jan. 1968), pp. 8-9; and "French Policy in the Middle East," *The World Today*, vol. 24 (May 1968), p. 214.

[37] Jacques Soustelle, interviewed in Paris, May 27, 1969; and Jean Daniel, "Prophet of the Arab World? De Gaulle and the Jews," *Atlas*, vol. 15 (Feb. 1968), p. 23.

[38] Jean Renou, since 1959 chief of the Department of Foreign Relations (Interior and Public) of the French Commissariat for Atomic Energy, interviewed in Paris, June 16, 1969.

braking trend could be discerned after 1959, existing agreements were allowed to run their course.[39]

Electronics, particularly medical electronics, was one field where Israel could have contributed to joint efforts with France for by 1965 it was already relatively advanced in this field. The electronics division of IAI (Elta), formed in 1962, had acquired a worldwide reputation for its developments in radar and airborne fire control and work on ship automation systems, as well as industrial control systems. Elta produced advanced flight instruments for the Magister, in addition to new avionics packages—airborne radar test equipment, communications equipment, medical defibrillators, pulse monitors, cardiac pacemakers, and transistorized radio compasses and nuclear test equipment.[40] An Israeli professor of experimental physics admitted to a visiting United States Senator that "advanced European industry had benefited more" from Irsaeli research on magnetism, laser beams, optical spectroscopy and advanced electronics, "than had Israel's young industry." [41]

The decline of French interest in collaboration with Israel was probably in part due to changing circumstances. At first France had sought mutual cooperation with Israel on arid zone research and desalination, but, with the loss of the Sahara, this need and interest sub-

---

[39] Interview cited. This view runs counter to the opinion of General Gaston Jean Lavaud, President of the *Conseil d'Administration* of the *Office Nationale d'Etudes et de Recherches Aérospatiales* (ONERA) (1963-1965), interview cited; and General André Martin, interview cited. See *Ha-Arets* and *Jerusalem Post,* April 17, 1963.

[40] Cecil Brownlow, "Israel Aircraft Planning Major Reshuffle," AWST, vol. 80 (June 15, 1964), p. 104; see also JOMER, vol. 13 (March 13, 1964), pp. 12-13; and *New York Times,* April 23, 1971.

[41] *Ibid.,* April 24, 1967.

sided. France had itself begun an activist era in science around 1958, exploding its first bomb in 1960. As it sought to forge an international system of scientific and technological alliances that could effectively balance American expertise, supplementing national programs with cooperation through the Common Market and bilateral arrangements, France had less need of the kinds of skills and limited finances Israel could offer and more need of the financial and technological resources that could be obtained through European-scale efforts. This was especially true after 1966, once the technology gap had become a major issue in Europe. Correspondingly, from 1962, Israel turned increasingly to European agencies, the United Kingdom, and the United States for help in desalination projects. Finally, one must also consider the role of the United States. General Paul Ely blamed American pressure for the decline in French cooperation with Israel, for France could benefit from United States advances in research only if it refrained from passing on the information received. This, and de Gaulle's notion of sovereignty, might explain why France continued to permit nuclear technicians to work in Israel, but closed the doors to further joint efforts within France.[42]

[42] Almost all the individuals interviewed who had visited Israel up to 1969, and the author, were eye-witnesses to the presence of French technicians at the Dimona installation throughout the 1960s.

VIII

The Collapse of the Alliance

IF SHIM'ON PERES had been the architect of the partnership with France under the Fourth Republic, it was Ben Gurion who bound Israel to the Fifth. The Israeli Premier was as Gaullist as de Gaulle in his suspicion of United States' involvement in world and Arab affairs and in his distaste for American arms policies. Throughout his long tenure he operated in a Gaullist manner, limiting debate and making major policy decisions, although he did at the same time allow his assistants in the defense establishment wide latitude at the operational level.[1] Ben Gurion's replacement with Levi Eshkol in 1963 and Shim'on Peres' eventual removal from government in 1965 were bound to have an effect on relations with France, especially as the events coincided with an ongoing domestic debate concerning the role of the defense establishment in Israeli politics.

Since the Lavon affair of 1960, the workings of the Defense Ministry and the secret services were the object of violent controversy. The Ministry wielded immense

[1] This chapter relies heavily on interviews with Mordechai Bar-On, formerly Chief Educational Affairs Officer of the Israel Defense Forces, in Jerusalem, July 22, 1969; Shim'on Peres, Deputy Minister of Defense (1959-1965), in Tel-Aviv, July 31, 1969; and General Paltiel Makleff, Director of Elta, Electronics Industries, at Israel Aircraft Industry near Lydda, August 14, 1969.

power in industry, science and technology.[2] Under the direction of Shim'on Peres, it had pioneered the new aviation industries, and the Board of Directors of Bedek, Israel Aircraft Industry, included Peres and Colonel Moshe Kashti of the defense establishment. While the Ministry was the major client of Israel's science and technology and, next to *Histadrut* (General Federation of Labor) and the civil service, Israel's chief employer, the Weapons Development Authority was involved in the mechanical, chemical, physics, and electronics industries. As Ben Gurion sought to insulate the defense establishment from criticism in order to preserve its role as an instrument of nation-building, he, Moshe Dayan, and Shim'on Peres became the focus of concern about the issue of civilian control over the military.

The danger was not so much from too much power in one person's hands, but of partisan politics in defense and security affairs. In particular, the need for political bargaining in order to form a government coalition could threaten the momentum of decision-making just at the point where decisiveness was at a premium. When Ben Gurion resigned on January 31, 1961, the price demanded by Ahdut ha-'Avodah for its cooperation in a new cabinet was the establishment of a ministerial security committee under the Premier. It was composed of the Ministers of Foreign Affairs, Finance, Agriculture (Mapai), Labor (Ahdut ha-'Avodah), and Interior (National Religious Party). While the committee's power of investigation was circumscribed in that only those officers and officials authorized by the

[2] See Amos Perlmutter, "The Institutionalization of Civil-Military Relations in Israel: The Ben Gurion Legacy and Its Challengers (1953-1967)," *Middle East Journal*, vol. 22, no. 4 (1968), pp. 422-423; and p. 415.

Defense Minister might appear before it, and it lacked policy-making authority, this advisory body could request information on and discuss all aspects of security, from military planning and operations to arms purchases and weapons development, on the initiative of the Defense Minister, the cabinet, or a member of the committee.[3] In contast to the situation in France under the Fifth Republic, where centralization of defense matters reduced avenues open to Israel, decentralization in Israel opened France-Israel relations to the vagaries of coalition politics—a process that could only have deleterious effects when discretion, maneuverability, and rapid decisions were essential to success.

When Ben Gurion lost control of the situation and resigned in June 1963, he was replaced by Levi Eshkol as Premier and Defense Minister. In contrast to Ben Gurion, who considered himself an expert on military matters, Eshkol relied more heavily on his Chief of Staff. As Finance Minister prior to 1963, he had often intervened in defense matters, cutting the budget—especially for nuclear research. However, as Defense Minister, Eshkol regularly complied with his army chief's requests for expensive new weaponry and continued to expand the defense establishment's scientific and industrial empire.[4]

Nonetheless, only one month after Eshkol took office

---

[3] See J. C. Hurewitz, "The Role of the Military in Society and Government in Israel," *The Military in the Middle East. Problems in Society and Government*, Sydney Nettleton Fisher, ed. (Columbus: Ohio, 1963), p. 91.

[4] See Perlmutter, *Civil-Military Relations*, pp. 424, 429; *ibid.*, "The Israeli Army in Politics: The Persistence of the Civilian over the Military," *World Politics,* vol. 20 (July 1968), pp. 606-643; and Nadav Safran, *From War to War. The Arab-Israeli Confrontation, 1948-1967* (N.Y.: Pegasus, 1967), pp. 305ff.

dissension appeared which had its roots in defense policy. Minister of Agriculture Moshe Dayan threatened to resign in an unsuccessful attempt to set up a permanent Mapai advisory panel within the cabinet security committee, while those who had opposed Ben Gurion attempted to keep Shim'on Peres off the committee.[5] Foreign Minister Golda Meir had long been angered at Peres' independence in foreign relations with France and Germany and sought this opportunity to curtail his influence.[6] Eshkol tended to favor a neutral position with a slight shift toward the United States and with looser ties with Germany than Ben Gurion advocated.[7] Shim'on Peres felt that Eshkol had relatively little understanding of Europe or of France and that he tended to ignore the importance of sentiment in Israel's relationship with France. Eshkol, said Peres, felt that the French were basically only interested in the financial benefits that accrued from the sale of arms.[8] In a Kneset speech June 25, 1963, Peres argued that Israel should build a political and security policy along parallel lines with France. The advantage of French aid, said Peres, was its openness and the fact that France made no political conditions nor any attempt to supervise the use of weapons it sold.[9]

A struggle for control over the Mapai Executive Com-

[5] *Jerusalem Post,* July 19, 22, Sept. 5, 1963.

[6] See Jon Kimche and Dan Bawly, *The Sandstorm. The Arab-Israeli War of June 1967: Prelude and Aftermath* (N.Y.: Stein & Day, 1968), pp. 62ff.

[7] Ze'ev Katz, "Eshkol's 'Winds of Change'," *New Outlook,* vol. 7 (July/Aug. 1964), pp. 16-19; see also *Jerusalem Post,* March 20, April 6, 1964.

[8] Peres, interview cited.

[9] See Shim'on Peres, "Outlines for an Israeli Foreign Policy," *New Outlook,* vol. 6 (Sept. 1963), pp. 14-19.

mittee ensued, leading to the resignations of Dayan and Ben Gurion in late 1964, and in May 1965 Shim'on Peres left his post as Deputy Minister of Defense. The three created a new party, *Rafi* (Israel Workers List), which attempted to challenge Eshkol's control, accusing him of harming Israel's security by encouraging politics within the Defense Ministry. In addition to apparent feuds within the Ministry and the security services, unrest was also apparent within the atomic energy authority throughout 1966 and 1967, and, according to Ernst Bergmann, Israel's scientific policy regarding France was one of the factors involved.[10] Eshkol, who was attacked for his weakness and indecisiveness in this sphere and for his unwillingness to devote funds to research, retaliated by having a law passed making retired public servants liable to three years in prison for unauthorized disclosures of official information. He then assumed leadership of the Atomic Energy Commission personally, replacing Bergmann, who disagreed with Eshkol's negative attitude toward extensive foreign contacts.[11]

Because the changeover from the Ben Gurion regime coincided with the decline in ties with France, it is tempting to overstate Eshkol's role in the process. It is true that many Frenchmen in political life felt he was less of a statesman than Ben Gurion and that he allowed Israel's foreign policy to lie dormant. Baron Edmond de Rothschild, for example, decried Eshkol's neglect of Africa, his misunderstanding of France, and, more seriously, his lack of awareness of Israel's need for good

[10] Ernst Bergmann, former Chairman of the National Committee for Space Research; head of the Defense Ministry's Scientific Department, interviewed in Jerusalem, July 29, 1969.

[11] See *New York Times* and *Jerusalem Post,* March 31, 1967.

public relations.[12] However, when it came to policy-making, the differences between Ben Gurion and Eshkol were more a question of style than of substance. Eshkol has been accused of overinvolvement in defense matters, but, in the last analysis, it is the right of the Prime Minister to be involved in the affairs of the defense establishment. Eshkol, because he was more interested in details than Ben Gurion, simply made his presence felt more at the operational level. Ben Gurion, for example, had held weekly meetings to keep in touch with defense matters, but he did not require the military to consult with other organs of government on security questions. Eshkol, on the other hand, insisted that the Defense Ministry coordinate its activities closely with the Ministry for Foreign Affairs.[13] While it is true that the ministerial security committee, created in 1961, had wider powers under Eshkol than during his predecessor's tenure and suffered from a resulting loss of decisiveness, this was rarely felt in relation to foreign policy with France. In the last analysis, about all that can be said with any degree of certainty is that internal political developments in Israel further aggravated strains already apparent within the alliance with France. France's diminishing interest in Israel played a larger role than did any penchant for disengagement on Eshkol's part.

France continued to display coolness in its economic relations with Israel during the latter's negotiations with the Common Market. Israel had sought an agreement with the EEC ever since early 1959, for almost one-third of its exports by 1960-1961 went to the Com-

[12] Interviewed in Paris, July 1, 1969.
[13] Bar-On and Makleff, interviews cited.

mon Market countries.[14] It was expected that by 1970 Israel would feel the full impact of Common Market tariffs and would be particularly vulnerable if Britain joined. Ben Gurion raised the issue in his talks with de Gaulle and again asked for French support in November 1961. Israel had no success, however, despite pressure from influential quarters. Moreover, since cease-fire negotiations with the FLN in Algeria coincided with the Brussels meeting of the EEC ministerial council in April 1962, it seemed doubtful that France would risk sponsoring Israel at that time. Senator André Monteil recalls that the *Alliance France-Israël* organized public meetings, conferences and a press campaign to mobilize public opinion, while Michel Debré personally intervened with de Gaulle.[15] Maurice Schumann, Chairman of the National Assembly Commission for Foreign Affairs, also appealed for support of Israel's bid in the name of the UNR, the Socialists, Radicals, MRP, and Independents.[16] Finally persuaded, General de Gaulle and the Prime Minister's office managed to overcome Quai d'Orsay opposition to action on Israel's behalf.

In September 1962 talks were initiated after unofficial French insistence that Israel's economy was threatened by the EEC. Although negotiations with the EEC failed to produce full association for Israel they did result on November 26, 1962, in tariff and quota concessions on

[14] *The Middle East Record,* vol. 2, 1961, pp. 82-85; 301; *Jerusalem Post,* Nov. 16, 17, 23, 1961; Feb. 25, 1962; Dec. 12, 1967; Oded Remba, "Israel and the European Economic Community," *Midstream,* vol. 8 (Sept. 1962), pp. 22, 28-29; and the *Middle East Economic Digest* (London), Oct. 12, 1967, p. 696.

[15] Senator André Monteil, interviewed in Paris, June 20, 1969.

[16] *The Jewish Observer and Middle East Review* (JOMER), vol. 11 (March 2, 1962), pp. 5-6; (March 9, 1962), p. 4; (March 30, 1962), p. 3.

some forty groups of items and duty-free entry for goods manufactured from raw materials imported into Israel from Common Market countries. On August 16, 1963, Israel became the first non-OECD member admitted to the scheme for the application of international standards to fruits and vegetables, and, with support from Paris, the EEC Council of Ministers offered Israel a twenty percent tariff suspension for three years on twenty-three products and concessions on fifteen others. There were still problems concerning oranges, eggs, and semi-finished goods. Finally, on May 9, 1964, the Council of EEC Ministers instructed the EEC Commission to conclude a trade agreement with Israel, effective July 1, 1964.[17] The agreement covering thirty-seven products included substantial tariff cuts on grapefruit, avocado pears, and twenty-three other items; Italy agreed to ease its quota on bromides (Israel was the main EEC supplier of bromides), and France its quota on orange juice. There was also a promise of negotiations if Israel citrus exports to the EEC fell. One main difficulty left unresolved was Israel's desire for concessions on goods manufactured from imported raw materials. Hoping for better advantages, Israel continued to press for association with the EEC. Although initially the Council of Ministers had hesitated to pursue a closer relationship with Israel, it reported favorably on the prospect on June 10, 1967.[18]

While France did not oppose any of the concessions granted by the EEC, its official support for Israel could not compare with the staunch attitude of Belgium and the Netherlands. Most sources agree, however, that this

[17] See *Bulletin of the European Economic Community,* no. 3 (Brussels: 1964), p. 62; and no. 7 (1964), pp. 14-17.

[18] See *Jerusalem Post,* June 3, Oct. 5, 14, 1966.

disinterest reflected France's preoccupation with North Africa and de Gaulle's overall hesitations with regard to the EEC, rather than any negative policy decision concerning Israel.[19] The two countries had simply diverged to the point where France no longer felt a need to protect Israel's economic interests.

Paris continued to serve as a neutral meeting-ground however. Levi Eshkol and Ismet Inonu met there in July 1964. Golda Meir and the Lebanese President were simultaneously in the French capital, suggesting the possibility that France might mediate on the Jordan waters dispute. Although there is no evidence of French intervention, Lebanon did ultimately "delay" action on the diversion scheme. Couve de Murville promised to speak to Moscow on behalf of the status quo in the Middle East, and an agreement was signed whereby dual citizens could serve in either the French or Israel army.[20] When Israeli spy Eli Cohen was captured and executed by Syria in 1965, France made several attempts to intercede. But these and similar episodes were really only superficial amenities.

Expressions of support for Israel emanating from Paris were less and less enthusiastic, despite the reassurances that occasionally appeared in the press of both nations.[21] Eshkol's trips to the French capital did little

[19] Pierre Gilbert, Ambassador to Israel (1953-1959), interviewed in Paris, June 11, 1961; Pierre Maillard, Deputy Counsellor to the Secretariat General of the President (1959-1964), interviewed in Paris, June 24, 1969; General Pierre Billotte, Vice President of the UNR group in the National Assembly (1962-1966), interviewed in Paris, May 29, 1969; and Ya'akov Tsur, Ambassador to France (1953-1959), interviewed in Jerusalem, Aug. 13, 1969.

[20] JOMER, vol. 15 (Feb. 4, 1966), pp. 3-4; *Jerusalem Post,* June 3, 1964.

[21] See André Scemama in *Le Monde,* Oct. 21, 1965.

to revive dying French ardor. Despite a reiteration of the formula, "Israel, our friend and ally," during Eshkol's 1964 visit, and a reputed guarantee to protect Israel "even if it meant destroying Cairo," relations were no longer as intimate as they had been.[22] Moreover, the French press dwelled on political dissension within Israel and cited Ben Gurion's criticism of Eshkol for his reliance on United States guarantees for Israel's security.[23]

When the Prime Minister, following his return from Paris, assured the Kneset that Israel would continue to benefit from scientific collaboration with France, Quai d'Orsay circles were reported deeply resentful at his "indiscretion."[24] An exaggerated amount of publicity accompanied the signature in the same year of an agreement to cooperate on oceanography and arid zone research; yet enthusiasm for the projects was never mutual. France even minimized the importance of such accords. Seemingly taking their cue from the government, French scientists were cool to specific proposals that Israel advanced.[25] Instead, it was the United States that devoted one million Israeli pounds for a joint marine radioactivity research project in the eastern Mediterranean, and Israel increasingly sought closer collaboration with European organizations such as the Vienna Atomic Energy Commission, Euratom, and the European Molecular Biology Organization.

Finally, in 1965, a French minister reportedly told

[22] *The Economist,* vol. 212 (July 25, 1964), p. 347; Joel Marcus, "The Rift Between Israel and France," *Midstream,* vol. 14 (Jan. 1968), p. 41; *Jerusalem Post,* June 19, 28, 1964.

[23] *Le Monde,* June 30, 1964; and *Ha-Arets,* March 26, 1965.

[24] *The Economist,* vol. 212 (July 25, 1964), p. 347.

[25] See *Jerusalem Post,* June 6, July 5, 8, 10, 1964; April 15, 1965; Sept. 8, 1967.

a western diplomat that the Elysée had lost confidence in Israel's future, while Moshe Dyan in turn admitted that

> Israel's position today . . . is established by various international organizations, such as the North Atlantic Treaty Organization and the Common Market, "and not by the Suez-Sinai alliance, which is now seen as no more than a passing episode." [26]

Despite continued good will between the defense establishment and strategic industries, developments within the governmental structure of both countries and the changing role of France in regional politics increasingly weakened the alliance. Under General Charles Ailleret, named Chief of Staff in 1961, the annual staff level meetings between the two armed forces were discontinued.[27] However, Generals Jacquier and Grossin affirmed that collaboration continued between the secret services, which in France reported directly to the President. Exchanges of intelligence on Africa and the Arab world lasted at least until 1966 and, according to the former intelligence chiefs, France had a continuing interest in Algeria, a fear of both Egyptian and British intentions at Suez, and a desire to keep Lebanon and Syria calm. French officials respected Israeli intelligence particularly when it came to analyses of 'Abd al-Nasir

[26] Dayan, cited in *New York Times,* Oct. 30, 1966. See also Ben Porat, "Israël Fait Son Autocritique," *L'Arche,* no. 130 (Dec.-Jan. 1968), pp. 31-32, 57. See also 'Abd al-Nasir in Peter Calvocoressi et al., *Suez Ten Years After. Broadcasts from the BBC Third Programme* (London & Frome: Butler & Tanner, 1967), p. 57.

[27] General of the Air Force André Martin, Chief of the Interarmy General Staff (1961), Inspector General of the Air Force (1963-1967), interviewed in Paris, June 12, 1969.

and the Russian role in the area. Israel, for its part, was anxious to obtain from France additional, precise tactical information on the deployment of Arab troops.[28]

Because of its own foreign policy aims, France preferred discretion as to the scope and content of its ties with Israel and was bound to resent anything which drew attention to those ties. Israeli publicity, while geared primarily to the political struggle between Eshkol and Ben Gurion, nonetheless exerted pressure on Franco-Arab relations. Dayan's *Diary of the Sinai Campaign,* which appeared in 1965, Bar-Zohar's official biography of Ben Gurion, and Ya'akov Tsur's memoirs, which followed in 1966, revealed details of earlier French assistance to Israel. Their publication, in addition to having been part of Israel's ongoing internal political debate, was probably also inspired by a desire to embarrass France in its rapprochement with the Arabs, to shore up a fading romance, or to prod France into renewed obligations.

Although close contacts continued with the French aircraft industry until Shim'on Peres left the government in 1965, his successor as Director-General of the Defense Ministry, Dr. Zvi Dinstein, aroused French ire by clumsily capitalizing on those ties. Sensational reports leaked to the press in 1966 told of a "new agreement" whereby France "will place important orders for components as well as precision instruments which will be made in Israel" for absorption by the local market or for export, with an undertaking by France not to

[28] General Paul Grossin, Director-General of the *Service de documentation extérieure et de contre-espionnage* (1957-1962), and General Paul Jacquier, his successor (1962-1966), interviewed in Paris, June 25, 1969.

manufacture those parts itself.[29] The French Defense Ministry was quick to call these reports a muddle of fact and fiction, pointing out that, first, France and Israel had cooperated in military, industrial, and various other fields for a number of years and, second, that Israel was already producing components for French arms industries. Now France merely undertook to offset Israeli purchases by ordering Israel-made components in an amount equivalent to twenty-five percent of military sales to Israel. Third, no new access to French knowledge was envisioned in view of the already considerable "existing mutual access" in many fields. Fourth, Israel's participation in French military production was not unique since other—mainly European—countries cooperated with the French arms industries, and Israel products were accepted by many countries in partial payment for arms orders. Finally, no conflict with Arab interest in purchasing French arms was foreseen. The French concluded with the accusation that

> A complete misunderstanding of the issue was shown by the attempts in various newspapers to link France's orders of components from Israel with her desire to reduce her dependence on American equipment. This is so out of proportion as to require no further comment.[30]

It is true, as pointed out above, that the French government had earlier decided to let Israel fabricate arms in order to ease the exchange deficit and that Israel was manufacturing parts of shells, tanks, airplanes, and

[29] *Le Monde,* March 9, 1966; cf. *Jerusalem Post,* March 7, 1966; *Yediot Ahronot,* March 6, 1966; and *Ma'ariv,* March 6, 1966, which refers to cooperation with Israel solely on the Dassault Mystère-20.

[30] Cited in JOMER, vol. 15 (March 18, 1966), pp. 6-7.

doing repairs on the Super-Mystère for the French Air
Force. However, there is evidence that cooperation
ceased where competition began. In 1961, Israel began
to enter the executive transport field with major modifications on the Convair 240. Its low labor costs enabled
IAI to offer a competitive selling price.[31] The same
year plans were being drawn for a six or nine-passenger
light twin-jet executive transport, the B-101C. The airframe was to be built in Israel and ferried to the United
States for delivery, or licensing arrangements would be
made. Wind tunnel testing would be done in France
and the CSF (*Compagnie Générale de Télégraphie
San Fil*) of France, which shipped airborne radar to
Israel and which licensed IAI to produce a transistorized
radio compass for the Magister, would manufacture the
electronic equipment.[32] In 1964, IAI suddenly aban-
doned the B-101C project because of "parallel" plans
in other countries and its inability to get financial
support for the project.[33] The fact that Dassault had
just decided to enter the executive transport market
was more than a coincidence.

In 1965, perhaps in partial compensation for IAI's
"cooperation" in withdrawing the B-101C, Israel was
awarded a flap subassembly contract for the Dassault
Mystère-20 twin-jet executive aircraft.[34] Thereafter, IAI

[31] *Aviation Week and Space Technology* (AWST), vol. 74
(April 10, 1961), p. 117.

[32] Erwin J. Bulban, "Israeli Aircraft Surveying B-101C Market,"
ibid., pp. 108-110; *ibid.* (March 6, 1961), pp. 87-91; *Business Week*,
Dec. 1, 1962, pp. 61-62; Arnold Sherman, "Israel Aircraft Considers Private Financing for B-101C Development," AWST, vol. 77
(July 23, 1962), p. 71.

[33] Cecil Brownlow, "Israel Aircraft Planning Major Reshuffle,"
ibid., vol. 80 (June 15, 1964), p. 105.

[34] *Ibid.*, vol. 89 (July 8, 1969), pp. 73-76.

confined itself to projects overlooked by United States and European firms such as the Arava Stol, a twenty-two passenger twin-engine propeller-driven plane particularly suited to non-industrial countries. The Arava Stol, powered by a Turboméca Astazou-16 engine or a Canadian PT A-27 powerplant, was to be manufactured from raw materials imported from the United States and would eventually be produced in a military version as well.[35]

General Lavaud revealed that the Dinstein agreement had included a provision to help Israel toward the gradual fabrication of French planes from component parts.[36] Publicity about these arrangements infuriated the Quai d'Orsay, as did erroneous reports appearing in the press in September 1964 that General Itshaq Rabin was negotiating in Paris for the Mirage IV atomic bomber. Israel was actually interested in purchasing the Mirage V series, a stripped-down cheaper version of the Mirage III particularly suitable for good climates.[37] French negotiators, however, according to Lavaud, began to feel somewhat more reserve on the part of Israel and, particularly after 1965, saw Israel's

[35] See *The Israel Digest*, vol. 14 (June 11, 1971); and on the Arava's inaugural flight, April 9, 1970, see *New York Times*, April 10, 1970.

[36] General Gaston Jean Lavaud, President of the *Conseil d'Administration* of the *Office Nationale d'Etudes et de Recherches Aérospatiales* (ONERA), interviewed in Paris, June 12, 1969.

[37] See *Jerusalem Post* and *Le Monde*, Jan. 7, Feb. 11, Sept. 15, 18, 1964; and Safran, *From War to War*, Appendix B, p. 444. The Mirage III is a single-seat all-weather interceptor with advanced electronics which allow for low-altitude flying, computer bombing, and fire control. The Mirage V is considered competitive with the United States Northrop Aviation F-5 and costs, on an average, between $1.3 and $1.5 million.

new option of purchasing American aircraft as a threat to business.[38]

Despite Israel's 1966 orders for the Mirage V and its purchase of the Super Frelon, the French arms industry must have been reluctant from a purely commercial point of view to see their exclusive customer buy elsewhere. Israel lost interest in the AMX-30 tank, once Washington offered a less expensive means of reinforcing Zahal's armor: United States M-48 Patton tanks were delivered via West Germany in accordance with a 1964 agreement.[39] The French also noted that American cooperation with Israel on nuclear desalination lessened the chances that Israel might purchase another French reactor. Finally, because Israel rejected the French Triton trainer in 1966, several other air forces turned it down as well. All this coincided with a series of Israeli moves to lessen its dependence on France in the aerospace field.

The IAI-Potez agreement had prohibited the sale of the Magister to former French colonies, and each sale had to be negotiated separately, with Potez receiving royalties from every export. Beginning in 1962, Israel attempted to penetrate the African market and to satisfy African needs for a bush-type craft with export models of the Magister which could be readily converted from jet trainers to ground attack fighters.[40] IAI also built its own jigs, ground handling equipment, modification kits, and tooling for the Magister, which was superior in some ways to the original and was simplified to re-

[38] Lavaud, interview cited.

[39] J. C. Hurewitz, *Middle East Politics: The Military Dimension* (N.Y.: Praeger, 1969), pp. 477-479; *Jerusalem Post*, July 1, 1963; see also *New York Times*, Dec. 5, 1966.

[40] For details, see Brownlow, "Israel Aircraft," p. 107.

flect a lower rate of production. The fuselage was built in a single horizontal jig rather than three separate vertical sections which, according to the French design, had to be joined. This saved four assembly jigs overall. Optical tooling replaced the mostly manual tooling in the French model; two starter generator units (one for each engine) replaced the single unit of the French design, saving weight and eliminating the gear box in the middle. Other modifications included larger ailerons for augmenting roll-rate, and the use of glass fiber in the airframe (tail cone, engine intakes, opaque parts of the canopy), to facilitate manufacture and save ten percent in weight below the original design.

Georges Volland has admitted that Potez was largely unaware of the changes made by IAI, and, apart from the *Boîte Bedek* accessory units developed in Israel and purchased by Potez (considered a relatively minor contribution), none of the modifications was placed on the French assembly-line.[41] Moreover, manufacture of the parts designed for the Magister was not undertaken by the French firm, but by the Breeze Corporation of New Jersey.[42] Without French approval or foreknowledge, the Israelis loaned two Magisters to Uganda prior to sales negotiations at the governmental level. Meanwhile, Nigerian trainees were in Israel receiving instruction in airframe, engine, and Douglas DC-3 maintenance, possibly as a prelude to further sales.[43]

In 1965, IAI's Engineering Division purchased a new $400,000 jet test cell to check the Snecma Atar-9 powerplant for the Mirage III, eliminating the cost of air

[41] Interviewed in Paris, June 17, 1969.

[42] AWST, vol. 76 (Jan. 8, 1962), pp. 59-65; Brownlow, "Israel Aircraft," p. 105.

[43] AWST, vol. 82 (Jan. 18, 1965), p. 101.

freight to France for service and overhaul and reducing ground time. IAI also pioneered a way to test aerodynamic shapes without a wind tunnel and developed a "clean room" for testing guidance systems, further increasing its aerospace independence. In 1965, Elta, the electronics division of IAI, set up a plant to make Servo mechanisms and hydraulic systems for aircraft and joined with an American firm, Austin Instruments, Inc. of Syosset, New York, for the manufacture of precision gears in Israel.[44] Elta, incidentally, had produced a defibrillator which was being sold through French outlets.[45]

By the mid-1960s it was apparent that the tacit alliance was crumbling even in the one sphere that had shown the greatest stability—military and technological cooperation. Despite French opposition to international inspection of its facilities or those of countries with which it had bilateral agreements, and despite initial Israeli reluctance to permit American inspection of the Dimona reactor, the Eshkol government began to allow informal visits by AEC representatives in 1964. On July 13, 1966, Israel and the United States agreed to transfer inspection authority over the research reactor at Nahal Soreq to the International Atomic Energy Commission. Eshkol's actions were part of a larger dispute within the defense, scientific, and political establishments, revolving around Israel's nuclear option. Professor Bergmann had resigned as Chairman of the IAEC, and as head of the research and planning division of the Defense Ministry and scientific adviser to Prime Minister Eshkol because he felt that the Premier was less sympathetic to long-term scientific-defense planning

[44] *Business Week,* Oct. 7, 1967, p. 127.
[45] *Jerusalem Post,* Feb. 26, 1964.

than Ben Gurion had been. Bergmann decried the lack of funds for research and development and deplored the risks incumbent in Israeli dependence on foreign weapons sources or American guarantees.[46]

It is apparent that Eshkol was ranged against the more activist members of both the scientific and defense establishments. While in the early 1960s military leaders were generally optimistic that the balance of power would not shift against Israel for fifteen years or so, they became more pessimistic toward the middle of the decade.[47] Given the qualitative developments in the Middle East conventional arms race, Israel, they argued, might find itself forced to obtain atomic arms as the most economical security choice. The defense budget constituted an enormous burden for Israel, particularly since German reparations payments had been completed and in view of increased barriers to exports to the EEC, and the growing burden of debt servicing.[48]

Fearing that the USSR might give Egypt nuclear weapons, Israeli leaders wanted to keep open all options as a deterrent, without actually developing an atom bomb.[49] Israel may well have accumulated a plutonium stockpile without testing or deciding to fabricate a weapon and, as Leonard Beaton asserts, Israeli scientists would no doubt have "mastered the theoretical basis of

[46] Interview cited; see also *New York Times,* May 14, 1966.

[47] See Leonard Beaton, "Must the Bomb Spread? The Case of India, Egypt and Israel," JOMER, vol. 15 (Jan. 14, 1966), pp. 10-11.

[48] See *The Military Balance 1968-1969* (London: Institute for Strategic Studies [ISS], 1968), and William B. Bader, *The United States and the Spread of Nuclear Weapons* (N.Y.: Pegasus, for the Center of International Studies, Princeton, 1968), p. 91. Defense expenditures totaled $498 million in 1967, $628 million in 1968. The 1966 defense budget was 23% of the total budget. Cf. Hurewitz, *Middle East Politics,* pp. 106-107.

[49] Bader, *U.S. and the Spread of Nuclear Weapons,* p. 93.

plutonium separation and the design of plutonium bombs" just in case that knowledge were needed.[50] Now, too, for the first time Israel had a delivery capacity in the A-4, although the missile and electronics industries might also have been able to provide an important delivery system.

Israel signed the partial test ban treaty which France had refused to sign, but there is little evidence that France in any way resented Israel's actions. Israel, like many small nations, does not have adequate territories in which to test, and underground testing is not feasible. As for the nonproliferation treaty which the United States wanted, if Israel refused to sign, holding out for a bilateral defense treaty with the United States as its price, it could keep its options open and its Arab adversaries uneasy.[51]

Eshkol appears to have concentrated his efforts on creating a bargaining position vis-à-vis the United States by holding out Israel's nuclear option in the hopes of obtaining clear-cut security guarantees. The activists would have preferred to exercise that option. Dayan, for example, was reported opposed to denuclearization as long as the Arab world refused to recognize the State of Israel. Together with Shim'on Peres, he pleaded with the Premier to preserve Israeli ties with France and to create a nuclear capacity jointly.[52] Eshkol ignored them.

[50] *Must the Bomb Spread?* (Middlesex: Penguin for the ISS, 1966), p. 81.

[51] See Bader, *U.S. and the Spread of Nuclear Weapons,* pp. 61, 94; and *New York Times,* Nov. 20, 1968.

[52] See *Le Monde,* May 12-18, 1966. Bergmann, in the interview cited, maintained his belief that Israel could produce an independent nuclear capacity, but he underlined a crucial shortage of technicians. See Bader, *U.S. and the Spread of Nuclear Weapons,* p. 91; and Simha Flapan, "Swords Across the Sea," *Atlas,* vol. 8 (Sept. 1964), p. 90.

IX

The End of Illusions: The Six Day War and Its Aftermath

AS EVENTS moved toward a new Arab-Israeli confrontation in 1967, General de Gaulle remained silent during the series of crises that preceded the outbreak of hostilities.[1] Some observers felt that he was trying to preserve his impartiality because he hoped eventually to be called upon to mediate the dispute. As if to underscore de Gaulle's position, Hervé Alphand, Secretary General of the Foreign Ministry, was careful to signal his country's nonalignment in regional affairs at a conference of French ambassadors to Middle East countries held in Beirut on May 11.[2] Tensions heightened during the month, and, following the troop mobilizations along the Egypt-Israel border, the Egyptian takeover on May 21 of UNEF positions at Sharm al-Shaykh, and the closing of the Gulf of 'Aqabah to Israeli shipping on May 22, the Israel government decided to send Minister for Foreign Affairs Abba Eban to the three western capitals to garner support. If Britain, France, and the United States could give assurances of diplomatic action to overturn Egypt's blockade, then, it was hoped, Israel might be able to avoid a recourse to arms.

Eban arrived in Paris on May 24 and met with Gen-

---

[1] For an excellent analysis of the Six Day War, see Nadav Safran, *From War to War. The Arab-Israeli Confrontation, 1948-1967* (N.Y.: Pegasus, 1969), pp. 266ff.

[2] *Le Monde*, May 12, 1967.

eral de Gaulle. While no complete record of the conversations has been made public, and there is some question of what actually was said during their thirty-five minute meeting, most sources agree that the interview was a cold one. Israeli officials referred to General de Gaulle's sharp warning against initiating hostilities as a "dictat" and said that the General seemed ill-disposed toward Israel at the outset. Evidently de Gaulle and Eban had completely opposing views as to the seriousness for Israel of the present situation. Eban explained the menace to Israel posed by the concentration of Arab troops along its borders, described the increased acts of terrorism and sabotage actively encouraged by the Arab governments, and most essential, outlined the threat posed by Egypt's closing of the Gulf of 'Aqabah. Finally, he reminded de Gaulle of France's 1957 commitment to view any attempt to close the Strait of Tiran as a *casus belli*.

De Gaulle rejected Eban's contention and made it quite clear that France would not aid Israel in forcing open the Gulf of 'Aqabah. He feared, given the world situation, that a local conflict thus engendered might lead to global warfare. Moreover, he advised Israel that France would not favor any purely western action but would work for an accord supported by the four major powers. He warned Israel not to be the first to make war. Eban retorted that, given Israel's precarious strategic position, the war had already begun and Egypt had fired the first shot when it closed the Strait of Tiran. The interview terminated on a note that ended once and for all any illusions that Israel's favored relationship with France had survived.[3]

[3] The above account of the Eban-de Gaulle conversations relies on interviews with several confidential sources in the

As the crisis entered its final phase, General de Gaulle suspended deliveries of war matériel, first unofficially on June 3, then officially on June 5. The Six Day War and Israel's overwhelming victory seemed to reaffirm his view that Eban had exaggerated the menace Israel faced, hardening his stand and leading to his condemnation of Israeli aggression and expansionism at a press conference November 27, 1967 and his unfortunate recourse to a racial stereotype in denouncing the Jews as "an élite people, self-assured and domineering." A complete ban on January 3, 1969, on all military supplies to Israel followed a reprisal raid on the Beirut airfield; France continued to refuse to deliver the fifty Mirage Vs ordered in 1966, even after Israel completed payments in April 1968.

In his correspondence with former Premier Ben Gurion, December 30, 1967, de Gaulle admitted to having earlier made solemn promises with regard to Israel:

> . . . and you cannot doubt that, if necessary, we would have been opposed to its being annihilated, as guaranteed by our official conversations of former times and by the fact that in them I had publicly called Israel a "friendly and allied State." [4]

Yet his statement during the November press conference that he had assured Abba Eban in May that France would come to Israel's aid in the event of an Arab attack is not supported by any evidence. At most such

---

Israel Ministry for Foreign Affairs and the Israel Embassy in Paris. My information generally agrees with the version published by *Ma'ariv* correspondent, Samuel Segev, in *Israël, Les Arabes et Les Grandes Puissances, 1963-1968*, trans. by Gabriel Roth (Paris: Calmann-Levy, 1968), pp. 98ff.

[4] "Ben Gurion and De Gaulle: An Exchange of Letters," trans. by Hillel Halkin, *Midstream*, vol. 14, no. 2 (1968), p. 25.

promises were made after the de Gaulle-Eban interview at lower echelons and without any binding commitment.[5] Moreover, de Gaulle had not honored the obligations undertaken by the Fourth Republic; he remained vague on the extent to which France might support an effort to keep open the Gulf of 'Aqabah and expressed reservations about a United States-Great Britain attempt to challenge the Egyptian blockade.[6] In a statement of noncommitment, he not only refused to sign a declaration on 'Aqabah but issued a stern warning against the use of force.[7] Worse, from the Israeli point of view, he linked the issue of the Gulf of 'Aqabah to the settlement of the Arab refugee problem.[8] When one considers the limitations of a defense policy based on nuclear weapons and France's weakness in conventional forces, there were few courses of action open to de Gaulle. But had he acted differently, it is possible the Six Day War might never have happened. By taking even a minimal diplomatic stand, he would have helped eliminate many of the misundertsandings and certain of the miscalculations that propelled the protagonists toward war.

De Gaulle's actions were clearly motivated primarily by a desire to disassociate France from American policy, particularly in southeast Asia. According to Gaullist theory, the Soviets were menacing the Middle East through their Arab clients in response to American involvement in Viet-Nam. Second, the General wished to strengthen and extend French influence in the

[5] See Segev, *Israël*, p. 101.

[6] *Le Monde*, June 4-5, 1967.

[7] See *New York Times*, May 25, 1967, and *Le Monde*, June 3, 1967.

[8] See *New York Times*, June 1, 3, 1967.

Middle East, especially with regard to the French position in Algeria and a widening market for arms sales.
Third, he hoped to secure France's oil supply independently of other western powers. Fourth, he wished
to ensure French participation in any big power settlement concerning the region and to prevent any increase
in the radicalism of the "progressive" Arab states which
might result from a complete western ouster from the
area. He hoped also to counter a heightened United
States presence in the region. French official circles had
been aware of the precise Israel plans for occupying the
Golan heights, which aimed at posing a threat to
Damascus rather than preventing guerrilla activity.[9]
This was probably an additional reason for de Gaulle's
actions, for France had always placed Syria and Lebanon
in a reserved category when dealing with Israel security
planners. The relative level of Israeli enmity against
Syria, as opposed to Egypt, was a barometer in France-
Israel relations. Finally, there is the psychological element and de Gaulle's pique: he seemed to have re-
proached Israel for going to war despite his warning,
and quite possibly he neither foresaw the consequences
of events in 1967 nor the rapidity of Israel's victory.[10]

[9] Eric Rouleau, "French Policy in the Middle East," *The
World Today*, vol. 24 (May 1968), pp. 209-218.

[10] It has been brought to the author's attention by Nicholas
Wahl that Nahum Goldmann of the World Zionist Organization
and certain French diplomats have suggested that de Gaulle
was enraged at having been lied to by Israeli officials. While
there may have been a misunderstanding of Eban's intent, it
seems unlikely that Eban could have made any promise not
to open hostilities. Logic dictates against it, given the Israeli
security situation which made a preemptive strike imperative
and given also the tenor of Eban's remarks to de Gaulle reported
above. However, it was probably not until June 1 that Eban
himself became absolutely convinced that there was no hope

De Gaulle's principal error was that he refused to recognize the depth of pro-Israel feeling that had penetrated France and the extent to which Frenchmen would insist that Israel be succored in its hour of need. By his failure to do so, he had called into play a whole medley of forces which he was to decry as "the Jewish lobby" or "Israeli influences." Once again Israel threatened to become enmeshed in internal French politics. Fifty-six percent of these polled pronounced themselves pro-Israel on June 6, 1967, against twenty percent who were pro-Arab and twenty-eight percent who favored neither, with fourteen percent having no comment. In September 1967, the figures were sixty-eight percent pro-Israel, six percent pro-Arab, sixteen percent neither, and ten percent no comment. Fifty-four percent blamed the Arabs for starting the war, six percent blamed Israel, and four percent had no comment.[11]

Through the organizations of Jewish war veterans or deportee groups, pressure was brought to bear on the government, while the committees for solidarity with Israel held public meetings and demonstrations to dramatize their stand, enlisting prominent non-Jewish personalities as members. The strength of Jewish families in French finance, the press, advertising, and public relations eased their task.[12] To illustrate the

---

for diplomatic action to break the blockade on the part of the United States and other maritime powers. Thus it is possible that his hopes on May 24 that Israel might yet avoid a military confrontation may have been misinterpreted by de Gaulle as an assurance Israel would do so.

[11] The public opinion poll conducted by *L'Institut Français d'Opinion Publique,* reported in *Le Monde,* Oct. 29-30, 1967.

[12] Interviews in Paris with Solomon Friedrich, Director-General of the *Alliance France-Israël,* June 18, 1969; and Baron Edmond de Rothschild, July 1, 1969.

change in popular feeling as this process rapidly accelerated after the June war, the France-Israel Solidarity Fund collected $12 million in 1967, which totaled as much as the donations of the entire fifteen-year period previously.[13] The General was ill-disposed toward such manifestations of double allegiance by French Jewry as contrary to the essence of French nationalism and contrary to the spirit of French patriotism. Jews had begun to mobilize around the issue of support for Israel in the campaigns of Gaullist candidates from 1965 on, and after 1967 one can see a transfer of allegiance on the part of Jewish voters. Ultimately the crystallization of their discontent, in addition to other major forces of protest which expressed themselves in the referendum of April 27, 1969, were to force de Gaulle to resign.

Although it would be wrong to emphasize the point unduly, leading figures in French aeronautics were powerful political personalities and of Jewish origin. For example, Marcel Dassault, who built the industrial empire that restored French aviation supremacy, carried great weight in Fifth Republic government circles as one of the biggest contributors to the Gaullist party funds. Joseph Szydlowski, whose brother was one of the founding members of Qibbutz Kinneret, was owner of Turboméca, manufacturer of engines for helicopters and Fouga Magister jet trainers; Chairman of Rolls Royce-Turboméca Ltd. of London; and member of the board of SFERMA (*La Société Française d'Entretien et de Réparation Aéronautique*), a subsidiary of the government-controlled Sud Aviation. Szydlowski had visited Israel several times, and his company had a long history of close relations with the Israel defense establishment. De Gaulle could not have looked with favor at opposi-

---

[13] *Jerusalem Post,* Oct. 4, 1967.

tion to his policies emanating from such a key industry where even private firms work intimately with, and are ultimately controlled by, the government.[14]

It was particularly irksome to the General to find wholesale disobedience to his dictates within the government and even among his closest supporters and in areas vital to the national defense. The military establishment and the defense-related industries continued to evade the embargo on arms to Israel. On the eve of the war, large-scale arms shipments, including missiles, were ferried to Israel by French military transports, while twenty Mystère IIIs were loaned to the Israel Air Force.[15] Spare parts, replacements, "defensive matériel" and "low offensive capacity matériel" evaded the restrictions as well, until finally, by the end of 1967, only the Mirages remained under embargo.[16]

[14] French airframe companies generally share production, and the bulk of Dassault production is carried out by the state-owned Sud Aviation, which is under the triple tutelage of the Ministries of War, Finance, and Transport. Snecma and Hispano-Suiza are partially government-controlled, and at times both Turboméca and Dassault have had reason to fear nationalization. See *Aviation Week and Space Technology* (AWST), vol. 86 (Jan. 16, 1967), p. 35; and *The Economist*, vol. 213 (Oct. 10, 1964), p. 179. See also *Flight, Aircraft, Spacecraft, Missiles*, vol. 75 (June 12, 1959), pp. 795-798; and vol. 77 (June 17, 1960), pp. 829-830; 837-846.

[15] See *The National Review*, vol. 19 (July 25, 1967), pp. 782, 784; and Safran, *From War to War*, p. 442; David Kimche and Dan Bawly, *The Sandstorm. The Arab-Israeli War of June 1967: Prelude and Aftermath* (N.Y.: Stein & Day, 1968), p. 130, note; AWST, vol. 87 (July 31, 1967), pp. 26-28; *Le Monde*, June 22-28, 1967; *Jerusalem Post* weekly, July 31, 1967.

[16] *Press Conference of Georges Pompidou, President of the French Republic at the Elysée Palace, July 10, 1969* (N.Y.: Ambassade de France, Service de Presse et d'Information), No. 1270, p. 4.

In part, the industry's reactions were undoubtedly motivated by fears that the embargo would inhibit future arms sales abroad, particularly once Israel completed the Mirage V payments on April 16, 1968, and France still appeared determined to keep both the planes and the $65 million paid.[17] A major appeal in the purchase of French equipment had always been its apolitical character. Dassault and Sud Aviation suffered as Belgium, Denmark, Switzerland, and other prospective customers hesitated to place orders. Dassault tried to get the embargo lifted, making both "informal" and "formal" protests, while the aerospace industry as a whole made "at least two formal protests" to the French government.[18]

It would be an exaggeration, however, to claim as did the Paris correspondent of the *Jerusalem Post* on October 4, 1967, that "France's aircraft industry which depended on Israeli orders is now threatened by a serious recession by the embargo [which] is hurting its own manufacturing and technological potential." Despite an initial wariness after the war, Brazil, Argentina, Nigeria, the Netherlands, Belgium, and Pakistan soon bought French arms. Rewards from the Arab world followed as Iraq in February and April 1968 spent $150 million for fifty-two Mirage Vs and seventy AMX-30 tanks to be delivered in 1970; Saudi Arabia ordered AML-90s for about $200 million and light armored cars for $96 million, with delivery scheduled for 1969.[19] French sales agents were negotiating with

---

[17] *New York Times,* March 4, 1970. On an agreement to terminate Israel's order, see *ibid.,* Feb. 7, 1972.

[18] *Dun's Review,* vol. 91 (April 1968), pp. 61-62; AWST, vol. 88 (April 22, 1968), p. 22.

[19] See *The Military Balance 1968-1969* (London: Institute for Strategic Studies [ISS], 1968), pp. 58-59; AWST, vol. 88 (Feb.

Chile, Venezuela, and Argentina; Australia was reported ready to switch its production licenses to the Mirage V; New Zealand was thought about to choose the Dassault jet; and South Africa ordered thirty special Mirage III Zulus, continued to purchase the Alouette and Super Frelon helicopters and Panhard armored cars, and was reported anxious to buy the civilian Falcon to replace Britain's blockaded Beagle.[20]

Much of the French success was due to tempting payment terms and offset agreements. Moreover, the government promised additional support and subsidies for export sales in the wake of the June 1968 strikes, and these actions were likely to stifle any further industry objections at the loss of Israeli business. Those who mourned the loss of Israel's exclusive relationship with French aviation had to reconcile themselves to the fact that that exclusiveness had disappeared well before 1967. Ironically, Israel's success with French aircraft had boosted export orders, and Israel ranked only ninth in importance out of a dozen countries that purchased French aircraft in 1961, after the Federal Republic of Germany, Argentina, Australia, Belgium, Brazil, the United States, Finland, and India, and ahead of Sweden and Switzerland. France had even been able to penetrate the Arab market in 1965-1966, and by 1966, Australia, South Africa, and the United States made forty-three percent of all French aerospace purchases.[21]

12, 1968), pp. 55-56; (Feb. 26, 1968), pp. 16-17; vol. 87 (Dec. 18, 1967), p. 19; *Dun's Review, loc. cit.*

[20] See Francis Hope, "De Gaulle's African Balancing Act," *New Statesman* (Jan. 12, 1968), p. 34.

[21] *Interavia*, vol. 16, no. 5 (1961), p. 596; vol. 17, no. 9 (1962), p. 1080; AWST, vol. 74 (June 5, 1961), p. 21; vol. 86 (May 29, 1967), pp. 84-91; vol. 88 (June 17, 1968), pp. 18-19; Robert E. Farrell, "French Score in Drive to Widen Market," *ibid.*, vol. 74 (March 13, 1961), pp. 280-281, 283-285; and "French Nuclear,

With General de Gaulle's resignation as President of the Fifth Republic in 1969, there was a great deal of speculation whether his successor, Georges Pompidou, would deviate from the General's Middle East policies. From all evidence, Pompidou faithfully followed the lines of policy established by his predecessor. He sought to make France available as an alternative force in the area—to balance out the superpowers and fill the vacuum in the Arab world resulting from American support for Israel. In addition to earlier sales of Mirages and Panhard armored gun carriers to Iraq in 1967 and 1968, France reportedly began delivering to several Arab nations, surface-to-air rockets designed for defense against low-flying planes.[22] After a fourteen-year blacklisting by the Arab boycott organization, the *Société Nationale d'Etudes et de Construction de Moteurs d'Aviation* (Snecma), which makes jet engines for Dassault planes, submitted documentary proof that it had severed all dealings with Israel.[23] In the past Dassault had resisted and resented Arab boycott demands.

Obviously France was hardly suffering in its aeronautical exports, despite an initial thirty-seven percent loss of business after the embargo, which had hurt not only the aviation and electronics industries but shipbuilding as well. By 1970 France had recovered, however, and could boast an export total of $453 million—

Space Work Moves Toward Major Goals," *ibid.,* vol. 80 (March 16, 1964), pp. 270-275; J. F. Simon, "France's Flourishing Exports," *The Aeroplane and Astronautics,* vol. 101 (Dec. 14, 1961), pp. 763-764. See also AWST, vol. 84 (April 11, 1966), p. 34.

[22] *New York Times,* June 8, 1970.

[23] *Ibid.,* Dec. 28, 1970.

an increase of 11.5 percent over 1969.[24] Arms exports totaled nearly ten percent of all sales; more than one-fourth of all manufactured equipment was exported. Sales negotiations were particularly successful in Latin America and South Africa. Some twenty-six countries were purchasing the Mirage, the Fouga, and Alouette, AMX tanks, armored cars, gunboats, and sea-to-sea missiles. France was also evidently repeating its earlier pattern of seeking international cooperation for research and development. South Africa, for example, was supposedly paying three-fourths of the development costs of the Cactus surface-to-surface missile.[25]

France cut into traditional American markets in its role as independent arms purveyor. The biggest coup, and greatest irritant both in terms of American policies and the Middle East military balance, came with the disclosure in January 1970 that Libya had purchased 110 French Mirages after canceling an order for British jets. While France offered reassurances that the aircraft would be used for self-defense only and not be available for transfer to third parties, the participation of UAR officials in the Libyan negotiations and Libya's membership in the proposed federation with Egypt boded ill for stability in the local arms race.

French policy was motivated not only by the desire for greater weight in regional affairs but also by the simple economics of arms sales and expected return benefits from oil rich countries. Libyan oil constituted approximately seventeen percent of French oil imports in 1970, while France, after losing out in North

---

[24] Ambassade de France, Service de Presse et d'Information, *France,* April 1, 1971; and *Christian Science Monitor,* Jan. 19, 1971.

[25] See C. L. Sulzberger in *New York Times,* Feb. 21, 1971.

Rumaila, won some concessions in southern Iraq for its government-owned *L'Enterprise de Recherches et d'Activités Petroliers.*[26]

With France no longer serving as the major supplier of modern weaponry to Israel, the United States was forced to fill the vacuum. It was ironic that the Americans, after long resisting the role, had become by 1967-1968, the world's principal arms supplier and, although British sources had opened, practically Israel's sole outside source of sophisticated equipment. This carried certain disadvantages for the United States, which found itself increasingly isolated from the more radical states of the Arab world. The Americans were faced with a de facto division of the area, with USSR-supported Arab clients able to use American support for Israel as a justification for their continued hostility to the United States. As former American clients such as Turkey and Iran moved to normalize relations with the Soviet Union and to diminish their dependence upon Washington, it seemed as if the United States' position in the area would deteriorate further as long as the Arab-Israel problem remained acute.

Israel's first direct purchase of American weapons had been in 1962-1963, when the Hawk missile launchers were made available. As noted above, Israel bought the Hawk not because of cooling French ardor but because of Israel's changing weapons needs. After 1965 Israel was making large-scale purchases of American arms, including some 200 M-48 Patton tanks; 80 A-4 Skyhawk bombers purchased in early 1966 at a reported cost of $52 million; 80 Hawks; and some 50 F-4 Phantom fighter-bombers, sold by the Johnson administration in December 1968 at a cost of approximately $3-4 million

---

[26] See *France,* April 1, 1971, on French oil imports.

apiece, additional Skyhawks and Hawk missiles having been approved earlier in the year.[27]

One has only to compare the composition of the Israel Air Force in 1968 and 1971 to see the change. In 1968, a majority of the 273 combat aircraft in Israel's air arm were of French manufacture with only 48 A-4 Skyhawks in service. The backbone of the combat force was still the 65 Mirage IIIs, 15 Super Mystères, 35 Mystère IVs, 45 Ouragans, and 65 Magisters.[28]

Faced with continuing losses averaging forty to fifty jets a year in the war of attrition on the Suez front, Israel had desperate need of a plane suitable for the kind of defense role the Skyhawk could not fulfill. Since 1968 both the Johnson and Nixon administrations agreed to sell a total of 80 Phantoms plus six reconnaissance models. Deliveries started in the fall of 1969 and were reportedly completed by 1971. Thus, on April 20, 1971, the *New York Times* assessed Israel's air strength as being based upon 70 F-4s, 100 A-4s, 50 Mirage IIIs, 20 Mystère IVs, and some 150 miscellaneous older jets. The benefit offered by the greater sophistication and maneuverability of American aircraft may have been offset by their higher cost as compared to their French counterparts and the likelihood that the United States may have placed some restraints on their use.[29] Unlike the French who, after the Suez episode, were careful to

[27] *New York Times,* Oct. 25, 1967; Oct. 13, 1968; March 8, 1970; Feb. 7, 1972. Military credits from the 1950s to 1967 were reported in the neighborhood of $24 million. Nonmilitary aid in agricultural commodities totaled about $30 million annually. See *ibid.,* Aug. 4, 1967.

[28] *Ibid.,* Oct. 13, 1968.

[29] The Mirage V Snecma engine had been considered weak and troublesome. Dassault, however, was generally able to produce a prototype for 50% less than any American company.

divorce military cooperation with Israel from political and diplomatic aims, the United States generally tended to use military aid as a political instrument. There was the constant possibility that the American government would hold up future deliveries to obtain Israeli concessions in the negotiations underway for reopening the Suez Canal and for Israeli withdrawal from the occupied territories. Whether or not this would enhance prospects for peace in the region remained unclear. While the United States might pressure Israel into temporary concessions, without some permanent settlement of the larger issues which met with Soviet acquiescence, Israel might merely be placed in what it conceived of as an untenable position militarily. In the past, when it considered itself threatened Israel had countered with the first military blow.

Conscious of the dangers inherent in its reliance on the United States, Israel continued to develop an independent deterrent by strengthening its aeronautics and electronics industries. Since the French arms embargo of January 1969, Israel's weapons manufacture had increased by fifty percent, with special emphasis on airplane armaments, small computers, electronics and communications systems, explosives, fuses, aerial bombs, and rocket propellants.[30] In May 1970, the Gabriel, a sea-to-sea missile, made its appearance in the Israeli arsenal. The first major weapon to be developed entirely in Israel, the Gabriel was designed to overcome some of the weaknesses of the Styx. For example, it was only eleven feet long, in comparison to the twenty-foot Styx, so that a missle boat could carry more than a

[30] On Israeli arms sales abroad, see *New York Times,* Nov. 25, 1967; April 23, 1971; January 14, 1972; and *Le Monde,* June 22-23, 1969.

Styx-equipped vessel. The Gabriel had a secret guidance system, a twenty-mile range at supersonic speeds, and a low-level trajectory. It was probably one of a planned series of missiles which reportedly entered the final development phase around 1964.[31]

Israel pressed ahead in atomic research and, in the summer of 1970, the old argument of just how close Israel had come to attaining a nuclear capability was revived. By early 1968, Israel was said to possess nearly thirty pounds of weapons-grade plutonium. In 1969 exports generally argued that Israel was unlikely to develop an atomic bomb and could not do so in less than twelve to eighteen months. Yet one year later most American observers assumed that Israel had either atomic weapons or the components available for ready assembly.[32] Reports also circulated—accompanied by Israeli denials—that in 1968 Premier Levi Eshkol had asked for nuclear bomb racks to be installed in the Phantoms purchased, and that President Johnson had refused. Then there was the matter of the twenty-five French built surface-to-surface MD 620 missiles (also designated in some press reports as the MD 660) produced for Israel by Dassault. The two-stage solid-fuel missile could carry a 1,000-1,200-pound warhead 280 miles and its use seemed to make little sense without nuclear armament. Reports also mentioned newly constructed plants, presumably part of the Bedek complex,

[31] *Jewish News* (Newark, N.J.), May 22, 1970; *New York Times,* May 6, 1970.

[32] Cf. Leonard Beaton, "Why Israel Does *Not* Need the Bomb. A Report on the Real Nuclear Standing of Egypt, India and Israel," *The New Middle East,* no. 7 (April 1969), pp. 7-11; and *New York Times,* July 18, 1970.

for the manufacture of solid propellant fuel and missile engines, mobile erector platforms, and test facilities.

Other concrete signs pointed to Israel's growing independence in the aviation field. Shim'on Peres was a particular advocate of the view that Israel should, and could, begin producing its own military planes in two to three years. It could accomplish this with a newly purchased American factory and the cooperation of several French firms. An agreement was signed July 4, 1967, with French industrialist Joseph Szydlowski to establish Turboméca-Israel, a jet engine factory. This was Szydlowski's own personal protest against de Gaulle's embargo on arms to Israel following the June war. He had originally intended to manufacture helicopters and jet trainers in West Germany for local consumption and export.[33] Potez also signed a new agreement in June 1968 for twenty-five Magister jet trainers, expected in service in 1968.[34] IAI also acquired production rights to manufacture the seven-passenger twin-jet Commander, formerly produced by Rockwell-Standard Corporation of Oklahoma. Since Pentagon approval was needed for the sale and Israel acquired at the same time a marketing outlet in the United States, there was every indication that links with the American air industry were likely to increase.[35]

In addition to the Arava Stol, which had its inaugural flight on April 9, 1970, and the Commodore (the redesigned Jet Commander), there were reliable reports that Israel would—by early 1971—have ready a

[33] *Jerusalem Post,* July 5, 1967.

[34] *The Military Balance 1968-1969,* p. 58; and an interview in Paris with Georges Volland of Potez-Fouga, June 17, 1969.

[35] *Business Week,* Oct. 7, 1967, p. 127; *Jerusalem Post,* Sept. 14, 1967.

prototype jet fighter designed for combat missions, bombing, and ground support. Essentially an improved version of the Mirage, the plane could go into production within eighteen months after the completion of the prototype.[36] These reports were given added credence at the time by the disclosure that a Swiss aeronautical engineer, Alfred Frauenknecht, had been convicted of selling Israel blueprints for the tooling for the Mirage III-SX, currently manufactured for the Swiss Air Force under French license by Sulzer Brothers Co. of Switzerland. Two new factories for the production and reconditioning of jet engines were opened in 1971: Misco Beit Shemesh, which produced components for jet aero-engines, gas turbines, and electronic computers; and Turbochrome Ltd., which conditioned and coated jet engine parts of local and foreign airlines.[37]

Since 1967 Israel has been attempting to forge even closer ties with Germany, while a curious rapprochement with Rumania has been in progress. Although there is too little information available to attempt a detailed analysis of those ties at this time, in many respects one is reminded of the genesis of the France-Israel alliance, which occurred while France was something of a pariah, embarked on an independent course within the western camp. Rumania is in a somewhat analogous position within the Soviet bloc. While a complete parallel may not be tenable, one might also note that, under Golda Meir's premiership, Israel has experienced a return to more centralized leadership and a reduction in the factionalism characteristic of the Eshkol period. This might make it easier for Israel to pursue new avenues for unorthodox diplomacy.

[36] *New York Times,* April 10, 1970.
[37] See *The Israel Digest,* vol. 14 (July 9, 1971), p. 2.

Can one discern any remnant of the special ties that had characterized France-Israel relations before 1967? The "gunboat affair" might raise the question whether the old pattern of tacit, direct military connections might not have persisted despite political disengagement. Israel had initially purchased twelve gunboats as missile launchers at a cost of $2 million apiece after the German arms shipments ceased in 1965.[38] France had not outbid other competitors, but the Israel Embassy reportedly argued that political considerations should outweigh pecuniary advantage. After a visit by Cherbourg Mayor Dr. Jacques Hébert to Jerusalem, the order was placed with the *Chantier de Constructions Mécaniques de Normandie,* which secured a loan to cover the two-thirds of the costs outstanding.

Five boats were delivered in 1968, and two more were spirited away just as the total embargo was imposed after the January 3, 1969, Beirut raid. When the remaining five completed gunboats slipped out of Cherbourg in December 1969 and made their way to Israel, it was obvious that high government officials were implicated in the subterfuge. Not only had the Mayor and the press of Cherbourg withheld news of the boats' departure, but evidence pointed to complicity within the government in the matter of the dummy company that had been established to shield Israel's intentions. The Interministerial Commission on Arms Sales had approved an export permit for the boats without close scrutiny and without restrictions as to third-party transfers.

The French navy must have been involved, especially if one considers the general irritation that branch

---

[38] *New York Times,* Feb. 2, 1970.

of the armed forces had long felt in the face of General de Gaulle's bias in favor of the *force de frappe* and subsequent shortchanging of the navy. The navy was also most likely to be concerned about the Soviet build-up in the Mediterranean and anxious to have its old friend and ally strong at the eastern end. Lower level officials, military and civilian, would also have had to be involved to ensure Israeli success in the venture. Doubtless the Ministry of Finance was anxious to receive full payment for the boats to cover its loan to the Cherbourg builders and thus likely to go along with the plot. There, such old friends of Israel as Jacques Piette could be found in high positions. Whatever the case, the "gunboat affair" led to the dismissal of the two men involved in the interministerial commission's approval of the sale: General Bernard Cazelles, Secretary General of the National Defense Council, and Louis Bonte, an aeronautical engineer, head of the foreign section of the government arms agency. The incident led Michel Debré to admit the difficulty of imposing a total embargo.[39] Fragmentation was evidently still a reality in the French government, and sympathies for Israel undoubtedly persisted at various levels. The situation, however, was if anything more analogous to that obtaining in the immediate postwar period, before the rise of the tacit alliance.

At the beginning of 1970 there were few members of Pompidou's inner circle who might conceivably have favored a pro-Israel policy. Léo Hamon, the government spokesman, and Maurice Schumann—both of Jewish origin—Albin Chalandon, Minister of Equipment and Housing, and Robert Vivien, Under Secretary of State for Housing, had been identified as supporters of Israel. But it was unlikely they carried anywhere

---

[39] *Ibid.*, Jan. 22, 1970.

near the weight of Michel Debré or Chaban-Delmas, neither of whom displayed any signs of favoring a resumption of the tacit alliance. Occasionally the pro-Israel Senator André Monteil, of the Foreign Affairs Committee, Paul Stehlin in parliament, or Michel Poniatawski, Secretary General of the Independent Republicans, might question the government's stand on Middle East issues. However, their voices were faint on the whole, and the French public seemed reconciled to a neutral, even pro-Arab position. There were also fears that since de Gaulle's infamous press conference, the large-scale dismissal of Jewish civil servants and radio and television personalities, and the demonstrations that met Pompidou during his 1970 visit to the United States, anti-Semitism might once again become an issue in France, and, at the time, there seemed to be a flood of virulent anti-Jewish books and articles and anti-Semitic demonstrations at the universities. Pompidou was widely quoted as saying that Israel should cease being a "racial and religious state" and seemed to be warning the 550,000 Jews in France—the largest Jewish population in Western Europe—to choose carefully between loyalty to France and support for Israel. The implication was that the issue was one of dual and incompatible loyalties.

Pompidou also continued to follow de Gaulle's diplomatic example with regard to regional affairs, projecting France's image as a potential mediator in the Arab-Israel dispute, while often striking what appeared to the Israelis at least, as a pro-Arab stance in key Security Council votes. As de Gaulle had done, Pompidou consistently pressed for Israeli withdrawal from occupied territories, opposed Israel's "administrative" unification of Jerusalem, and evinced a reluctance to condemn outrightly either hijackings by Arab guerrillas or sabotage within Israel, on the grounds that such terrorism might be called legitimate action by an occupied people against a foreign power. At the same time the French President rejected Israeli demands for direct negotiations with the Arabs, arguing for some four-power guarantees as a solution to the regional issues and insisting that the inclusion of France was indispensable to such a solution.[40]

France also continued to place obstacles in Israel's path as the latter sought special trading arrangements within the EEC. Instead, France had been spearheading efforts to open contacts between the EEC and Lebanon and Egypt. Only in February 1970 was a preferential five-year trade pact completed, as a result of a Netherlands-inspired compromise.[41]

The tacit alliance was a fact of Middle East politics from 1956 to 1967. Once it disappeared, one might have expected major changes in the position of the regional contenders in the Arab-Israel dispute and in their relations with outside powers. Yet, because the relationship had been withering over a period of years, the final break merely accelerated and consolidated trends already in progress. There were no new radical departures from patterns already apparent in the mid-1960s. While France supported Israel during the 1950s and early 1960s, it did have some measure of influence in Middle East affairs, if only by proxy. By military disengage-

[40] See Ambassade de France, Service de Presse et d'Information, *Statement Delivered by His Excellency Jacques Kosciusko-Morizet, French Permanent Representative to the United Nations Before the General Assembly on October 30, 1970,* no. 1474.

[41] For details, see *New York Times,* Feb. 23, June 30, 1970.

ment from Israel, it had hoped to gain greater maneuverability for its diplomatic activities. There is little evidence, however, that France has been able to play a meaningful role in the area.

While there were scattered reports in 1970 of French successes in having dissuaded Iraq from intervening in Jordan, of having negotiated for the release of airplane hijacking hostages, and of having arranged the release from prison of some eighty Egyptian Jews, France seemed to have relatively scant influence on any of the more important regional issues. Moreover, for each gain as in Libya or Iraq, there seemed to be setbacks, as in the Iraqi oil concessions or in Lebanon, where a prominent representative of the French state-owned oil company was asked to leave in reaction to difficulties over irregularities in French-sponsored community projects. In short, while French actions could still have nuisance value for its western allies, and while at the regional level French actions might be of importance to individual states on a bilateral basis, there was little evidence of any third force being created.

Pompidou seems to have decided to concentrate on the Mediterranean and Europe and to leave aside de Gaulle's ambition for a global role. He may have been as effectively in charge of foreign policy as de Gaulle had ever been, but he lacked his mentor's prestige. He could demand a voice in regional affairs, but no one seemed to be listening. Of course it is unfair to blame the French President entirely in assessing the success or failure of French ambitions, for in any possible Middle East scenario, ranging from open hostilities to an eventual peace settlement, it is difficult to find a meaty role France can play. Ultimately, the starring parts will belong to the superpowers, and one can safely assume that, if any lessening of tensions is achieved, it will be due primarily to mutual superpower accommodation.

Since the Six Day War there has been an increasing polarization of the Middle East as the superpowers augmented their individual regional commitments. While Russia tightened its relations with the "progressive" Arab states, particularly the UAR, the United States was forced to assume greater responsibilities in the region, despite the fact that it was hampered by having become more closely involved in support for Israel. The sinking of the Israeli destroyer *Eilat* on October 21, 1967, by a Soviet-made missile; the introduction into the Egyptian arsenal of Sam II and III missiles which were manned by Russians; the arrival of Mig-23 and Su-11 aircraft; the growing numbers of Russian advisers in the army and air force at battalion and squadron level; continuing massive arms shipments; and the expanding Soviet naval presence in the Mediterranean, all raised fears for the security of western interests in the eastern Mediterranean. These fears were aggravated by the 1971 USSR-UAR treaty which legalized a continued Soviet military presence in Egypt, providing for coordination between the two powers to "eliminate any threat" to the peace. Although Egyptian relations with the USSR have since cooled somewhat, the extent of Soviet influence cannot be discounted.

With the heightened polarization of the Middle East into USSR-supported states and United States clients, superpower involvement not only meant that any regional settlement would inevitably be tied to unresolved worldwide Cold War issues such as the Viet-Nam war, but implied the danger that the superpowers might be drawn directly into the regional conflict. Meanwhile, the escalating arms race threatened to radicalize the Arab-Israel dispute even further for newer and more devastating weapons were introduced on a larger scale. As Israel sought to reduce its dependence upon the United States, there was the ever-present threat of further qualitative escalation. De Gaulle may well have been right in hoping to balance these forces and to serve as a mediating third choice. Unfortunately, after having abruptly ended the tacit alliance with Israel, France was no closer to achieving its aims in 1972 than it had been in 1967.

Conclusions

The Tacit Alliance: A Peculiar Relationship

THE TACIT alliance between France and Israel was a peculiar arrangement between two states whose interests ran parallel for a time, then diverged. While it reflected some of the principal aspects of an alliance, in many respects it differed from the normal patterns of international politics. Alliances are essentially military arrangements based on reciprocity or interdependence. In an unequal alliance, the stronger partner will usually guarantee the security of the weaker in exchange for some form of political support or subordination, strategic advantage or economic benefits. Military support was indeed at the core of the France-Israel relationship, but there was no express commitment or structure, nor was it apparently envisaged that France might actively defend Israel—although the extent of actual commitments made during and after the Suez crisis will have to be reevaluated when the official record is more substantially opened to the public. Instead, France undertook to provide Israel with the military means with which it could secure its own destiny.

French friendship for Israel was initially expressed in terms of modern equipment, tanks, and jet aircraft for the Israel Defense Forces and, ultimately, a nuclear option. What made the alliance unique and unlikely to be repeated was the fact that close cooperation evolved between the two defense establishments and their intelligence networks, between the Israel Air

Force and the French aviation industry, in space, nuclear science, and missile technology. These special ties extended the life of the relationship beyond the period of convergent national political interests. However, as international politics became increasingly dominated by the scientific nation-state and as France attained an independent nuclear capacity and advanced technology, it needed the broader resources which were available through European cooperation. The value of scientific collaboration with Israel was therefore undermined, particularly once the technology gap and fears of American scientific domination became a major issue in France. Yet progressive disengagement in the political sphere, apparent from the late 1950s, was never completely followed by military and technological disengagement until the events of 1967.

Israel's contributions were of course limited by its human and material resources and undoubtedly both countries would have eventually achieved the same scientific advances acting alone. Nonetheless, cooperation proved useful for France at a decisive stage in its postwar development. First, the timing of Israel's need for arms had coincided with the French industry's need for expansion. After 1956 Israeli purchases made it possible for France to develop weapons systems at reasonable costs, exploiting economies of scale. This was less crucial for ground equipment than for the some three hundred French aircraft on which the Israel Air Force was almost exclusively built. General Lavaud has testified that Israel's orders could cut one-third off the assembly-line price of French planes.[1]

---

[1] General Gaston Jean Lavaud, President of the *Conseil d'Administration* of the *Office Nationale d'Etudes et de Recherches Aérospatiales* (1963-1965), interviewed in Paris, June

Conclusions

Accurate statistics on the terms of payment and actual costs of major weapons systems are almost non-existent, but even at the height of their cooperation, France could never afford to give Israel as favorable terms on arms purchases as, for example, the USSR gave the UAR. With defense expenditures constantly rising, Israel was an important source of revenue for any arms supplier. Between 1955 and 1967, Israel spent more than an estimated $600 million for arms from France, including $75 million for the Dimona reactor.[2] This matches the figures given by Pierre Gallois of Dassault—NF 1 milliard from 1958 to 1962 and NF 1 milliard from 1962 to 1967, including research and development on the Dassault MD 620 missile and the undelivered Mirages, or approximately $400 million.[3] The escalating costs of the weapons systems is illustrated by comparing the price of the first Matra rocket launchers sold Israel, about NF 600 ($120 apiece), with the price in the late 1960s, when Matra missiles added twenty percent to the cost of aircraft, or between $30,000 and $50,000.[4] The Mystère was about half the price of the Mirage.

12, 1969; and *Aviation Week and Space Technology* (AWST), vol. 64 (March 12, 1956), pp. 304-309; vol. 65 (Dec. 24, 1956), p. 31.

[2] J. C. Hurewitz, *Middle East Politics: The Military Dimension* (N.Y.: Praeger, 1969), p. 442; and Nadav Safran, *From War to War. The Arab-Israeli Confrontation, 1948-1967* (N.Y.: Pegasus, 1967), p. 228.

[3] General of the Air Force Pierre Gallois (ret.), Commercial Director of the *Société des avions Marcel Dassault* since 1958, interviewed in Paris, June 10, 1969. These figures may, if anything, be somewhat understated.

[4] Marcel Chassagny, President and Director-General of the *Société des Engins Matra* since 1937, interviewed in Paris, June 16, 1969.

It is one of the ironies of the tacit alliance that, while Israel could offer France relatively little in the realm of technology during the first half-decade, by the time it had advanced in military technology to the point where it could make a major contribution, the relationship was unilaterally ruptured by France. By 1967 the Israel defense industries had, for example, developed a new special concrete blasting bomb for use on enemy runways during low-level attacks.[5] This bomb was fitted with retroactive rockets to give a vertical descent, and thus ensured maximum destruction of the airfields during the June war. Matra later advertised its own "bombe freinée," with broad hints that this was the bomb that had won the Six Day War.

As for cultural and economic ties, they were surface reflections of the underlying strength or weakness of the tacit alliance. Although it might be interesting to study the economic relations between the two countries and the obstacles which arose as a result of the special nature of Israeli socialism and the unique character of the French capitalist, the purely economic aspects of the France-Israel tacit alliance are relatively unimportant. There was an extremely narrow rationale for close economic ties.[6] After 1962, once French responsibilities and influence in North Africa had diminished, larger quantities of Israel citrus were imported, but the only other considerable Israel export to France was polished diamonds. In addition, France bought small quantities of industrial products—chemicals, medicines, paints,

[5] AWST, vol. 87 (July 17, 1967), p. 85.

[6] The following relies upon interviews in Paris with Menahem Meir, Economic Counsellor of the Israel Embassy, May 27, 1969; François Perreire of the Rothschild Bank, July 3, 1969; and Baron Edmond de Rothschild, July 1, 1969.

textiles, and clothing and, in the agricultural sector, token amounts of eggs.

Although France was not Israel's main supplier, it nontheless derived considerable economic benefit from the Israel market. Production inputs and investment goods were the two largest categories, but the long list of French exports to Israel included food and live animals, beverages and tobacco, crude and synthetic rubber, wood, textile fabrics, fertilizers and minerals, petroleum products, chemicals, medicinal products, manufactured goods, printed matter, machinery, appliances, vehicles, aircraft, and aircraft parts.

In the few instances where economic relations were particularly successful and close during the period under review, it seems a case of personal, pro-Israel biases in key industries or financial circles. The long-term credits granted Israel for ship-building led to closer ties between the two merchant navies and important contracts from the French point of view. It is significant that a leading role in this development was played by the French Minister for Foreign Trade, Gilbert Grandval (later Minister of Labor as well), a former Secretary General of the French Merchant Navy. Grandval was one of the two Jewish ministers in Pompidou's cabinet—the other being Minister for Industry Marcel Maurice Bokanowsky. However, when later Israeli contracts were awarded to Japanese firms which offered easier terms, some of Israel's friends were alienated, causing further strains in the relationship with France.

On the Israel side, it was those industries largely under the aegis of the defense establishment which managed to strengthen their contacts with France. One example is the electro-chemical field, where French investment and technical cooperation remained high despite threats of the Arab boycott. Another is the electronics industry after the early 1960s, where lower research and development costs gave Israel a competitive advantage in the export of computer software for use in French nuclear research projects. In 1966, a joint engineering planning company was set up to exploit Israel patents and expertise, but, as it turned out, Israel suffered an economic recession shortly after the agreement was signed and was hard-put to produce sufficient quantities of goods even to fulfill the quotas in the bilateral trade agreement. Finance Minister Michel Debré, in a gesture of good will, hosted an economic mission to study ways of expanding Israeli trade with France, but little came of it before the Six Day Arab-Israeli war.

Avenues for and interest in French investment in Israel were limited despite tax concessions available to firms with subsidiaries or branches abroad and government guarantees for investments with state insurance against losses caused by the Arab boycott. French fiscal problems and currency restrictions, moreover, created a situation where investment was either curtailed or had to be effected in a round-about way. Although the Tel-Aviv Investment Authority deals with approved government investments, private French investments will not appear in their records and were few and far between in the years under investigation. The largest private French financial interest in Israel belonged to Edmond de Rothschild's group, but his affairs were handled by a Swiss organization. France ranked below the United States, Canada and the sterling bloc countries, Latin America, Italy, and Switzerland in approved foreign investment in Israel. In 1964, for example, the United

States and Canada represented a total of $28.5 million out of $55.4 million total foreign investment, the sterling bloc $7.5 million, and France $0.7 million— just ahead of Germany with $0.5 million and Denmark and Sweden with $0.1 million.[7] Prior to the Arab-Israel war, out of nearly four hundred Israeli agreements with foreign companies for licenses and patents, only twelve were with France; not one French company or bank had permanent offices in Israel.[8]

Only after the Six Day War and a series of economic conferences held in August 1967, April 1968, and June 1969, did prospects appear brighter for greater French investment in Israel and wider trade exchanges. Indeed economic ties between France and Israel gave evidence of being profoundly revised.

Most Israeli transactions with France were paid for in cash in United States dollars. Importers were not allowed to accept credit, and exporters did not give credit, so that it is useless to investigate the government role in extending credits as a factor in the relationship. Agricultural products provided the mainstay of Israel trade and were exchanged on normal commercial terms, i.e. payment in cash in thirty days. One useful avenue for further investigation is the extent of commercial ties with French Africa, particularly in comparison to English-speaking Africa. Although there has been some Israeli cooperation with French companies in exports to Africa, generally Israeli trade with the former French territories has lagged behind that with the former British dependencies.

To ascertain what common interests could have prompted France to seek an alliance with Israel despite

[7] *Entreprises,* Dec. 18, 1965. Dossier spécial.
[8] *Le Patronat Français,* 1966.

the very narrow potential for any special ties between the two states, and to understand how the unique combination of military, technological, and scientific ties which lay at the center of the tacit alliance could have been fostered, often at variance with the foreign policy of the two partners, it was necessary to consider the France-Israel relationship within the context of the changing domestic, regional, and international systems. As international and regional politics created a timely conjunction of different but compatible interests which began to draw France and Israel together by 1952, the political systems of the future allies facilitated and even accelerated the process. Domestic politics were particularly responsible for the tone of the relationship, for despite its military focus the tacit alliance was not a typical defense contract conducted through normal diplomatic channels. Its implied nature and almost clandestine methods of operation were largely due to the segmented internal structure of the Fourth Republic.

Despite the round-robin of shifting portfolios and government changes in France, there was actually little turnover in a few key positions and the frequent interchange of functions took place among a group of some fifty core *ministrables* who had considerable influence. With long tenure in office they could build solid power bases and pursue their own policies with some continuity. The Radical Maurice Bourgès-Maunoury, who played such a prominent role in the alliance with Israel, was almost continually in office from 1947 on, during which time he held key portfolios twelve times in ten years in one of the defense posts or in the Interior Ministry, and served as Prime Minister in 1957-1958.

The key or senior cabinet portfolios were the Ministries of Foreign Affairs, Finance, Defense, Interior, and Justice, one of which the Prime Minister often held. In addition, there was the Vice President of the Council of Ministers and a Minister of State without portfolio, who usually dealt with special problems. Thus a fairly small group of politicians within the bureaucracy and defense establishment was involved in effective decision-making, and these elements, rather than the traditionalists of the Quai d'Orsay, were able to assess the role Israel could play as a proxy or pawn in French political, military, and strategic calculations. The tacit alliance was, in effect, their creation.

Under Charles de Gaulle a certain momentum carried over from the Fourth Republic into the Fifth, but by 1962, the main architects of the relationship with Israel had disappeared from the scene. Because the Middle East was fairly low in the list of French priorities, despite de Gaulle's reserved sphere of control over foreign policy, Quai d'Orsay influence over a whole range of issues was strengthened. In certain increasingly narrow political spheres, protection of Israel's interests fit into the scheme of world affairs envisaged by de Gaulle, but French interests were forcefully reasserted, sometimes to the detriment of Israel. However, the special relationship was forced to adjust less to the international politics of the French President—many elements of which were carried over from the Fourth Republic—than to his personal politics and the internal power struggle which his actions occasioned. As de Gaulle increasingly centered responsibility in the presidency at the expense of all other institutions, subordinating parliament, the politicians, and a rebellious army, centralization of the command structure of the military establishment reduced avenues of access to the French system for Israel interests, and, correspondingly, possibilities for cooperation decreased. When defense-related ties with Israel were "commercialized" or "institutionalized," direct contacts were again at the core, but this time between the defense establishment of Israel and the French military industries. Thus a whole range of pressure group interests existed within France which could benefit from support for Israel, and the key industries, allied with the military, were able to exercise an important role in orienting and actually conducting a pro-Israel foreign policy. This counterbalanced the prevailing tendency to centralization and pro-Arab influences at the Quai d'Orsay. As long as de Gaulle did not immediately terminate commitments to Israel or countermand existing tendencies, the alliance withered only slowly.

In Israel the situation was almost the reverse of that in France although the changes that took place were nowhere nearly so dramatic. Until 1963, the Israel government operated under a cohesive cabinet and strongly centralized leadership with David Ben Gurion as Premier. He conceived of weapons needs as the first priority, and, unhampered by conventional niceties of state-to-state relations, he allowed the defense establishment to exploit openings for direct contact with key individuals in the fragmented French decision-making apparatus. Responding quickly to developments with a unity of purpose and a minimum of official decision-making and diplomatic fuss, he permitted the unorthodox relationship to raise few problems for the normal functioning of Israel's system.

When Ben Gurion held both portfolios as Premier and Minister of Defense, his interest in security received primary consideration. He was effectively able to insulate the defense establishment from coalition politics because of his leadership of Mapai, his acknowledged expertise in military matters, and his method of independent decision-making. Meanwhile, the influence of the defense complex extended into spheres normally reserved for civilian institutions so that a crisis was probably inevitable once Eshkol took office. Eshkol not only lacked Ben Gurion's charisma and close identification with the defense establishment, but he had different views of defense and foreign policy priorities.

There is little doubt that the changes in Israel aggravated the strains already apparent in the alliance with France as Israel suffered from indecisiveness and coalition politics and as the guardians of a pro-French orientation revoked their support for Eshkol. However, to blame the Eshkol government for the erosion of ties with France would be far from warranted. Of the two domestic systems, French politics exercised the greater influence, for there was more continuity in the Israel system. France had already begun to move away from its ally as early as 1958, and, by the time Eshkol succeeded to the premiership, the process had begun to accelerate. To a certain extent, Eshkol responded to the French disengagement by following Ben Gurion's lead in seeking closer ties and weapons from the United States. Although this in turn caused further strains in the alliance, it is hard to see what alternatives were available.

There was a very narrow range of agreement where Israel served French political purposes under the Fourth and Fifth Republics. It became apparent shortly after the Mollet government fell in 1957 that diverging regional interests would make a continuing complete identification of interests impossible. As the Israelis persistently sought reassurances, they confused platitudes with hard reality and seemed to be conducting diplomacy in the press so far as the French were concerned. Whether they sought to ease their own sense of isolation or tried at the same time to exert pressure on the French, they undermined the very nature of the alliance. Publicity threatened to prejudice the reassertion of traditional French interests in the Arab world and opened a whole range of security questions and unorthodox procedures to public and government scrutiny. It would be particularly interesting to analyze information policies in this regard, especially with reference to Israel's apparent failure to distinguish between internally and externally oriented information. Where the alliance relationship became a controversial issue in domestic politics—in France in 1961 and after 1967, and in Israel after 1963—it aggravated internal civil-military tensions and added to strains in the accord.

As overt political support from France disappeared, Israel tried to shift the emphasis in the relationship to broadened technological and scientific cooperation and cultural activities. However, this policy was ineptly executed, possibly because Israel had not yet reached a sufficiently high level of technology. Israel leaders also tended to ignore all signs of political disenchantment as long as the supply of essential arms continued. The failure to recognize the dangers implicit in accepting short-sighted military goals as the barometer of the relationship was, in essence, the failure of tacit diplomacy. Because the relationship with France was not conducted through the regular foreign affairs channels, but by military purchasing agents and defense strategists, there was less accuracy in assessing overall long-range policies. Once the centralizing tendency of the Fifth Republic and the loss of decisiveness of the Eshkol regime became apparent, the tacit alliance had to become a formal, orthodox, binding diplomatic understanding, or decline. By relying on the strength of its existing technological and military ties with France, Israel overstressed the influence of such factors in international relations and ignored the fact that nations first and foremost act in accordance with their own political priorities.

The international and regional systems did not remain stable in the period under review. First, postwar Anglo-French hegemony gave way to the formality of tripartite diplomacy. Then, as British power weakened and American responsibility grew, the entrance of the Soviet Union into the area brought about the period of four-power rivalry which preceded the Suez crisis. With the end of Anglo-French illusions of influence in the region, American supremacy in the post-Suez period remained unchallenged until United States-Soviet competition in the 1960s dominated and polarized the Middle East. French efforts to erect a third force had not shown much success by 1967, for the superpowers remained unchallenged. Meanwhile, at the regional level, the Arab states were being split into revolutionary-radical and conservative camps, each supported by a superpower. At the same time, the Arab-Israel dispute had become increasingly intractable.

Despite a growing tendency for the Middle East to operate as an autonomous regional system in which the actions of the great powers were mutually paralyzing, there was constant interaction between international and regional politics in the evolution of the alliance. It thrived during multipower competition and regional flexibility, disintegrating as regional politics became rigidly polarized and dominated by the superpower conflict. Generally, international rivalries aggravated the local problems and were a catalyst for the major transformations that took place. Britain and the United States, for example, were largely responsible for initiating an arms race in the Arab-Israel zone as a result of the Baghdad Pact negotiations. The Soviet Union responded with the Egyptian arms deal and introduced big power competition, spurring multilevel arms races throughout the region. Modern weapons technology created its own foreign policy imperatives severely limiting Israel's freedom of choice in foreign affairs and making the need to obtain equipment and support for defense against Arab hostility the prime factor. Given the escalating arms race and rise in the technological level of weaponry, it was logical that Israel should seek to widen its sources of armaments and to create, as far as possible, an independent national deterrent. Once Egypt embarked on a missile program in 1961-1962, Israel was forced to turn to the United States for an anti-missile defense system unavailable elsewhere. The United States decision to make advanced weapons available to Israel coincided with France's reentry into Middle East politics after the Algerian settlement, and with French efforts to widen its export market by selling the latest equipment to the Arab states. This in turn reinforced the trend toward greater Israeli independence from the French aeronautics industry and decreased French dependence upon the Israeli market.

International politics were of prime consideration for France and conditioned its behavior toward Israel. Essential French interests lay outside the region, and the alliance was central to French policy only during the Algerian war from 1954 to 1962, but even then only secondarily. Certain continuous threads, however, are evident in French actions, such as the desire not to be excluded from any privileged relationship between the United States and Britain and the need for independence from the United States in defense matters. Particularly after Suez, the French relationship with Israel could be viewed as an attempt to encroach on an American sphere of influence, although the degree to which Washington's approval of French policies was implied remains to be documented. The only major shift in French attitudes came with regard to the presence of the USSR in the Mediterranean: whereas the Fourth Republic rejected the possibility, de Gaulle accepted the reality and sought instead to spearhead a third world force in order to reduce rigid bipolarization of the region. Both his championship of Israel and rapprochement with the Arab states clearly furthered his claim to leadership of the noncommitted world.

In some respects the French role in regional politics is reminiscent of the nineteenth-century European state system's preoccupation with the balance of power. No longer a colonial force after the war, France sought a means of exercising influence in regional and thereby global affairs. In order to counteract British power, it found common cause with Israel in opposition to plans for Greater Syria, while in the intra-Arab struggle for primacy among Iraq, Syria, and Egypt, Israel was used to maintain an equalization of power. Once 'Abd al-Nasir's revolutionary mission aggravated the Algerian rebellion and radicalized regional politics, it threatened to upset the regional balance in Egypt's favor. France was then propelled by common enmity to 'Abd al-Nasir into a military and political partnership with Israel at Suez.

From 1959 on, however, the change in the regional system ultimately forced the allies apart. Once the cause of Arab unity and Arab nationalism led Egypt to accept the necessity for long-range plans geared to the eventual elimination of Israel, Israel was forced to seek advanced and highly sophisticated defense weapons systems of American manufacture. Moreover, its acquisition of greater independence in defense was bound to break its exclusive relationship with France. Faced in 1967 with the realization that informal ties are a luxury afforded only by the secure, Israel reverted to its earlier pattern of defensive behavior, which placed a premium on independent activism and self-dependence. As it moved toward the acquisition of a national deterrent free from outside allegiances or restraints, this raised the specter of further escalation of the arms races. Viewed in this light, de Gaulle's violent reaction to the sweeping Israeli victory in the 1967 Arab-Israel war and subsequent courting of Iraq, Libya, and Lebanon in particular, seem less the aberration of a particular individual than part of a continuous thread of policy designed to redress regional imbalances of power. His attempt to maintain a neutral position by supporting both a rapprochement with the Arabs and continued aid to Israel could be interpreted as a desire to be the *puissance médiatrice* or balancer of power in the Middle East. However, as the chance for regional peace became more remote, France's ability to maintain the middle ground and mediate an amiable settlement became less feasible.

Faced with an almost rigidly complete superpower polarization of the Arab world, France was forced to make a choice. De Gaulle became dealigned with Israel and realigned with certain Arab states in the hope of offering a third choice to offset regional disequilibrium. In the final analysis he was following the same line of policy which for eleven years had equilibrated regional imbalances by strengthening Israel as a counterforce to the influence of Egypt and the radical, revolutionary regimes within the Arab-Israel zone.

The balance of power game was supposed to deter aggression, and in this sense France ultimately failed—first to prevent the threat of open hostilities to Israel and then to forestall Israel's preemptive action. The nature of the alliance was partly to blame for its failure. For Israel, the alliance was the key to its defense. Unless the Arab states discontinued their basic assumption regarding Israel's right of survival, force and the exercise of power would be the kingpin of Israel's relations with the Arab world in its search for security. Armaments in turn would be the central issue determining Israel's relations with the major powers. As long as its military needs were met, Israel accepted the unorthodox nature of the "special relationship," hoping it would prove as permanent and as strongly rooted in sentiment as the Anglo-American entente.

For France, however, the alliance was a limited arrangement—at least once de Gaulle came to power, for the General argued that nations have no friends, only interests, and that alliances are only temporary. In the nineteenth century Britain had taken a similar view and enjoyed relative freedom to adjust to situations and devise ways of applying a tacit general guarantee of lesser states because its alliances were temporary ad hoc arrangements entered into for a particular crisis. The analogy is not without basis, for even geographically there is a similarity between Britain's insular position vis-à-vis Europe and France's location with regard to the Middle East.

An alliance can only remain vigorous where convergent and complementary interests are stronger than any conflicting or potentially conflicting ones. Rarely is there ever complete solidarity among allies, for even with respect to the identification of a common enemy, no two states will ever always see the same degree of threat implied in the policies of a third. Alliances, therefore, do seem to be vulnerable to divergence and dissolution and, as de Gaulle had suggested, can only be temporary. This would be especially true for a tacit arrangement where the insecurities of the more dependent state are compounded by the absence of a well-defined guarantee. The keystone of an alliance is confidence in the behavior of the partners. Once the feeling of solidarity is undermined, a threatened state might well lose its trust in the reliability of promises and commitments made by its ally where they are not formalized by a written agreement.

If Israel had had a written, formal alliance, instead of an amorphous tacit arrangement, it might have felt less insecure and isolated in the face of the Egyptian blockade, the increasing Egyptian troop concentrations in Sinai, the threat of a Jordan-Syria alignment and the entrance of Iraqi troops into Jordan—and ultimately averted a preemptive war. Yet the ties between Israel and France had never been formalized, even during the period when the Mollet government was in power. Bar-Zohar has suggested that neither Israel nor France was anxious for a written engagement—Israel because it would have meant association with a colonial power, France, because a treaty with Israel would have damaged the French image in the eyes of the Arabs. According to this view, the Quai d'Orsay was motivated by a desire for eventual rapprochement with the Arabs.[9]

[9] See *Gesher 'al ha-Yam ha-Tikhon. Yahasei Tsarfat-Israel, 1947-1963* (Bridge over the Mediterranean. France-Israel Rela-

Pierre Maillard of the Quai d'Orsay has argued—with cogency—that a formal pact would have added little to the relationship where France was concerned, since an alliance is only as good as the moral commitment behind it.[10] Actually, an overt alliance would have provided both sides with some strange bedfellows. Although the two governments were profoundly reluctant to allow the relationship to become an issue in domestic politics, the strongest pressure for a formal pact came from the extreme Right—in Israel from Menahem Begin and the Herut Party and in France from the *ultras* and their supporters in the army. Moreover, Jacques Soustelle's later role in domestic French politics and his involvement in the OAS no doubt embarrassed the movement for a formal alliance.

From the Israeli point of view, the issue of a written alliance probably never took shape at the decision-making level, although Ben Gurion did seek to have official assurances wherever possible. Ben Gurion himself had resisted Kneset discussion of the issue for "reasons of state," denying that negotiations were being or ever had been conducted toward a written treaty. The government position was that "we are content with the effective co-operation and mutual friendship between Israel and France," while officials repeated Ambassador Pierre Gilbert's quip that "An affair for a Frenchman is

---

tions, 1947-1963; Tel-Aviv: 'Am ha-Sefer, 1964), pp. 183-184, 210. Actually the Suez invasion and not the Algerian war most severely damaged French interests in the Arab world. Relations were normalized by the 1958 accords between France and Egypt. Economically, France never regained its privileged position in Egypt and Syria, however, because trade was diverted primarily to the Communist bloc.

[10] Interviewed in Paris, June 24, 1969.

better than marriage." [11] As long as Israel needs were
met, there seems to have been a general feeling that
there was no harm to the alliance remaining tacit and
implied, instead of formal and written. When cooperation later broadened into an almost symbiotic relationship in military and scientific fields, many Israelis were
convinced such cooperation was sufficient to preclude
any need for an orthodox treaty. Yet despite repeated
French assurances that ties with Israel belonged in
the realm of "ethics more than interests," and that an
unwritten alliance would last longer, there can be little
doubt that Israel would have responded positively had a
formal pact actually been offered. [12] A written alliance
would not only have had a beneficial psychological
effect by easing Israel's fear of isolation, but by stating
specific commitments and intentions it could have ultimately stabilized the relationship and avoided the kind
of unrealistic expectations by both parties which contributed to its breach and the subsequent bitterness
which characterized France-Israel relations after 1967.

[11] Ben Gurion, cited in *Jerusalem Post,* Jan. 1, 1957. For
disclosures of secret negotiations by a member of the French
Socialist delegation, see *ibid.,* Dec. 26, 1956. See also State of
Israel, *Divrei ha-Kneset,* 3rd Kneset, Nov. 18, 1957, pp. 182-183,
for interpellation by Esther Raziel-Neor of Herut and reply by
Ben Gurion. Gilbert, cited in *The Economist,* vol. 191 (May 16,
1959), supplement, p. 7.

[12] See *Jerusalem Post,* Feb. 25, April 13, 1958.

Bibliography

French Sources

The following individuals were interviewed in Paris on the dates given in parentheses next to their names.

Admiral Maurice Amman (June 26, 1969)
    Director of the cabinet of the Naval General Staff (1955-1959).

Confidential Source (June 14, 1969)
    Attached to the General Staff of the Minister of Defense; served in Indochina; Deputy to General Paul Ely, Chief of Staff of the Armed Forces; Chief of Staff attached to General Charles de Gaulle.

General André Beaufre (June 13, 1969)
    Served in Algeria (until August 1956); Commander of land forces during Suez invasion; supported nuclear deterrent for France.

General Pierre Billotte (May 29, 1969)
    Gaullist Deputy in the National Assembly (1951-1955); Minister of National Defense and the Armed Forces (1955-1956); Deputy and Vice President of the Gaullist UNR group in the National Assembly (November 1962-February 1966); Minister of Overseas Departments and Territories (1967).

Maurice Bourgès-Maunoury (June 23, 1969)
    Deputy Minister of National Defense (1951); Minister for Armament (1953); Minister of the Armed Forces (January-February 1955); Minister of Interior (February 1955-January 1956); Minister of National Defense and the Armed Forces (February 1956-June 1957); Prime

Minister (June-November 1957); Minister of Interior (November 1957-April 1958).

General Raymond Brohon (June 26, 1969)
Served in Indochina (1954); Commander of the Air Force in the Middle East (1956); Chief of Staff attached to the Secretary of State for Air (1957); Director of Sud Aviation; Secretary General of SFERMA (*Société française d'entretien et de réparation de matériel aéronautique*) (1964); President of the *Société d'exploitation et de construction aéronautiques*.

Maître René Cassin (June 3, 1969)
Member of the Constitutional Council since 1960; President of the *Alliance Israélite Universelle*.

Curtis Cate (several conversations, May and June 1969)
Writer.

General Maurice Challe (June 2, 1969)
Chief of the General Staff of the Secretary of State for Air (1951); General of the Air Force, Chief of Staff of the Armed Forces (1955); General of the Air Force (1958); Commander-in-Chief of French forces in Algeria (December 1958-April 1960); participated in Algiers coup of April 21-25, 1961; condemned by military tribunal May 31, 1961; pardoned in 1967. Was military organizer of Suez expedition, partisan of European and Atlantic integration. Employed by Zim Israel Navigation Company.

Marcel Chassagny (June 16, 1969)
President and Director-General of the *Société des Engins Matra* since 1937; since 1968 President of *L'Union syndicale des industries aéronautiques et spatiales*.

Jean Clémentin (several conversations, May and June 1969), Journalist, *Le Canard Enchaîné*.

General Paul Ely (June 5, 1969)
General of the Army (1953); Chief of Staff, President of the Committee of Chiefs of Staff (1954-1956); served in Indochina (1956-1958); Chief of Staff of the Army and President of the General Staff of National Defense (1959-1961); involved in negotiations with the Israelis prior to Sèvres agreement.

Solomon Friedrich (June 18, 1969)
Director-General of the *Alliance France-Israël;* and of the *Comité de Solidarité Française avec Israël;* associated with the Herut Party.

General Pierre Gallois (June 10, 1969)
Retired from Air Force (1957); Commercial Director of the *Société des avions Marcel Dassault* since 1958; theoretician of the nuclear deterrent.

Albert Gazier (July 2, 1969)
Minister of Social Affairs (1956-1957; June-November 1957). Considered a confidant of Guy Mollet; sent to London prior to Suez invasion.

Pierre Gilbert (June 11, 1969)
Ambassador to Israel (1953-1959).

Confidential source, cabinet of Resident-General of Algeria.

Gilbert Grandval (June 30, 1969)
Resident-General of France in Morocco (June-September, 1955); Secretary General of the Merchant Marine (1958-1962); Secretary of State for Trade (April-May 1962); Minister of Labor (May-November 1962; December 1962-January 1966); President of the *Compagnie des Messageries Maritimes* since 1966.

Professor Alfred Grosser (June 12, 1969)
Supervised Michael Bar-Zohar's dissertation (*Bridge over the Mediterranean. France-Israel Relations 1947-1963*) at the *Institut d'études politiques.*

General Paul Grossin (June 25, 1969)
> Director-General of the *Service de documentation extérieure et de contre-espionnage* (SDECE) (1957-1962); attached to Prime Minister Guy Mollet (February 1956-June 1957); member of the Superior War Council (1957).

General Augustin Guillaume (correspondence with author, June 23, 1969)
> Chief of General Staff of the Armed Forces (1954-March 1956).

General Paul Jacquier (June 25, 1969)
> General of the Air Force; Director of SDECE (1962-1966).

General Pierre Koenig (June 16, 1969)
> Victor of Bir Hakeim, 1942 (Libyan campaign); served in Tunisia (1941-1943); Vice President of the Superior War Council (1950-1951); Minister of National Defense and the Armed Forces (June-August 1954; 1955); President of the *Alliance France-Israël* and the *Comité de Solidarité Française avec Israël* since May 1967.

General Gaston Jean Lavaud (June 12, 1969)
> Chief of General Staff attached to the Minister for Armament (1952); attached to the Ministry of National Defense (1956-1957); Technical Counsellor in the cabinet of the Minister of Defense and the Armed Forces (1956); Chief of Staff of the Army (February 1959); Ministerial Delegate for Armament (April 1961); President of the *Conseil d'Administration* of *L'Office Nationale d'Etudes et de Recherches Aérospatiales* (ONERA) (1963-1965); member of the *Conseil de l'Etat*. Partisan of the nuclear deterrent.

Pierre Maillard (June 24, 1969)
> Chief of the Levant Desk at the Quai d'Orsay (1954); Deputy Counsellor attached to the Secretariat General of the President (1959-1964); Deputy Secretary General of National Defense (May 1964-November 1968).

Colonel Louis Mangin (correspondence with author, July 2, 1969)

> Served in cabinets of the Minister for National Defense and the Prime Minister (1956-1960). A confidant of Maurice Bourgès-Maunoury.

General André Martin (June 12, 1969)

> General of the Air Force; Chief of the General Staff under Minister of the Armed Forces Guillaumat (1958-1959); Chief of the Interarmy General Staff (1961); Inspector General of the Air Force (1963-1967); second in command to Maurice Challe; involved in pre-Suez planning.

Jules Moch (June 2, 1969)

> Minister of Interior (1947-1950); Vice President of the cabinet; Minister of Defense (1950-1951); Minister of Interior (May 1958); Minister of Public Works and Transport in the second cabinet of de Gaulle after World War II; and also under Gouin, Bidault, Ramadier; Minister of National Economy and Reconstruction in 1947; member of the United Nations delegation (1947, 1951-1960); Permanent Representative of France to the Disarmament Commission (1951-1961).

André Monteil (June 20, 1969)

> Secretary of State for the Navy (1950-1951; June-November 1954); Senator (since 1959); President of the Senatorial Commission for Foreign Affairs, Defense and the Armed Forces (since 1968); member of the French Committee for Solidarity with Israel.

Roger Nordmann (June 17, 1969)

> Dassault aircraft company, St. Cloud.

General Maurice Perdrizet (June 18, 1969)

> Representative of *L'Office français d'exportation de matériel aéronautique* in Israel.

Bibliography

François Perreire (July 3, 1969)

    Chairman of the Eilat Oil Pipeline Company; the Caesarea Development Corporation; President of the Chamber of Commerce France-Israel; President of the European Delegation of the Economic Conference; President and Director-General of the *Compagnie Financière* (Rothschild Group).

Jacques Piette (June 6, 1969)

    Former deputy; President and Director-General of the *Société nationale de constructions aéronautiques du Nord* (1951-1955); member of the French delegation to the General Assembly (1956); Inspector General of the National Economy (since 1959).

Jean Renou (June 16, 1969)

    Since 1959 head of the Department for Foreign Relations (Interior and Public) of the Commissariat for Atomic Energy.

Emile Roche (June 26, 1969)

    President of the *Conseil Economique et Social de France* (since 1959); President of the European Committee for the Development of Israel (since 1962).

Baron Edmond de Rothschild (July 1, 1969)

    President for Europe of Israel Bonds; President of the Israel European Company (ISROP); Administrator of the *Compagnie Financière*.

Jacques Soustelle (May 27, 1969)

    Deputy, Fourth Republic; Governor General of Algeria (1955-1956); Minister of Information (1958-1959); Ministerial Delegate for Atomic Affairs (1959-February 1960). Involved with the OAS (secret army organization) in opposition to de Gaulle's policies in Algeria. President of the *Alliance France-Israël* (1957).

Albert Stara (June 5, 1969)

    Revisionist organization.

General Paul Stehlin (June 28, 1969)
Chief of the Air Force General Staff (March 1960-September 1963); Vice President of the Superior Council of the Air Force (1962-1963); Counsellor of State on Extraordinary Service (September 1963-March 1964); Deputy of the National Assembly (since June 1968). A nuclear theoretician.

Abel Thomas (July 3, 1969)
Deputy Director of the cabinet of the Minister of National Defense (1948-1949); Technical Counsellor to Defense Minister Jules Moch (1950-1951) and Minister of Armament Bourgès-Maunoury (1952); Chief of the *Service Economie de Guerre* at the permanent Secretariat General of National Defense (1953-1956); Director of the cabinet of Bourgès-Maunoury as Minister of Industry (1954); Deputy Director of his cabinet as Interior Minister (1955-1956) and Defense Minister (1956-1957) and Deputy Director of his cabinet as Prime Minister (June-November 1957); and as Interior Minister (1957-1958); presently Director-General of SEDAM (naval aerogliders) and associated with the Rothschild group.

Raymond Triboulet (June 13, 1969)
Minister Delegate in charge of Cooperation (1962-1966); Deputy, National Assembly; President of the *Groupe d'Amitié "France-Israël"* within the National Assembly.

Georges Volland (June 17, 1969)
Potez-Fouga. Personally involved in arranging for clandestine shipments of Fouga Magisters to Israel on the eve of the Six Day War.

ISRAEL SOURCES

Yehoshua' Almog (Jerusalem, July 28, 1969)
Department for International Cooperation, Ministry for Foreign Affairs.

Bibliography

Ya'akov Aviad (Paris, May 22, 27, 1969)
Israel Embassy.

Avraham Avihai (Jerusalem, several conversations, July-August 1969)
Formerly with the Prime Minister's Office.

Colonel Mordechai Bar-on (Jerusalem, July 22, 1969)
Formerly Chief Educational Affairs Officer, Israel Defense Forces.

Menahem Begin (Jerusalem, August 12, 1969)
Head of Herut Party; Minister without Portfolio.

David Ben Gurion (Tel-Aviv, July 30, 1969)
Prime Minister and Defense Minister (1948-1953: 1955-1963).

Professor Ernst Bergmann (Jerusalem, July 29, 1969)
Chairman of the National Committee for Space Research; former head of the Defense Ministry's Scientific Department and in charge of Israel's atomic energy program; resigned in opposition to Levi Eshkol's policies (1966).

David Catarivas (Jerusalem, July 16, 1969)
Ministry for Foreign Affairs.

Zvi Dar (New York, May 2, 1969)
Defense Ministry.

Walter Eytan (Paris, June 19, 1969)
Ambassador to France (since 1959)

Azriel Harel (Jerusalem, July 15, 1969)
Deputy Director, Department for International Cooperation, Ministry for Foreign Affairs. Former Ambassador to Malawi.

General Paltiel Makleff (Lydda, August 14, 1969)
Director of Elta, Israel Electronic Industries, at Israel Aircraft Industry near Lydda.

Bibliography

Menahem Meir (Paris, May 27, 1969)
Economic Counsellor, Israel Embassy.

Confidential source, Prime Minister's office.

General Aharon Nachshon (Bet Shemesh, July 18, 1969)
Director-General of Bet Shemesh Engines, Ltd., firm established by Joseph Szydlowski of Turboméca.

Confidential source, Ministry of Defense.

Shim'on Peres (Tel-Aviv, July 31, 1969)
Director-General, Ministry of Defense (until 1959); Deputy Minister of Defense (1959-1965); Minister without Portfolio (1969).

Ben Porat (telephone conversation, August 6, 1969)
Journalist, *Yediot Ahronot.*

Ya'akov Schachar (Jerusalem, August 5, 1969)
Ministry of Finance and Commerce.

Yoel Sher (Jerusalem, July 15, 1969)
Department for International Cooperation, Ministry for Foreign Affairs.

Yael Vered (Jerusalem, August 7, 1969)
Ministry for Foreign Affairs.

Ya'akov Tsur (Jerusalem, August 13, 1969)
Ambassador to France (1953-1959).

Yoram Ziv (telephone conversation, August 4, 1969)
Assistant Director-General, Ministry of Finance and Commerce.

Public Documents

République Française. French Embassy. Press and Information Service, New York. *Major Addresses, Statements and Press Conferences of General Charles de Gaulle, May 19, 1958-January 31, 1964.*

————. *Ibid. French Foreign Policy: Official Speeches and Communiques 1966* (1967).

————. *Journal Officiel de la République Française. Débats Parlementaires. Assemblée Nationale. Compte Rendu.*

————. Ministère des Finances et des Affaires Economiques. *Annuaire Statistique de la France.*

————. *Ibid. Statistiques et Etudes Financières.*

OECD. *Geographical Distribution of Financial Flows to Less Developed Countries, 1960-1964* (Paris: 1966).

————. *The Flow of Financial Resources to Developing Countries in 1961* (Paris: 1963).

OEEC. *The Flow of Financial Resources to Countries in Course of Development 1956-1959* (Paris: 1961).

State of Israel. Central Bureau of Statistics. *Statistical Abstract of Israel.*

————. *Divrei ha-Kneset.*

————. Ministry for Foreign Affairs Information Division. *Facts About Israel.*

————. *Ibid. Israel's Programme of International Cooperation* (Jerusalem: 1967).

————. *Government Yearbook.*

United Nations. *General Assembly Official Records.*

————. *Security Council Official Records.*

————. Document A/AC. 105/L.13. *Review of national and co-operative international space activities.*

————. Document A/AC.105/26. *Space Activities and Resources* (Sales No. 65.I.14).

————. Documents A/3268 and A/3269, November 3, 1956. *Letters from representatives of France and United Kingdom to Secretary General.*

————. Food and Agriculture Organization. *FAO Trade Yearbook* (Rome).

————. Department of Economic and Social Affairs. Statistical Office of the United Nations. *Yearbook of International Trade Statistics* (New York).

United States Government. Department of State. *United States Policy in the Middle East, September 1956-June 1957, Documents* (Washington: GPO, 1957).

BOOKS

Abi-Mershed, Walid. *Israeli Withdrawal from Sinai, 1956-57.* Beirut: Institute for Palestine Studies, 1966.

Alwan, Mohamed. *Algeria Before the United Nations.* New York: Speller, 1959.

Ambler, John Steward. *Soldiers Against the State. The French Army in Politics.* Garden City: Doubleday, 1968.

Aron, Raymond. *De Gaulle, Israël et Les Juifs.* Paris: Plon, 1968.

————. *The Great Debate. Theories of Nuclear Strategy,* trans. by Ernst Pawel. Garden City: Doubleday, 1965.

Azeau, Henri. *Le Piège de Suez (5 novembre 1956).* Paris: Laffont, 1964.

Bader, William B. *The United States and the Spread of Nuclear Weapons.* New York: Pegasus, for the Center of International Studies, Princeton, 1968.

Bar-Zohar, Michael. *Gesher 'al ha-Yam ha-Tikhon. Yahasei Tsarfat-Israel, 1947-1963* (Bridge over the Mediterranean. France-Israel Relations, 1947-1963). Tel-Aviv: 'Am ha-Sefer, 1964.

————. *The Armed Prophet; A Biography of Ben Gurion,* trans. by Len Ortzen. London: Barker, 1967.

Beaton, Leonard. *Must the Bomb Spread?* Middlesex: Penguin, for the Institute for Strategic Studies (ISS), 1966.

Beaton, Leonard, and Maddox, John. *The Spread of Nuclear Weapons.* New York: Praeger, for the ISS, 1962.

Beaufre, André. *Dissuasion et Stratégie.* Paris: Colin, 1964.

Bidault, Georges. *Resistance. The Political Autobiography of Georges Bidault,* trans. by Marianne Sinclair. London: Weidenfeld & Nicolson, 1967.

Billotte, Pierre. *Le Temps du Choix.* Paris: Laffont, 1950.

Bourdeillette, Jean. *Pour Israël.* Paris: Seghers, 1968.

Bromberger, Merry and Serge. *Les Secrets de l'expédition d'Egypte.* Paris: Aymon, 1957.

Buchan, Alastair, ed. *A World of Nuclear Powers?* Englewood Cliffs: Prentice-Hall, 1966.

Cairns, John. *France.* Englewood Cliffs: Prentice-Hall, 1965.

Calmann, John. *European Co-operation in Defence Technology: The Political Aspect.* London: ISS, 1967.

Calvocoressi, Peter. *International Politics since 1945.* New York: Praeger, 1968.

———. *World Order and New States: Problems of Keeping the Peace.* New York: Praeger, 1962.

———, et al. *Suez Ten Years After. Broadcasts from the BBC Third Programme.* London & Frome: Butler & Tanner, 1967.

Campbell, John C. *Defense of the Middle East. Problems of American Policy,* rev. ed. New York: Praeger, 1960.

Challe, Maurice. *Notre Révolte.* Paris: Cité, 1968.

Chantebout, Bernard. *L'Organisation Générale de la Défense Nationale en France Depuis la fin de la Seconde Guerre Mondiale,* vol. 26. Bibliothèque Constitutionnelle et de Science Politique. Librairie Générale de Droit et de Jurisprudence. Paris: 1967.

Childers, E. B. *The Road to Suez: A Study of Western-Arab Relations.* London: MacGibbon & Kee, 1959.

Churchill, Randolph S. *The Rise and Fall of Sir Anthony Eden.* London: MacGibbon & Kee, 1959.

Crozier, Michel. *The Bureaucratic Phenomenon.* Chicago: Chicago University Press, 1964.

Dayan, Moshe. *Diary of the Sinai Campaign.* New York: Harper & Row, 1965.

DePorte, A. W. *De Gaulle's Foreign Policy 1944-1946.* Cambridge: Harvard, 1968.

Duhamel, Georges. *Israël. Clef de l'Orient.* Paris: Mercure de France, 1957.

Dulac, André. *Nos Guerres Perdues.* Paris: Fayard, 1969.

Eden, Anthony. *The Memoirs of Anthony Eden: Full Circle.* Boston: Houghton-Mifflin, 1960.

Ely, Paul. *Mémoires. Suez . . . le 13 Mai.* Paris: Plon, 1969.

Epstein, Leon D. *British Politics in the Suez Crisis.* Urbana: Illinois, 1964.

Eytan, Walter. *The First Ten Years: A Diplomatic History of Israel.* London: Weidenfeld & Nicolson, 1958.

Finer, Herman. *Dulles over Suez. The Theory and Practice of His Diplomacy.* Chicago: Quadrangle, 1964.

Frutkin, Arnold W. *International Cooperation in Space.* Englewood Cliffs: Prentice-Hall, 1965.

Furniss, Edgar S., Jr. *De Gaulle and the French Army. A Crisis in Civil-Military Relations.* New York: Twentieth Century Fund, 1964.

————. *France Troubled Ally. De Gaulle's Heritage and Prospects.* New York: Harper, 1960.

Gilpin, Robert, Jr. *France in the Age of the Scientific State.* Princeton: Princeton University Press, 1968.

Giniewski, Paul. *Israël devant l'Afrique et l'Asie.* Paris: Durlacher, 1958.

Goldschmidt, Bertrand. *L'Aventure Atomique. Ses Aspects Politiques et Techniques.* Paris: Fayard, 1962.

de la Gorce, Paul-Marie. *The French Army. A Military-Political History,* trans. by Kenneth Douglas. New York: Braziller, 1963.

Gottmann, Jean. *Etudes sur l'Etat d'Israël et le Moyen Orient.* Paris: Colin, 1959.

Grosser, Alfred. *La Politique Extérieure de la Ve République.* Paris: Seuil, 1965.

Halpern, Ben. *The Idea of a Jewish State.* Cambridge: Harvard University Press, 1961.

Harkabi, Yehosafat. *Nuclear War and Nuclear Peace,* trans. by Yigal Shenkman. Jerusalem: Israel Program for Scientific Translations, 1966.

Haskins, Caryl P. *The Scientific Revolution and World Politics.* New York: Harper, 1964.

Hershlag, Z. Y. *Introduction to the Modern Economic History of the Middle East.* Leiden: Brill, 1964.

Hoffmann, Stanley, et al. *In Search of France. The Economy, Society and Political System in the Twentieth Century.* New York: Harper, 1963.

Bibliography

Hurewitz, J. C. *Middle East Politics: The Military Dimension*. New York: Praeger, 1969.

Institute for Strategic Studies [ISS]. *The Military Balance 1966-1967*. London: 1967.

———. *The Military Balance 1968-1969*. London: 1968.

———. *Strategic Survey 1966*. London: 1967.

———. *Strategic Survey 1967*. London: 1968.

Israel and the United Nations. New York: Manhattan, for the Carnegie Endowment for International Peace, 1956.

Johnson, Paul. *The Suez War*. New York: Greenberg, 1957.

Juin, Marshal and Massis, Henri. *The Choice before Europe*. London: Eyre & Spottiswoode, 1958.

Kagan, Benjamin. *Combat Secret pour Israël*. Paris: Hachette, 1963.

Kash, Don E. *The Politics of Space Cooperation*. Lafayette: Purdue University Press, 1967.

Kimche, Jon and David. *Both Sides of the Hill. Britain and the Palestine War*. London: Secker & Warburg, 1960.

Kimche, David, and Bawly, Dan. *The Sandstorm. The Arab-Israeli War of June 1967: Prelude and Aftermath*. New York: Stein & Day, 1968.

Kohl, Wilfrid L. "The French Nuclear Force and Alliance Diplomacy, 1958-1967." Unpublished Ph.D. dissertation, Columbia University, 1968.

Kowitt, Sylvia. "The Influence of the Military Establishment on Israeli Politics." Unpublished M.A. thesis, Columbia University, 1961.

249

Kulski, W. W. *De Gaulle and the World: The Foreign Policy of the Fifth French Republic*. Syracuse: Syracuse, 1966.

Lapierre, Jean-William. *L'Information sur l'Etat d'Israël dans les grands quotidiens français en 1958*. Paris: Centre National de la Recherche Scientifique, 1968.

Laufer, Leopold. *Israel and the Developing Countries: New Approaches to Cooperation*. New York: Twentieth Century Fund, 1967.

Le Procès de Raoul Salan. Compte Rendu Stenographique: Paris: Michel, 1962.

Le procès des généraux Challe et Zeller: textes complets des débats réquisitoires-plaidoiries, annèxes. Paris: Nouvelles Editions Latines, 1961.

Liska, George. *Nations in Alliance: The Limits of Interdependence*. Baltimore: Johns Hopkins, 1962.

Love, Kennett. *Suez: The Twice-Fought War. A History* (N.Y.: McGraw Hill, 1969).

Meinertzhagen, Richard. *Middle East Diary 1917-1956*. London: Cresset, 1959.

Miller, J. D. B. *The Politics of the Third World*. London: Oxford, for the Royal Institute of International Affairs (RIIA), 1967.

Mollet, Guy. *Bilan et Perspectives Socialistes*. Paris: Plon, 1958.

Nutting, Anthony. *No End of a Lesson. The Story of Suez*. London: Constable, 1967.

Peres, Shim'on. *Hashlav ha-Bah* (The Next Phase). Tel-Aviv: 'Am ha-Sefer, 1965.

————. *David's Sling. The Arming of Israel*. London: Weidenfeld & Nicolson, 1970.

Perlmutter, Amos. *Military and Politics in Israel. Nation-Building and Role Expansion.* London: Cass, 1969.

Pickles, Dorothy. *The Fifth French Republic. Institutions and Politics,* 3rd ed. New York: Praeger, 1966.

Porat, Ben and Dan, Uri. *Mirage Contre Mig.* Paris: Laffont, 1967.

Ra'anan, Uri. *The USSR Arms the Third World: Case Studies in Soviet Foreign Policy.* Cambridge: M.I.T. University Press, 1969.

Rapport Jeanneney. La Politique de Coopération avec les pays en voie de développement, no. spécial 201. Paris: La Documentation Française, 1964.

Regards sur l'Alliance France-Israël. Paris: Service d'Etudes et Liaisons, d'Information et de Propagande, 1957.

Rémond, René. *La Droite en France de la Première Restauration à la Ve République.* Paris: Aubier, 1968.

Reynaud, Paul. *The Foreign Policy of Charles de Gaulle. A Critical Assessment,* trans. by Mervyn Savill. New York: Odyssey, 1964.

Ridley, F., and Blondel, J. *Public Administration in France.* New York: Barnes & Noble, 1965.

Robertson, Terence. *Crisis. The Inside Story of the Suez Conspiracy.* New York· Atheneum, 1964.

Rosecrance, R. N. *Problems of Nuclear Proliferation. Technology and Politics.* Security Studies Paper No. 7. Los Angeles: California, 1966.

Rosner, Gabriella. *The United Nations Emergency Force.* New York: Columbia, 1963.

Rustow, Dankwart A. "Problems of United States Defense Policy in a World of Nuclear Proliferation. Israel—United Arab Republic." Unpublished manuscript.

Safran, Nadav. *From War to War. The Arab-Israeli Confrontation, 1948-1967*. New York: Pegasus, 1967.

Sayegh, Fayez A., ed. *The Dynamics of Neutralism in the Arab World: A Symposium*. San Francisco: Chandler, for the Council on International Perspectives, 1964.

Scheinman, Lawrence. *Atomic Energy Policy in France under the Fourth Republic*. Princeton: Princeton University Press, 1965.

Schoenbrun, David. *The Three Lives of Charles de Gaulle*. New York: Atheneum, 1966.

Seguev, Samuel. *Israël, les Arabes et les Grandes Puissances 1963-1968*, trans. by Gabriel Roth. Paris: Calmann-Levy, 1968.

Seligman, Lester G. *Leadership in a New Nation. Political Development in Israel*. New York: Atherton, 1964.

Servan-Schreiber, J.-J. *The American Challenge*, trans. by Ronald Steel. New York: Atheneum, 1968.

Soustelle, Jacques. *A New Road for France*, trans. by Benjamin Protter. New York: Speller, 1965.

Stehlin, Paul. *Retour à Zéro*. Paris: Laffont, 1968.

Stock, Ernest. *Israel on the Road to Sinai 1949-1956*. Ithaca: Cornell, 1967.

Thomas, Hugh. *The Suez Affair*. Liverpool: Weidenfeld & Nicolson, 1966.

Tournoux, J.-R. *Secrets d'état*. Paris: Plon, 1960.

Tsur, Ya'akov. *Prélude à Suez; journal d'une ambassade, 1953-1956*. Paris: Cité, 1968.

Wajsman, P., and Teissedre, R. F. *Nos Politiciens face au conflit Israélo-arabe*. Paris: Fayard, 1969.

Werth, Alexander. *The De Gaulle Revolution*. London: Hale, 1960.

Bibliography

Williams, Ann. *Britain and France in the Middle East and North Africa, 1914-1967*. New York: St. Martins, 1968.

Williams, Philip M. *Crisis and Compromise. Politics in the Fourth Republic*. Garden City: Doubleday, 1966.

———. *The French Parliament (1958-1967)*. London: Allen & Unwin, 1968.

Wint, Guy, and Calvocoressi, Peter. *Middle East Crisis*. Harmondsworth: Penguin, 1957.

Zidon, Asher. *Knesset. The Parliament of Israel*, trans. by Aryeh Rubinstein and Gertrude Hirschler. New York: Herzl, 1967.

ARTICLES

Aldrich, Winthrop W. "The Suez Crisis. A Footnote to History," *Foreign Affairs*, vol. 45 (April 1967), pp. 541-552.

Allemann, F. R. "L'Orient dans la pénombre," *Preuves*, vol. 8 (Sept. 1958), pp. 53-58.

Alvarez del Vayo, J. "New Anti-Israel Policy?" *Nation*, vol. 176 (June 13, 1953), p. 500.

"Atomic Energy Development in France during 1946-1950," *Nature*, vol. 165 (March 11, 1950), pp. 382-383.

Barjot, Admiral Pierre. "Reflexions sur les opérations de Suez 1956," *Revue de Défense Nationale*, vol. 22 (Dec. 1966), pp. 1911-1924.

Beaton, Leonard. "Must the Bomb Spread? The Case of India, Egypt and Israel," *Jewish Observer and Middle East Review* (JOMER), vol. 15 (Jan. 14, 1966), pp. 8-12.

"Address Before the Knesset by Prime Minister David Ben Gurion—February 21, 1957," *Middle East Affairs*, vol. 8 (April 1957), pp. 143-150.

Ben Gurion, David. "Israel's Security and Her International Position. Before and After the Sinai Campaign," *State of Israel Government Yearbook 5720* (*1959/1960*), pp. 9-87.

"Ben-Gurion and De Gaulle: An Exchange of Letters," trans. by Hillel Halkin, *Midstream,* vol. 14 (Feb. 1968), pp. 11-26.

Binder, Leonard. "The Middle East Crisis: A Trial Balance," *Bulletin of the Atomic Scientist,* vol. 23 (Sept. 1967), pp. 2-7, 33-37.

Bonte, General Louis. "The French Aerospace Industry. A Survey of Present and Future Prospects," *Interavia,* vol. 20 (June 1965), pp. 879-880.

Boutros-Ghali, B. "Middle Eastern Security Pacts," *Revue Egyptienne de Droit International,* vol. 13 (1957), pp. 31-39.

Brownlow, Cecil. "Egypt Plans Satellite Launch Within Year," *Aviation Week and Space Technology* (AWST), vol. 79 (Sept. 9, 1963), pp. 32-33.

————. "Israel Aircraft Planning Major Reshuffle," AWST, vol. 80 (June 15, 1964), pp. 104-108.

Bulban, Erwin J. "Israeli Aircraft Surveying B-101C Market," AWST, vol. 74 (April 10, 1961), pp. 108-110.

Cain, Charles W. "Israel's International Air Line," *Aeroplane,* vol. 88 (March 4, 1955), pp. 279-282.

Calvocoressi, Peter. "The Consequences of Suez," *The Listener and BBC Television Review,* vol. 76 (Aug. 18, 1966), pp. 229-231.

Caplow, Theodore, and Finsterbusch, Kurt. "France and Other Countries: A Study of International Interaction," *The Journal of Conflict Resolution,* vol. 12 (March 1968), pp. 1-15.

Catarivas, David. "Sept ans de relations entre Israël et les étas francophones d'Afrique," *Mois en Afrique,* no. 20 (Aug. 1967), pp. 29-41.

Catroux, General Georges. "La Mediterranée orientale, Foyer des Tensions Internationales," *Etudes Mediterranéennes* (Autumn 1958), pp. 27-35.

Chapman, Guy. "France, The French Army and Politics," *Soldiers and Governments,* Michael Howard, ed. London: Eyre & Spottiswoode, 1957, pp. 51-72.

Chauvet, Paul-Louis. "Israël et le Monde Moderne," *La Revue Littérature, Histoire Arts et Sciences des Deux Mondes* (Feb. 1960), pp. 422-435.

Chorin, Yehuda. "Israeli Citrus and the Common Market," *New Outlook,* vol. 9 (March/April 1966), pp. 25-31.

Daniel, Jean. "Prophet of the Arab World? De Gaulle and the Jews," *Atlas,* vol. 15 (Feb. 1968), pp. 21-26.

Decalo, Samuel. "Israeli Foreign Policy and the Third World," *Orbis,* vol. 11 (Fall 1967), pp. 724-725.

Ely, Paul. "Perspectives stratégiques d'avenir," *Revue de Défense Nationale,* vol. 14 (Nov. 1958), pp. 1631-1640.

———. "The Role of the French Army Today," *Réalités* (English edition; April 1961), pp. 45-47.

Eshkol, Levi. "Israël et le Marché Commun," *Revue Politique et Parlementaire,* no. 730 (Jan. 1963), pp. 3-11.

Farrell, Robert E. "French Nuclear, Space Work Moves Toward Major Goals," *AWST,* vol. 80 (March 16, 1964), pp. 270-275.

———. "French Score in Drive to Widen Market," *AWST,* vol. 74 (March 13, 1961), pp. 280-281; 283-285.

Faydeau, François. "Les Accords franco-égyptiens du 22 août 1958," *Orient* (Paris), no. 7 (1958), pp. 71-79.

Février, Georges. "The French Industry's Programme," *Interavia,* vol. 16 (May 1961), p. 596.

Fink, Donald E. "French Seen Acting to Bolster Economy," AWST, vol. 89 (July 8, 1968), pp. 18-20.

Flapan, Simba. "Swords across the Sea," *Atlas,* vol. 8 (Sept. 1964), pp. 85-90.

Fontaine, André. "Il y a dix ans la Guerre de Suez," *Le Monde,* Oct. 30-31, Nov. 1, 1966.

Fouchet, Paul. "Un nouvel aspect des relations internationales: La coopération technique," *Tendances,* vol. 14 (Dec. 1961), pp. 641-672.

Frank, L. A. "Nasser's Missile Program," *Orbis,* vol. 11, no. 3 (1967), pp. 746-57.

Furniss, Edgar S., Jr. "The Grand Design of Charles de Gaulle," *Virginia Quarterly Review,* vol. 40 (Spring 1964), pp. 161-181.

de Galard, J. "The French Aeronautical Industry—still standing firm," *Interavia,* vol. 20 (June 1965), pp. 859-866.

Galli, Elkana. "Franco-Israel Alliance Confirmed. Doubts Dispelled by the New York Times, JOMER, vol. 15 (Jan. 14, 1966), p. 7.

———. "Les grandes puissances et la paix au Moyen-Orient," *Evidences,* vol. 7 (March 1956), pp. 1-4, 48-49.

———. "The Franco-Israel Reality. Existing Agreements Expanded," JOMER, vol. 15 (March 18, 1966), pp. 6-7.

Gallois, Pierre M. "Power and Paralysis," *Orbis,* vol. 11, no. 3 (1967), pp. 664-675.

Ginay, Erel. "De Gaulle and Israel," *New Outlook,* vol. 11 (Jan. 1968), pp. 13-18.

Girardet, Raoul. "Civil and Military Power in the Fourth Republic," *Changing Patterns of Military Politics,* Samuel P. Huntington, ed. New York: Free Press, 1962, pp. 121-149.

Goldschmidt, Bertrand. "The French Atomic Energy Program," *Bulletin of the Atomic Scientists,* vol. 18 (Sept. & Oct. 1962), pp. 39-42; 46-48.

Gottlieb, Gidon. "Israel and the A-Bomb," *Commentary,* vol. 13 (Feb. 1961), pp. 93-99.

de Gramont, Sanche. "Nasser's Hired Germans," *Saturday Evening Post,* vol. 236 (July 13-20, 1963), pp. 60-64.

Grosser, Alfred. "General de Gaulle and the Foreign Policy of the Fifth Republic," *International Affairs,* vol. 39 (April 1963), pp. 198-213.

Hart, B. H. Liddell. "Strategy of a War," *Encounter,* vol. 30 (Feb. 1968), pp. 16-20.

Hayter, Teresa. "French Aid to Africa—Its Scope and Achievements," *International Affairs,* vol. 41 (April 1965), pp. 236-251.

Hereil, Georges. "L'aviation, son present, son avenir," *Revue Politique et Parlementaire* (Jan. & Feb., 1962), pp. 50-55; 53-58.

Heymont, Irving. "The Israeli Nahal Program," *Middle East Journal,* vol. 21, no. 3 (1967), pp. 314-324.

Hoagland, John H., Jr., and Teeple, John B. "Regional Stability and Weapons Transfer: The Middle Eastern Case," *Orbis,* vol. 9, no. 3 (1965), pp. 714-728.

Hohenemser, Christoph. "The Nth Country Problem Today," *Disarmament: Its Politics and Economics,* Seymour Melman, ed. Boston: American Academy of Arts and Sciences, 1962, pp. 238-276.

Hope, Francis. "De Gaulle's African Balancing Act," *New Statesman* (Jan. 12, 1968), pp. 33-34.

Hourani, A. H. "The Middle East and the Crisis of 1956," *St. Antony's Papers,* no. 4, Middle Eastern Affairs, no. 1. London: Chatto & Windus, 1958.

Howard, Michael, and Hunter, Robert. "Israel and the Arab World: The Crisis of 1967," *Adelphi Papers,* no. 41. London: ISS, 1967.

Hudson, G. F. "The United Nations Emergency Force: A Notable Precedent," *Current History,* vol. 38 (June 1960), pp. 327-331.

Hurewitz, J. C. "Origins of the Rivalry," *Soviet-American Rivalry in the Middle East.* New York: Praeger, 1969, pp. 1-17.

————. "Regional and International Politics in the Middle East," *The United States and the Middle East,* Georgiana G. Stevens, ed. Englewood Cliffs: Prentice-Hall, 1964, pp. 78-112.

————. "The Role of the Military in Society and Government in Israel," *The Military in the Middle East. Problems in Society and Government,* Sydney Nettleton Fisher, ed. Columbus: Ohio, 1963, pp. 89-104.

Katz, Ze'ev. "Eshkol's 'Winds of Change,' " *New Outlook,* vol. 7 (July/Aug. 1964), pp. 16-19.

Kelly, George A. "Algeria, the Army and the Fifth Republic (1959-1961): A Scenario of Civil-Military Conflict," *Political Science Quarterly,* vol. 79 (Sept. 1964), pp. 335-359.

————. "The Political Background of the French A-Bomb," *Orbis,* vol. 4 (Fall 1960), pp. 284-306.

Kemp, Geoffrey. "Arms and Security: The Egypt-Israel Case," Adelphi Papers, no. 52. London: ISS, 1968.

———. "Arms Sales and Arms Control in the Developing Countries," *The World Today,* vol. 22 (Sept. 1966), pp. 386-395.

———. "Controlling Arms in the Middle East: Some Preliminary Observations," *ibid.,* vol. 23 (July 1967), pp. 285-292.

Kimche, Jon. "La Politique Extérieure d'Israël," *Evidences,* vol. 6, no. 45 (1955), pp. 1-6, 39.

Kowitt, Sylvia. "Israel's Cooperation for Development," *New Africa* (Feb. 1963), pp. 11-13.

———. "Training for Managers of Developing Countries in Israel," *International Handbook of Management,* Karl E. Ettinger, ed. New York: McGraw-Hill, 1965, pp. 625-635.

Kreinin, Mordechai E. "Israel's Export Problem and its Policy Implications," *The Southern Economic Journal,* vol. 25 (Oct. 1958), pp. 202-212.

———. "Joint Commercial Enterprises as a Vehicle for Extending Technical Aid. Israel's Experiment in Afro-Asian Countries," *Social and Economic Studies* (Jamaica), vol. 12 (Dec. 1963), pp. 459-470.

Labrousse, Capitaine de Corvette H. "Les Menaces sur les Territoires Français et Anglais du Moyen-Orient," *Revue de Défense Nationale,* vol. 14 (June 1958), pp. 934-944.

Lambert, Mark. "The French Industry in 1962," *Flight and the Aircraft Engineer* (July 5 & July 12, 1962), pp. 11-14; 56-58.

Laqueur, Walter Z. "Israel's Great Foreign Policy Debate. The Crisis Mood Continues," *Commentary,* vol. 20 (Aug. 1955), pp. 109-115.

Lauru, Capitaine de Frégate. "A Propos de la Destruction de l' 'Elath'," *Revue de Défense Nationale,* vol. 24 (Jan. 1968), pp. 102-119.

Lavaud, Gaston Jean. "La Délégation Ministérielle pour l'Armement," *Revue Militaire Générale* (Dec. 1961), p. 617; (Jan. 1962), pp. 103-114.

Lazega, Max. "Quelques aspects de la politique israélienne," *Revue de Défense Nationale,* vol. 22 (July 1966), pp. 1027-1034.

Lehrman, Hal. "What Price Israel's Defense? The Middle East's New High Standard of Armaments," *Commentary,* vol. 22 (Sept. 1956), pp. 199-210.

———. "Washington's 'New Pacifism'. Morality and the Free World's Interest," *ibid.* (Dec. 1956), pp. 493-506.

Lentin, Albert-Paul. "Le Moyen-Orient à l'heure de l'unité arabe," *La Nef,* vol. 15 (Sept. 1958), pp. 49-52.

Lepotier, Admiral. "Pourquoi la force de frappe," *Revue de Défense Nationale,* vol. 16 (March 1960), pp. 413-420.

Levitte, Georges. "Impressions of French Jewry Today," *Jewish Journal of Sociology,* vol. 22, no. 22 (1960), pp. 172-184.

Lieber, Robert J. "The French Nuclear Force. A Strategic and Political Evaluation," *International Affairs,* vol. 42 (July 1966), pp. 421-431.

McElheny, Victor K. "Fundamental Biology at the Weizmann Institute," *Science,* vol. 148 (April 30, 1965), pp. 614-618.

———. "The French Bomb: How Much Technical Fallout," *ibid.,* vol. 147 (Jan. 1, 1965), pp. 35-36.

Manue, Georges R. "La Leçon de Suez," *Revue de Défense Nationale,* vol. 12 (Oct. 1956), pp. 1155-1164.

Marcus, Joel. "The Rift Between Israel and France," *Midstream,* vol. 14 (Jan. 1968), pp. 39-52.

Masannot, George S. "Sino-Arab Relations," *Asian Survey,* vol. 6 (April 1960), pp. 216-226.

Madden, Daniel M. "French Glory in the Holy Land," *America,* vol. 103, no. 21 (1960), pp. 552-555.

Mehrtens, Ruth. "Israel's Burgeoning Science-based Industries. Business Around the Globe. Report from Tel-Aviv," *Fortune,* vol. 77 (April 1968), pp. 61, 64.

Mendel, Wolf. "The Background of French Nuclear Policy," *International Affairs,* vol. 41 (Jan. 1965), pp. 22-36.

Messmer, Pierre. "The French Military Establishment of Tomorrow," *Orbis,* vol. 6, no. 2 (1962), pp. 205-216.

Metellus. "Politique de la France au Proche-Orient," *Politique Etrangère,* vol. 20, no. 6 (1955), pp. 677-688.

Peres, Shim'on. "Outlines for an Israeli Foreign Policy," *New Outlook,* vol. 6, no. 7 (1963), pp. 14-19.

Perlmutter, Amos. "The Institutionalization of Civil-Military Relations in Israel: The Ben Gurion Legacy and Its Challengers (1953-1967)," *Middle East Journal,* vol. 22, no. 4 (1968), pp. 415-432.

———. "The Israeli Army in Politics: The Persistence of the Civilian over the Military," *World Politics,* vol. 20, no. 4 (1968), pp. 606-643.

Pineau, Christian. "Dix ans Après. Si J'avais à refaire l'opération de Suez . . . ," *Le Monde,* Nov. 4, 1966.

Porat, Ben. "Israël Fait Son Autocritique," *L'Arche,* no. 130 (Dec.-Jan. 1968), pp. 31-32, 57.

Prittie, Terence. "Bomb Shop in the Nile: Target Israel," *Atlantic Monthly,* vol. 214, no. 2 (1964), pp. 37-40.

Remba, Oded. "Israel and the European Economic Community," *Midstream,* vol. 8 (Sept. 1962), pp. 20-33.

"Remise de la Médaille commémorative du Moyen-Orient," *La Revue Maritime,* no. 137 (Oct. 1957), pp. 1271-1273.

Reynaud, Paul. "De Sarajevo à Amman," *La Revue de Paris,* vol. 64 (June 1957), pp. 3-13.

Rondot, Pierre. "Politique Occidentale dans l'Orient Arabe," *Etudes* (June 1962), pp. 369-380.

———. "Vers un Orient San Liens?" *L'Afrique et l'Asie,* no. 4 (1963), pp. 41-46.

Rosenberg, Leonard G. "Industrial Exports: Israel's Requirement for Self-Support," *Middle East Journal,* vol. 12, no. 2, pp. 153-165.

Rouleau, Eric. "Au Moyen-Orient, diversification des amitiés dans la sauvegarde des intérêts nationaux," *Le Monde Diplomatique* (Jan. 1968), pp. 8-9.

———. "French Policy in the Middle East," *The World Today,* vol. 24 (May 1968), pp. 209-218.

———. "Le conflit israélo-arabe: l'affrontement soviéte-américain au Moyen-Orient explique la prise de position gaulliste," *Le Monde Diplomatique* (Aug. 1967), pp. 1, 9.

Sablier, Edouard. "La tension en Proche-Orient et la politique des grandes puissances," *Politique Etrangère,* vol. 21 (Jan.-Feb. 1956), pp. 21-26.

Samuelson, Robert J. "Israel Science Based Industry Figures Large in Economic Plans," *Science,* vol. 160 (May 24, 1968), pp. 864-867.

Sanders, Ronald, trans. "French Citizenship and Jewish Identity. A Discussion," *Midstream,* vol. 14 (Aug.-Sept. 1968), pp. 44-60.

Sherman, Arnold. "Israel Aircraft Considers Private Financing for B-101C Development," AWST, vol. 77 (July 23, 1962), p. 71.

Sidorsky, David. "The United States and Israel," *Current History*, vol. 34 (March 1958), pp. 158-165.

Simon, J. F. "France's Flourishing Exports," *The Aeroplane and Astronautics*, vol. 101 (Dec. 14, 1961), pp. 763-764.

Sitbon, Guy. "Peace in the Middle East," *Atlas*, vol. 7 (May 1964), pp. 291-296.

Spagnolo, J. P. "French Influence in Syria Prior to World War I: The Functional Weakness of Imperialism," *Middle East Journal*, vol. 23, no. 1 (1969), pp. 45-62.

"Sources of Conflict in the Middle East," *Adelphi Papers*, no. 26 (London: ISS, 1966).

Tandon, Yashpal. "UNEF, the Secretary-General and International Diplomacy in the Third Arab-Israeli War," *International Organization*, vol. 22 (April 1968), pp. 529-556.

Ullmann, Marc. "De Gaulle's Secret Diplomacy," *Interplay of European/American Affairs*, vol. 1 (Aug./Sept. 1967), pp. 38-41.

Verdier, Robert. "Le Moyen-Orient. Foyer de Guerre ou épreuve de coexistence pacifique," *Evidences*, vol. 8 (May 1956), pp. 1-5.

Vernant, Jacques. "La France et l'O.N.U. en 1960," *Revue de Défense Nationale*, vol. 16 (Nov. 1960), pp. 1857-1863.

————. "Vers une nouvelle stratégie diplomatique du Proche-Orient," *ibid.* (March 1956), pp. 359-364.

Wahl, Nicholas. "The French Political System," *Patterns of Government in Major Political Systems of Europe*, Samuel H. Beer & Adam B. Ulam, eds., 2nd rev. ed. New York: Random House, 1962, Part III.

Walsh, John. "France: First the Bomb, Then the 'Plan Calcul'," *Science,* vol. 156 (May 12, 1967), pp. 767-770.

―――. "Some New Targets Defined for French Science Policy," *ibid.* (May 5, 1967), pp. 626-630.

Wetmore, Warren C. "Israelis' Air Punch Major Factor in War," AWST, vol. 87 (July 3, 1967), pp. 18-23.

―――. "Stratocruiser to Drop Israeli Paratroops," *ibid.,* vol. 82 (Jan. 18, 1965), p. 101.

Windsor, P. "The Middle East and the World Balance," *The World Today,* vol. 23, no. 7 (1967), pp. 279-285.

Young, Judith H. "The French Strategic Missile Programme," *Adelphi Papers,* no. 38. London: ISS, 1967.

Zoppo, Ciro. "France as a Nuclear Power," *The Dispersion of Nuclear Weapons. Strategy and Politics.* R. N. Rosecrance, ed. New York: Columbia, 1964.

PERIODICALS

Aeronautics
The Aeroplane and Astronautics
Air Pictorial
Aircraft Engineer
America
L'Année Politique
L'Arche
Aviation Week and Space Technology
Bulletin of the Atomic Scientist
Bulletin of the European Economic Community
Business Week
Chronique de Politique Etrangère
Dun's Review
Economist
Encounter
Engineer

Bibliography

Entreprises
Esprit
Flight, Aircraft, Spacecraft, Missiles
Flying
Fortune
Interavia
International Financial News Survey
Israel Economic Forum
Israel Digest
Jewish Observer and Middle East Review
Jane's Fighting Ships and Jane's All the World's Aircraft
Missiles and Rockets
Nature
Near East Report
New Outlook
New Statesman
Newsweek
Notes et Etudes Documentaires
Nuclear Engineering
Politique Etrangère
Revue de Défense Nationale
Revue des Deux Mondes
Revue Militaire Générale
Sciences
United States Department of State Bulletin
Wall Street Journal
World Today

NEWSPAPERS

French

Le Figaro
France Observateur
France-Soir
La Vie Française
Le Monde

Le Patronat Français
Les Echos

Israeli

Davar
Davar ha-Shavuah
Ha-Arets
Ha-Boqer
Ha-Olam ha-Zeh
Jerusalem Post
Ma'ariv
Yediot Ahronot

Other

Daily Telegraph
Manchester Guardian
New York Times
Times (London)

Index

Israel, State of—Cont'd
Algeria, 58; arms and defense
policies, 22, 102, 108, 172-
173, 183, 185, 188, 204-206,
228, 231; civil-military relations, 170ff.; Defense Forces,
see ZAHAL; economic rela-
tions with other states, 134,
136, 220-221; and Europe, 21,
101, 150, 169, 173, 179;
Foreign Affairs and Security
Committee, 52; foreign policy,
173-175, 188; government, 51,
138, 170-175, 179, 225, 233;
Independence War, 13, 24,
29ff., 44; Ministry for Foreign Affairs, 3, 44ff., 53, 62,
79, 106-108, 175; Ministry
of Defense, 35, 44, 46, 48, 50,
52, 54-56, 62, 106, 108, 134,
147, 161, 174-175, 196, 224;
Ministry of Finance, 52; nuclear policy, 55-56; 115, 120ff.,
162, 165, 160ff., 172, 174, 184,
187-189, 204-205. *See also*
EEC, France, Germany,
NATO, United Kingdom,
United Nations, United States.
Israel Aircraft Industries (IAI),
55ff., 112ff., 171, 182ff., 204ff.
Israel Bonds, 95

Jacquier, Paul, 105
Jadid, Salah, 27
Japan, 219
Jeanneney Commission Report,
139
Jerusalem, 35, 44, 210
Jews, 99; in Algeria, 107, 140-
141; in Egypt, 212; in France,

195-196, 210; in Magrib, 63;
in U.S., 95, 140
Jewish emigration, 107, 131,
132, 141
"Jewish vote," 100, 196
Johnson, Lyndon, administra-
tion, 202, 203
Joliot-Curie, Fréderic, 115
Jordan, 9, 14, 21, 25, 27, 42, 59,
73-75, 139, 142, 212, 232
Joxe, Louis, 120

Kagan, Benjamin, 39-40
Kaiser-Ilin, 133
Kashti, Moshe, 171
Kersaint, 78
Khrushchev, Nikita 142
Kneset, 52, 161, 233
Koenig, Pierre, 39, 45, 56, 57,
118, 119, 125, 140

Lacoste, Robert, 59, 64, 72, 103
Laniel, Joseph, 99
Latin America, 141, 201
Laufer, Leopold, 151
Lavaud, Gaston-Jean, 66, 153,
154, 184, 216
Lavon, Pinhas, 45, 54-55, 170
Lazareff, Pierre, 98n.
League for the Independence
of the Arab West, 17
Lebanon, 6, 7, 9, 16, 21, 32,
42, 59, 102, 139, 142, 178,
180, 192, 194, 208, 211, 212,
230
Lejeune, Max, 72, 81, 119
Libya, 59, 142, 201, 212, 230
L'Information, 131
*Ligue Française pour la Pales-
tine Libre,* 33n.

Modern Middle East Series

1. Hirsch, Eva. *Poverty and Plenty on the Turkish Farm, A Study of Income Distribution in Turkish Agriculture.* New York: Middle East Institute of Columbia University, 1970. 313 pages.
2. Waterbury, John. *The Commander of the Faithful: The Moroccan Political Elite—A Study in Segmented Politics.* New York: Columbia University Press, 1970. 368 pages.
3. Allworth, Edward. *Nationalities of the Soviet East.* New York: Columbia University Press, 1971. 296 pages.
4. Yar-Shater, Ehsan, editor. *Iran Faces the Seventies.* New York: Praeger, 1971. 391 pages.
5. Greenwald, Carol S. *Recession as a Policy Instrument: Israel 1965-1969.* London: C. Hurst and Co., forthcoming.
6. Smolansky, Oles M. *The Soviet Union and the Arab East Under Khrushchev.* Lewisburg, Pa.: Bucknell University Press, forthcoming.

Library of Congress Cataloging in Publication Data

Crosbie, Sylvia K   1938-
    A tacit alliance; France and Israel from
Suez to the Six Day War.
        (The Modern Middle East series, v. 7)
        Bibliography: p.
        1. Israel—Foreign relations—France.
2. France—Foreign relations—Israel. I. Title.
II. Series.
DS119.8.F8C76   327.44'05694   73-18310
ISBN 0-691-07557-3